# DANCING WITH THE MUSES

A HISTORICAL APPROACH TO BASIC
CONCEPTS OF MUSIC

M. ZACHARY JOHNSON

PUBLISHED BY FASTPENCIL

Published by FastPencil
3131 Bascom Ave.
Suite 150
Campbell CA 95008 USA
info@fastpencil.com
(408) 540-7571
(408) 540-7572 (Fax)
http://www.fastpencil.com

Printed in the United States of America.

Second Edition

*to my students at the Mannes College*
*in the hope of encouraging you never to stop asking why*

Merry Christmas, Josh —
This book is on my short
list of the best books anybody
ever wrote about music.
Enjoy!
Eric and Terri

# Acknowledgments

Thank you, my wife Jocelyn, for your capacity for joy. Thank you to Shrikant Rangnekar, for shepherding this project into reality, for your expertise in mathematics, for teaching me about the music of India, and for your friendship. Thank you, Brian Horner, for your friendship and collaboration over the years, your thoughts on this book, and your role in promoting it. Thank you, Anna Franco and Dr. Stephen Siek, for your thoughts on the content of the book. Thank you, Marianne Ploger and Dr. Philip Lasser, for acquainting me with the Boulanger tradition, as well as for your own musical insights. I acknowledge a significant debt to the book "Counterpoint in Composition" by Felix Salzer and Carl Schachter. I also acknowledge a profound intellectual debt to the work of Charles Darwin and to the philosophy of Ayn Rand. I gained insight on the connection between these two from Dr. Harry Binswanger. Thank you, Lance Moore, Reid Ginoza, Glenn Martin, and Matthew Chung, for your observations on the first edition of the book, which helped me shape the second edition.

Graphics & Images: All graphics and images are the author's original creation, with the following exceptions: Cover image used under creative commons permission from art-wall-paper.com. Ch. 2: Pan flute image used by creative commons permission of Flickr user Marvin Ray; "The School of Athens" image used by creative commons permission from Flickr user JustinMN; the diagram of the siren is an adaptation of an illustration in Helmholtz's "On the Sensations of Tone," which is public domain. Ch. 3: the Debussy score, and the score of "Ut queant laxis" are public domain. Curwen's hand signs are adapted from Curwen's "Standard Course" which is public domain. Ch. 4: the image of the Parthenon is by creative commons permission of Yair Haklai via Wikimedia Commons; the image of the Erechtheum is by creative commons permission of Thermos via Wikimedia Commons. Ch. 6: the image of the David is used under creative commons permission from Flickr user jay8085. Ch. 9: Images of string partials and the staff notation of the overtone series are from Helmholtz's "On the Sensations of Tone" which is in the public domain. For the second edition, the images of Neumatic and Daseian music notation in Ch. 3 have been added; these are from Wikimedia Commons.

# CONTENTS

# PREFACE

*Dance of Apollo with the Nine Muses* by 16th century painter Baldassare Peruzzi graces the cover of this book. Apollo, the Greek god of reason and of music, is pictured dancing with the goddesses of the arts. The figures on the tips of their feet, lightly stepping; the flowing line of their arms and hands held in a wide, undulating ring; the fluid folds of the drapery and the rich coils of each figure's hair; the flourish of Apollo's quiver holding his bow and arrows; the mix of vibrant colors thrown into relief against the golden background—all these elements contribute to the theme of vital and joyous dynamic motion.

This book deals with precisely that: the phenomenon of living linear movement in music. It teaches:

1. melodic shape—its rise and fall—and melodic connection and coherence
2. the elements and basis of melody: interval, scale, and time
3. the art of combining lines in a musical fabric (polyphony)
4. the development of the harmonic system from the practice of polyphony

The book also deals with the error that has arisen from the harmonic way of thinking, which consists of inverting the hierarchy of knowledge, placing central trust and importance in the concept of chord, while neglecting what is actually first, primary and central to the subject: melodic line.

The method of this book is historical. It seeks to present the essentials of music, the basic concepts, in their proper order—which is the order in which mankind originally learned them.

However, history presents us with an overwhelming deluge of detail. Too often the subject causes us mentally to drown in a sea of minutia. We must sift through the facts of history to find the key turning points or milestones, and we must work to gain a broad perspective in order to embrace a wide range of relevant, interrelated facts. We must reduce the amount of material so that we can manage it mentally, but without losing completeness of understanding.

Therefore this book includes *only* the essentials of the subject, but *all* of them. Generally speaking, my test of what to include has been: the idea is a significant advance in our understanding of music which lasted for centuries and led to impressive practical results. Staying power and practical usefulness are signs of an idea being true and clear.

I take pride—in my classroom and in this book—in never resorting to the sentence "because I said so." Some teachers unfortunately have had a tendency to present the facts, concepts, and rules of music as a kind of authoritarian dogma, according to the pattern of religion, as though it were a revelation from God: "Accept it and learn it, because this is the material and that's that."

And yet every teacher of music theory using such a method experiences that decisive moment each semester when the class concludes once and for all that this content is nothing but baseless dogma and a total waste of time. Then their boredom becomes permanent and impenetrable.

I side with the students here: time should be spent only on things that are worthwhile. If there is no reason for something, it should not be done. (Of course, understanding music is not a waste of time when it is done right!)

Compounding this motivational issue, we live in a culture of subjectivist skepticism, of pervasive doubt and suspicion or outright rejection of the validity of knowledge. Getting over these motivational hurdles is the principal challenge confronting teachers today.

The historical method sweeps these problems aside. It shows at every step the realistic basis for ideas, their grounding in facts. Even for ideas that proved false, the method reveals why people thought the way they did.

Using history teaches the student not just the content, but its full meaning and context, including the answers to the questions: Where do these concepts come from? How did they come to be? Why are they what they are? Why are they worth knowing?

A further advantage of the historical approach is that it enables the presentation of knowledge as much as possible in the form of *stories*. Compared to a dry exposition of technicalities, stories are much easier to learn from. They take the curse of boredom off of the traditional material and make it vivid, engaging, and dramatic. To learn about the living, breathing men who discovered things, and how they did it and why, brings the knowledge within the student's ability to thoroughly understand and evaluate—and to enjoy and admire.

This book does not accept or embody a separation of the fields of knowledge. There is no division here between musical theory (technical concepts), music history (the facts of music in the past), and the philosophy of music (broad ideas about what music is and means, and how it relates to human life). The three are integrated and blended, not driven apart as specialties. Fields of knowledge do not exist as separate, independent bubbles of reality; they are merely different aspects of our knowledge of the one reality we perceive around us. They must be treated as such.

This book also takes a holistic view of cognition and emotion. Issues of both structure and expression are addressed in tandem throughout. I do not agree with the approach to music that treats it as pure structure devoid of emotional content, as though concepts of musical emotion were somehow baseless or illegitimate. Nor, obviously, do I condone an anti-intellectual, primal-emotion sort of habit. Our thinking about the subject must obey the fact that music is both intellect and passion.

The integrative, historical approach gives rise to some further original aspects of this book's content. The book gives a new, biologically-based theory of rhythm. It establishes both empirically and mathematically that the diatonic scale is not an arbitrary Western social construct, but a timeless, universal phenomenon natural to human music. It gives a new explanation of the way in which the fact of *volition*, mental goal-direction, is manifest in music —in the system of tonality. It provides a more realistic assessment than those traditionally offered of the role of the church in music history.

This book grows not only out of my research into music history but also out of my experience as a composer, writer, lecturer and listener. Most especially it grows out of my more than ten years of experience teaching music to pre-college students, first at the University of Michigan School of Music and then at the Mannes College in New York. This book is a compilation and expansion of the teaching materials I have created over the years for my students.

In teaching I've dealt with a wide range of ages, from first graders through college students. I've been able to see the continuous development of some students for many years running. This has helped me learn what questions come up when, and what students can understand at each stage of knowledge. It has helped me learn the most intelligible method and order of presentation, as well as what things are common to students despite their many differences.

The result, I hope, is a book that serves the youthful mind at any age. Its origin for and tailoring to teenagers makes the book a suitable source for understanding the basics for any interested person. Ironically, the student who masters this material will know far more than the graduates of most university degree programs.

So this book represents my own re-conceptualization and completion of the material provided by traditional curricula.

To readers who are musicians I say: you have to know all of this. To those who are not, I say: use the book to pursue the things which interest you and which you can follow. It is fine for the start of the learning process to be a glancing survey; that is how one develops an initial familiarity that serves as a base for later, more thorough understanding.

Be aware that the first chapter of the book deliberately throws everything at you at once. The purpose is not to overwhelm you or intimidate you, of course, but rather to give you a sense of how the ideas come together as a system—in other words, to give you the big picture. So don't expect to understand everything there immediately—just use it as an overview and introduction to the concepts and methods, with the idea in mind that you will be filling in detail to your understanding, and gaining clarity on the elements, as we go over the components one at a time. But in order to provide the overall framework, this holistic immersion comes first.

I hope you'll find that I bring the value of a composer's perspective to the subject, so that the ideas here are not just some fixed abstractions floating in the sky, but part of a dynamic understanding and learning process, undertaken for the practical reason of making something.

M. Zachary Johnson
*New York City, November 2010*

To hear audio examples relating to the content of the book, visit:
www.DancingWithTheMuses.com

For information about online music history and appreciation courses, taught by this author for homeschool students as well as adults, please visit:
www.MusicAtOurHouse.com

To engage the author for appearances as composer, conductor or lecturer—including for talks on this book—please contact:

Brian Horner
Sound Artist Support
www.SoundArtistSupport.com
bhorner@soundartistsupport.com
(615) 364-7656

# 1

## MELODIC SHAPE

In our youth when we are first personally captivated by music, when we have our first meaningful experience of it and our first strong response to it, we become immediately aware of two phenomena: melody and feeling. Emotion is an aspect or consequence of hearing the music, and the essential substance of the music is its melody. These are the two irresistible primaries.

Whatever the complexities or richness of the music we are struck by, and whatever emotion it arouses, its essential substance is a stringing-together of notes, a connection from one to the next and the next to form an overall coherent, memorable pattern.

To begin the study of music at the beginning, therefore, one must study how notes fit together over time. The first, most basic thing to study is the musical *line*.

A line is a succession of pitches that fit together. Its crucial attribute is its shape.

The best way to study line shape is to write short, simple examples using notes of uniform duration. We therefore turn to an old method of writing a "cantus firmus" or "fixed voice" of the sort that can later be used as a substrate to add other lines in harmony around it. But for now we concern ourselves only with the single line alone, to learn to shape it.

In composing a cantus firmus we deliberately abstract away from the element of rhythm to isolate and study how the pitches interconnect. Rhythmic elements can easily be added later, once one is familiar with how tones integrate in simple succession. But to introduce rhythm early on would introduce distracting complications.

The process of composing a cantus firmus should be looked at as both analytical and creative; it is a process of honing a malleable string of notes to bring it into an ideal form, like forming a shape from a mass of soft clay. Make a draft, analyze its strong points and its shortcomings, and revise based on the analysis, and continue in this way until the finished product is a nicely integrated little series of notes.

Here are three good "canti firmi" which illustrate the variety possible:

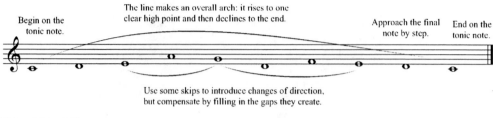

*1.1 A neatly integrated line.*

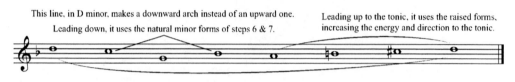

*1.2 Another good line, darker and stretching downward.*

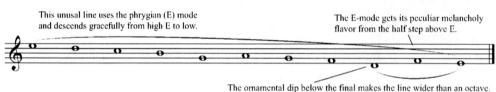

*1.3 A more unusual, but still beautifully coherent line.*

Certain rules will guide us to fulfill the purpose of creating a cantus firmus, which is a unified line on a simple level.

❋ The line should begin and end on the main note of the scale.
❋ For satisfying closure, approach the final note by step.
❋ The line should be 8-12 notes long. Shorter than that is insubstantial, longer becomes blathering.
❋ It should use no repeated notes, since they are rhythmic in nature.
❋ The melody should range within the span of an octave.
❋ Use enough changes of direction, but not too many. A line with so few notes works best if it changes direction about 3 to 5 times.
❋ The line should use only tones that belong to the scale you have chosen. The appropriate scales are those available using the white notes on the piano. The major mode is found beginning on C, the minor mode beginning on A. The modes beginning on D, E, F, and G

are also usable. In the minor mode, the melodic form of the scale (in which scale steps 6 and 7 are raised on the way up) is legitimately diatonic. These modes can be transposed to any starting note, but don't vacillate on the key once you have decided.

The shape of the line should be, in simplest essence, an arch. It should have a clear motion to a single goal note or climax and then away from it. It rises up to a high point, and then settles down to repose. (A downward arch is possible, but less common.)

However, we don't want a simple scale going up and then down again. We want our proto-tune to have unity in variety, not just unity. Therefore we must introduce some leaps and changes of direction. Planning the detailed shape of the line—its pattern of local peaks and valleys within the overall arch shape—is the most creative and imaginative aspect of this simple exercise.

The most important issue for coherence is to learn how to use leaps. Observe the problems that arise with the misuse of leaps.

1.4 *This disjunct array of pitches fails to make a coherent line.*

This "line" follows all the other rules, but is incoherent because of its use of leaps.

Stepwise motion is the basic, simplest type of melodic motion. It is what holds the line together and makes the backbone, the main structure. Steps provide simplicity and intelligibility; leaps introduce complexity and variety. Because they lend interest and richness, leaps are desirable. But because they can make the line incoherent, they must be controlled properly.

❋ Our line should contain 2-3 leaps. Fewer than that is too simple, more than that becomes incoherent.

❋ Avoid multiple leaps in the same direction in immediate succession.

❋ Leaps by dissonant intervals—seventh, tritone or augmented second—are too jarring and harsh to include in a simple exercise of this kind. (Be careful not to prominently outline these intervals using stepwise motion either, for the same reason, to avoid ugliness.)

The main idea is to mix the leaps in as smoothly as possible, to introduce them in such a way that they still integrate into the flow.

A leap opens a gap. It skips across a certain span of pitch and creates a need for the mind to receive the missing notes. A leap is like a question and to fill it in is like answering the question. Therefore fill in the gap created by a leap by using most or all of the missing notes as soon as possible afterward. This creates a cognitive pattern of opening and closing, of spreading apart and uniting together.

The strictest form of the rule for using leaps is: compensate for a leap by an immediate motion by step in the opposite direction.

Study the three good examples above (figures 1.1, 1.2 & 1.3) for their use of leaps.

When you leap to a note, that note is "off by itself" in a certain way. But if the note stands in stepwise relation to another note in the line, even if there are intervening notes, then it makes a connection. When there is no such stepwise connection, the note hangs over in the mind, it lingers as an incomplete element, as a loose end. Be conscious of what notes are hanging over as you create the line and work to tie up the loose ends. If unstable notes are left hanging, the line will not feel complete at the end. On the other hand if the loose ends are tied up, the line settles into completeness and closure in a satisfying way.

To show the stepwise note connections graphically, we can use extended beams. The beams here do not show rhythm, but cognitive connection. Only those notes that relate to one another by a stepwise relationship are beamed together. This enables us to see what the line components are and how they integrate (or don't). We apply this method to the first good line above (in C major, figure 1.1), and to the example above with the misuse of leaps (figure 1.4). Comparing the two in this way, we can see clearly why one line holds together while the other flies to pieces.

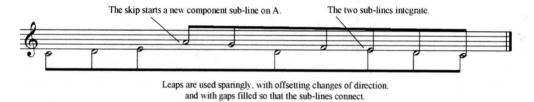

1.5 *Beams show the tightly interconnected nature of this line.*

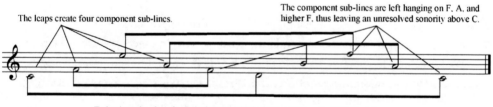

1.6 *Beams show the broken bits of connection in this poorly integrated bunch of notes.*

In the first example, the leap to A creates a new component sub-line, and the two line components proceed independently until they fuse by stepwise connection for the last three notes; this progression represents unity in variety. The second example opens a profusion of loose ends which are not tied up; this incoherent array represents variety without unity.

A line created using this method is a microcosm of larger principles of musical organization. It helps us understand musical coherence on a basic level.

The process of crafting these little lines is also a way of habituating good creative method. It develops auditory discrimination as well as analytical thinking about how music holds together.

Later we will use these lines as the basis for further musical study. The line will become a "fixed voice" and we will write other, new lines around it, introducing complexities step by step.

## ARISTOXENUS

The basic form of music throughout history has been the single melody, the *monophonic* or "one-voiced" style. We can be sure that in tribal life singing was often accompanied by percussive sounds such as hand claps or beats of a drum. Ancient written reports describe a practice of singing one version of a melody while simultaneously playing an ornamented version of the same tune on an instrument, which practice we call *heterophonic* or characterized by "diverse voices." But to whatever extent primitive man was able to use more than one note sounding at once, we are in the dark about it.

It was only late in history that men began to experiment with combining lines at the same time in the form of *polyphony* or "many-voices." (At least, it was only then that men became systematic about it and left a lasting record of it.) Initial, basic experiments were made and notated in Europe in the 9th century. A continuous gradual development of the art began toward the end of the 12th century, and polyphonic art came to its apex and full flowering during the Renaissance of the 15th-16th centuries.

It was very late indeed, after 1600, that the pattern of melody with harmonic accompaniment came definitely into being, and then only among a very small portion of the world's population in Western Europe. This style of music is called *homophonic* or "same-voiced" meaning that multiple voices move together in the form of changes of chord.

But essentially, by sheer percentage of time and number of people, nearly all of the world's music has been single-melody or just the slightest embellishment of it.

Yet few thinkers have paid much attention to melodic connections. Almost no one has treated melodic connection as the primary, central phenomenon of music. By comparison in the West a massive amount of attention has been paid, and a massive amount of theory formulated, to chords and their use—as in the academic tradition extending from Rameau's work in the 18th century (which we will learn about later on).

Let us therefore acquaint ourselves with what has been learned on the topic of melodic shape and the connections of notes over time.

The active-minded, rational, secular, conceptual culture of the ancient world, Greece, asked the question: What kind of note succession holds together, and what kind does not? What is a sequence that integrates into an emotionally powerful and memorable line—a melody?

In Greek thought we see the birth of the concept of melodic-perceptual integration in the concept "harmoniai." It is the root of our modern word "harmony" but for the Greeks it did not mean a fitting together of simultaneous notes, but of successive ones.

The most important treatment of the topic was in the work of Aristoxenus, a Greek musician-philosopher and a student of Aristotle who flourished around the year 335 BC. He wrote the definitive summary of the musical system and ideas of the golden age of classical Greece.

Aristoxenus attributed central importance to the subject of melodic coherence.

The standard translation of the title of his treatise *Armonika stoicheia* is "Elements of Harmony" because of the linguistic connection between the Greek and English words. But because of the difference in meaning of the Greek "Harmonia" (or *Armonika*) and the modern English "Harmony," the title would be more accurately and meaningfully translated "Elements of Melody."

In the preface of this treatise Aristoxenus observes that even the Greeks had very little theory on the subject for him to summarize and compile. Rather, he was forging new territory. He himself stresses that he provides only a rough, initial sketch of the issues involved. (But, I would add, that is where knowledge necessarily begins, since later refinements build upon the rough initial concepts.)

He defines the question of "whether there is a fixed principle that determines the synthesis of any given interval with any other, and under what circumstances scales do and do not arise from the syntheses."

"The subject of our study is the question: in melody of every kind what are the natural laws according to which the voice in ascending or descending places the intervals? For we hold that the voice follows a natural law in its motion, and does not place the intervals at random."

"There is a marvelous orderliness," he writes, "in the constitution of melody." "Of all the objects to which the five senses apply not one other is characterized by an orderliness so extensive and so perfect."

There is an analogy between speech and singing in that there is "a kind of melody in speech which depends upon the accents of words, as the voice in speaking rises and sinks by a natural law."

Nevertheless the two are different in kind. In ordinary speech, the voice moves with continually varying pitch, whereas in singing the voice sustains one point of pitch, one note, and moves by interval from one note to another.

"Harmoniai"—the synthetic connection of notes over time—requires more than a mere succession of notes. It requires not just any notes following one another, but a collocation or sequential linking according to a definite principle or law. Aristoxenus makes a strong distinction between a series of notes which fit together, versus a "faulty melody"—one whose notes fail to fit together, one whose notes fail to accord with the laws of "harmoniai" or melodic coherence.

"Though melody which accords with the laws of harmony [harmoniai] admits of many variations in collocating the intervals, there is yet one invariable attribute that can be predicated of every such melody, of so great importance that with its removal the [coherence of the line] disappears."

The key element of this is the way in which melody utilizes the *simple* intervals—by which he means the elementary perfect consonances.

Aristoxenus speaks of concords and discords, and as with all musical concepts he regards these as qualities of notes separated by a certain *melodic* distance. Concords, such as the fourth, are the basic structural elements of the musical scale; discords (such as the half-step) are secondary and coherence depends less on them. (The perfect intervals of the fourth and fifth, we shall see, are the basis of the scale system.)

He denounces the policy some had practiced, of attempting to divide the pitch spectrum into a series of equal intervals, using the smallest discriminable pitch relation as the basic unit. Such an approach is mere deduction based on an arbitrary assumption.

Rather, Aristoxenus asserts that the notes of the scale must be judged by hearing. "Our method rests in the last resort on an appeal to the two faculties of hearing and intellect. By the former we judge the magnitudes of the intervals, by the latter we contemplate the functions of the notes. We must therefore accustom ourselves to an accurate discrimination of particulars."

The message is: Don't just make up ideas spontaneously, *listen* and conceptualize what you hear.

Scales are not built using the smallest discriminable interval. They are not built using a series of equal intervals of any size. Nor is there an "a priori" rule that they should be unequal. One must judge by ear.

*"The apprehension of a melody consists in noting with both ear and intellect every distinction as it arises in the successive sounds—successive, for melody, like all branches of music, consists in a successive production. For the apprehension of music depends on these two faculties, sense-perception and memory; for we must perceive the sound that is present, and remember that which is past. In no other way can we follow the phenomena of music."*

In rejecting floating abstraction and arbitrary deduction in favor of attending to the sensible world and deriving knowledge from observation, Aristoxenus was a true and great proponent of the worldview of his teacher Aristotle.

The Greek philosophical perspective was rational, not subjectivist or relativist. Aristoxenus's insistence that we rely on hearing and intellect does not mean that any person can say anything he wishes about what his ear desires; it means that there is a scale of notes which is natural to human musical perception, a structure which is inherent in human music, and one must be sensitive to it. This natural structure allows for some variation and variety, but only within certain limits.

Aristoxenus proceeds to the proper construction of the musical scale, which is the basis of melody. The main principle is that the consonances form the structure of the scale, and the other notes are derived from, or in relation to, them.

*"Our next duty will be to determine the first and most indispensable condition of the melodious collocation of intervals. Whatever be the genus, from whatever note one starts, if the melody moves in continuous progression either upwards or downwards, the fourth note in order from any note must form with it the concord of the Fourth, or the fifth note in order from it the concord of the Fifth. Any note that answers neither of these tests must be regarded as out of tune in relation to those notes with which it fails to form the above-mentioned concords. It must be observed, however, that the above rule is not all-sufficient for the melodious construction of scales from intervals. It is quite possible that the notes of a scale might form the above-mentioned concords with one another, and yet that the scale might be unmelodiously constructed. But if this condition be not fulfilled, all else is useless. Let us assume this then as a fundamental principle, the violation of which is destructive of harmony [harmoniai, in the sense of melodic integrity]."*

We will learn the details of the Greek scale system later on. For now, we must emphasize the beginning in Western thought of the idea of melodic synthesis. It's an easy concept to take for granted today, but we should not if we want to understand the subject from the ground up.

In a subject that in the entire history of musical thought is totally unique to Aristoxenus, he addresses the issue of "continuity and consecution" of the notes of melody.

*"Continuity in melody seems in its nature to correspond to that continuity in speech which is observable in the collocation of the letters. ['For it is not every collocation but only certain collocations of any given letters that will produce a syllable.'] In speaking, the voice by a natural law places one letter first in each syllable, another second, another third, another fourth, and so on. This is done in no random order: rather, the growth of the whole from the parts follows a natural law. Similarly in singing, the voice seems to arrange its intervals and notes on a principle of continuity, observing a natural law of collocation, and not placing any interval at random after any other, whether equal or unequal."*

The idea of synthesis or coherence of line is the broad new basic concept that enabled the further development of music.

## FURTHER DEVELOPMENTS ON MELODIC SYNTHESIS

Three great innovators followed Arixtoxenus in advancing our knowledge of melodic shape and pitch connections. Let us summarize briefly for the sake of preliminary overview.

*Aristoxenus* of Ancient Greece founded the initial concept of "continuity and consecution" of melody, giving a systematic exploration of the concept of "harmoniai" or the fitting together of notes in series, and laid out the Greek scale system, which would come to be passed on to the Western World.

*Guido d'Arezzo*, an Italian monk of the 11th century, made important advances in the understanding of the musical scale, developing musical notation using a staff of horizontal lines, as well as a system of solfege syllables giving mnemonics for the notes of the scale.

*Johann Joseph Fux*, a Viennese composer and music teacher of the Enlightenment, codified the principles of polyphony—of combining lines in a musical fabric; he addressed the issue of line shape and created a step-by-step method for teaching the principles of polyphonic composition.

*Heinrich Schenker*, a Viennese pianist, teacher and theorist of the Romantic period, formulated a revolutionary new theory of the cognitive connections that the mind makes among notes sounding over time, and a method for notating these connections using an adaptation of music notation. His work was a culmination of man's understanding of linear synthesis.

These are the milestones in the subject of melodic shape and linear connection. We have seen some of the content already—the principles of the early part of this chapter draw upon the work of all four of these thinkers. We will discuss each further in due course.

Advances in neural science had relevance for music as well. These began most of all with the work of Charles Scott Sherrington, who founded the basis of our current understanding of the nervous system. His 1906 book *The Integrative Action of the Nervous system* was revolutionary. As David Levine wrote in a centennial article in the Journal of Neurological Sciences, "Sherrington's book... provided the conceptual framework for a century of research into the mechanisms of synaptic transmission and the neuronal discharges associated with perception and action."

Sherrington originated the conception that the nervous system is an integrating organ for sense-perception and action. His book's "goal was to explain how the nervous system welds a collection of disparate body parts and organs into a unified individual."

And he founded the concept of the *synapse*, the point of connection between two neurons, which is crucial to understanding the transmission of nerve impulses—and to understanding the fact that multiple neurons can fire into a single receptor neuron, thus integrating signals.

Sherrington himself did not deal with the subject of music, but his work enabled further advances in the science of musical perception.

In the field of philosophy, Ayn Rand pointed out the importance to music of the brain's sensory-integrating action in her 1971 essay "Art & Cognition":

*"We must remember that integration is a cardinal function of man's consciousness on all the levels of his cognitive development. First, his brain brings order into his sensory chaos by integrating sense data into percepts; this integration is performed automatically; it requires effort, but no conscious volition. His next step is the integration of percepts into concepts, as he learns to speak. Thereafter, his cognitive development consists in integrating concepts into wider and ever wider concepts, expanding the range of his mind. This stage is fully volitional and demands an unremitting effort. The automatic processes of sensory integration are completed in his infancy and closed to an adult.*

*"The single exception is the field of music..."*

*"Music is the only phenomenon that permits an adult to experience the process of dealing with pure sense data. Single musical tones are not percepts, but pure sensations; they become percepts only when integrated. Sensations are man's first contact with reality; when integrated into percepts, they are the given, the self-evident, the not-to-be-doubted. Music offers man the singular opportunity to reenact, on the adult level, the primary process of his method of cognition: the automatic integration of sense data into an intelligible, meaningful entity. To a conceptual consciousness, it is a unique form of rest and reward."*

These scientific and philosophical concepts will be part of the background of our discussion, as the framework for understanding the subject.

## TIMELINE OF THE DEVELOPMENT OF MUSIC THEORY

### BC

Greece

| | | |
|---|---|---|
| 500s | Pythagoras | (legendary) discovery of mathematical ratios of intervals |
| 400s | Socrates | thinking method: ask questions |
| ca. 400 | Plato | metaphysics of two worlds, high and low |
| 300s | Aristotle | logic, science, this-worldly philosophy |
| 300s | Aristoxenus | summary of Greek music theory, including scales; melodic synthesis |

### AD

Medieval Period

| | | |
|---|---|---|
| ca. 400 | Augustine | transforms Plato's philosophy into Medieval Christianity |
| ca. 600 | Gregory | organizes Christian church; (allegedly) collected church songs |
| ca. 800 | Charlemagne | unified Europe, temporarily revived learning and culture |
| ca. 900 | Unknown | first known polyphony, notated in *Musica Enchiriadis* (Handbook of Music) |
| ca. 1000 | Guido of Arezzo | staff notation, solfege; centered teaching on the major scale |

Renaissance

| | | |
|---|---|---|
| 1200s | Aquinas | infused Aristotelian philosophy into European thought |
| ca. 1440 | Gutenberg | the printing press |
| 1517 | Luther | Posts 'Ninety-five Theses,' initiating the Protestant Reformation |
| 1558 | Zarlino | *Le istituzioni harmoniche* (Institution of Harmony): rules of counterpoint including dissonance resolution, definition of triad, principle of tonality |
| 1500s | Palestrina | culmination of Renaissance polyphony |
| ca. 1605 | Monteverdi | asserted homophonic style, began practice of basso continuo; opera |

Enlightenment

| | | |
|---|---|---|
| 1687 | Newton | *Mathematical Principles of Natural Science* |
| 1700 | Christofori | invents the piano |
| 1701 | Sauveur | the overtone series |
| 1722 | Rameau | *Treatise on Harmony*, system asserting primacy of chord |
| 1725 | Fux | *Gradus ad Parnassum*, systematic counterpoint method |
| 1760s | Haydn | settles large-scale forms such as Sonata form |
| 1776 | Jefferson | Declaration of Independence |
| 1803 | Beethoven | *Eroica* Symphony – revolutionary new scope of expression |
| 1859 | Darwin | *The Origin of Species* – man's natural origin |
| 1863 | Helmholtz | *On the Sensations of Tone* – summary of science of music |
| 1877 | Edison | invents the phonograph |
| 1906 | Sherrington | *The Integrative Action of the Nervous System*; the synapse |
| 1920s | Schenker | levels of musical structure, concept of organic coherence, method of graphical analysis, re-asserts primacy of line |

Modern Era

| | | |
|---|---|---|
| 1781 | Kant | *Critique of Pure Reason*, system of philosophical Subjectivism |
| 1854 | Hanslick | *On the Musically Beautiful*, musical emotion as illegitimate (Formalism) |
| ca. 1900 | | beginnings of Jazz; principle of Africanism |
| 1912 | Schoenberg | *Pierrot Lunaire*; the principle of atonality; "liberation of the dissonance;" Serialism; principle of nihilism |
| 1913 | Stravinsky | *Rite of Spring* causes a riot in Paris; principle of primitivism |
| 1914-45 | | World Wars |
| 1956 | Chuck Berry | "Roll over Beethoven" – Rock 'n' Roll, lowbrow rebellion |

Information Age

| | | |
|---|---|---|
| 1920s | | use of radio becomes widespread |
| 1971 | Ayn Rand | *Art and Cognition* – neural integration applied to music |
| 1990s | | expansion of the Internet to the general public |

# 2

---

## INTERVAL

Melody does not move like the howling of wind or the wail of an ambulance siren, with continuously fluctuating changes of pitch. It consists of motion from one discrete point of pitch to another, from one tone to the next by a definite distance or interval.

Intervals differ in size, and each size produces in the mind a unique affective or emotional impression. We know musical relationships by measurement (whether implicit or explicit) and by the feeling they arouse in us. In other words, each interval has a cognitive aspect (perception of a certain distance) and an emotional aspect (a certain sense quality).

The beginning of our knowledge of musical distances must have been in prehistory when some intelligent early men sang, and paused to reflect on the distances between notes, noticing differences in the amount of tension they could feel in the voice when singing—differences which related to the audible change in a systematic way. However, feelings of vocal tension are fairly unspecific; without any other means of measurement this could give only the crudest initial idea of low versus high pitch, or notes near or far from one another.

The next crucial development was the formation of the distinction between a *step* and a *skip*. We can step or skip with our feet, and the same kind of movement can be observed in the vocal mechanism in singing notes. A fairly easy and gentle, incremental change of vocal tension makes a musical step. A greater movement of the throat, which has a subtly different feeling because of the activation of more tension in the vocal muscles, is a skip or a leap.

This distinction is important not only to tone production but also to tone perception. As we learned from writing our cantus firmus exercises in chapter 1, the ear makes connections between notes based on stepwise relationships. Two melody notes that are close to one another in pitch, which are at the distance of a step, connect in the mind in a much more complete way than skips. With a stepwise movement, the later note "swallows up" and comes to contain the preceding note; the auditory perception system folds the earlier note into the later one; an integration takes place. With a skip, both tones are retained in the mind, hanging there as separate strands waiting for further connection. Skips are integrated by the brain only by means of later stepwise connections. The distinction between a step and a skip is of great importance to our explicit understanding of musical perception.

The next development is a massive breakthrough, but one that took millennia to fully develop and solidify: the conception and formation of the musical *scale*.

The root of the word "scale" is Middle English *scole*, which meant "bowl." The word is akin to the Old Norse *skel*, which meant "shell." A bowl or shell was the item on each side of a balance, which was used to measure the weights of things. Balances indicated units of weight with an array or scale of marks.

The purpose of any scale is to measure something using a graduated series of uniform increments, thereby enabling man to do something with it. To scale a mountain is to ascend it incrementally, climbing using the necessary human means of one step at a time. The large project, the motion over a great span, is divided up into a series of manageable increments. This is what enables the climber to reach the apex.

The musical scale makes the intervals intelligible by putting them in a structured context or framework, and enables us to create pleasing and expressive melody.

The full understanding and layout of a scale could not be done from the voice alone. One can only get so far using this invisible organ inside the body, whose motions are known by means of fairly unspecific internal feelings.

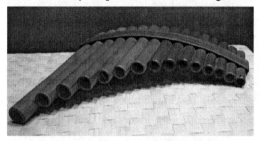

*2.1 The pan flute, like most musical instruments, gives a visual and tactile means of knowing the scale as an ordered series of increments.*

The settled development and conceptualization of the musical scale was possible only with the construction and playing of musical instruments. To make a pan flute, one has to know the proper lengths of the pipes, measure and cut them in the proper proportions, and then bind them together. The completed instrument shows visibly the series of increments from a short pipe to a long one, and one hears the same increments in the changes of pitch from one pipe to the next.

To make a transverse flute—a single tube with fingering holes to change the pitch—one has to know where to drill the holes. The holes must be measured out to the correct distance in order to produce the desired pitches. In playing the completed instrument, one puts the fingers in place and grasps how they stop the holes one by one in a series.

In order to make a plucked stringed instrument such as a lyre, one has to tune the strings in order to obtain the correct pitch. The string tension could be varied and adjusted by ear. But the finished instrument still shows the scalar series in a visual and tactile way as the player plucks one string then the next and the next to sound the notes in an incremental series.

With fingered stringed instruments, such as the precursors to the violin or guitar, there is not only the issue of the tuning of the string, but also (similarly to the transverse flute) the act of placing the fingers down one by one in a row to produce the notes of the scale. And the distance between one finger and the next had to be studied and gotten right in order to produce the correct series of increments, the correct pattern of whole and half steps.

All of these patterns from instrument making and playing confirmed and added to the familiarity with the scale men had from singing. The instruments added objectivity because they provided a visual-tactile perception of the same musical fact as in singing—and because the process included conscious, explicit physical-numerical measurement.

It was the construction and playing of instruments, beginning in ancient prehistory and continuing through high civilization, which enabled men to measure musical distances more precisely and to make finer conceptual distinctions. This in turn enabled an ever-growing understanding and control of the musical elements for expressive purposes.

In order to identify an interval, one simply counted the scale-steps. This, even today, remains our primary method of measuring pitch distance. A motion from one note up to the next in the scale is a second, up another is a third, up another is a fourth, etc. One counts the notes, the steps, not the spaces; the starting note is counted.

Next would have come an awareness that certain notes of the scale could be inflected; certain notes could be sung in a slightly lower version which still had the same place in the scale. For instance, from the first note to the second could be an ordinary wide step or a narrow one. This is the difference between the whole-step (a large or "major" second) and a small one (a small or "minor" second).

What are the notes that admit such a difference? The intervals of a 2nd, 3rd, 6th & 7th can be major or minor. The other notes of the scale (the 4th, 5th & octave) are more fixed and stable; they are not susceptible of smaller and larger sizes in the same way as the others.

It is also readily apparent upon hearing that the lowered forms of the notes, the minor notes, produce a darker emotional impression. The minor notes are more sultry or pained. The major ones are sunnier, brighter, lighter. This is a plainly audible, experiential fact, the explanation for which was discovered later.

Thus the growth of our understanding of music was made possible by the interaction of three elements: auditory perception, singing, and making and playing instruments. These three forms of action mixed together and influenced one another reciprocally, creating an upward spiral of knowledge, a virtuous cycle of learning.

The practices of instrument builders were never romanticized or thought of as historically important. The earliest builders worked informally by trial and error; later ones were tradesmen who passed on their knowledge to their apprentices; their knowledge was not written down in any form that has survived. Intellectuals, meanwhile, dismissed or ignored the practical knowledge of instrument makers as prosaic.

Instead, what captured the world's imagination and propagated for centuries right up to the present day, was the dramatic legend of a Greek thinker who was said to have stumbled upon the nature of musical intervals and had a sort of philosophical epiphany. The story does indeed teach valuable basic facts—the same facts instrument makers had known and used for thousands of years.

## PYTHAGORAS

Pythagoras, a Greek mathematician/philosopher born around 570 BC, founded a school of thought whose teachings bear his name. Among the school's doctrines is the familiar Pythagorean theorem, a formula interrelating the lengths of the sides of a right triangle.

According to this school, Pythagoras discovered the underlying mathematics of music when he overheard a blacksmith hammering metal, and recognized the musical intervals. This tale became a standard way of teaching intervals.

Around 200 AD, Nichomachus of Gerasa (a city in modern Jordan) wrote a book about how to tune strings to get musical notes, titled simply *Manual of Harmonics*. This is the earliest surviving source of the story.

*"One day [Pythagoras] was deep in thought and seriously considering whether it could be possible to devise some kind of instrumental aid for the ears which would be firm and unerring, such as vision obtains through the compass and the rule... or touch obtains with the balance-beam or the system of measures. While thus engaged, he walked by a [black]smith and... heard the hammers beating out iron on the anvil and giving off in combination sounds which were most harmonious with one another, except for one combination. He recognized in these sounds the consonance of the octave, the fifth and the fourth. But he perceived that the interval between the fourth and the fifth [the interval of a second or whole step] was dissonant.... Elated, therefore, since it was as if his purpose was being divinely accomplished, he ran into the smith and found by various experiments that the difference of sound arose from the weight of the hammers, but not from the force of the blows, nor from the shapes of the hammers, nor from the alteration of the iron being forged. After carefully examining the weights of the hammers and their impacts, which were identical, he went home.*

*"He planted a single stake diagonally in the wall in order that no difference might arise from this procedure or, in short, that no variation might be detected from the use of several stakes, each with its own peculiar properties. From this stake he suspended four strings of the same material and made of an equal number of strands, equal in thickness and of equal torsion [twisting]. He then attached a weight to the bottom of each string, having suspended each by each in succession. When he arranged that the lengths of the strings should be exactly equal, he alternately struck two strings simultaneously and found the aforementioned consonances, a different consonance being produced by a different pair of strings.*

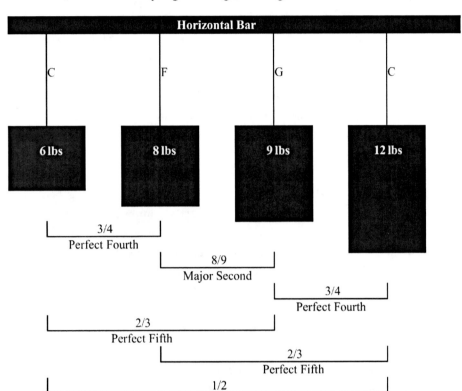

Pythagoras' Weighted Strings

According to legend, Pythagoras hung four identical strings from a horizontal bar;
he controlled the tension of each by attaching a different amount of weight.
When he plucked the strings, they sounded the perfect consonances.
He thereby showed the ratios physically present among the bodies making the sounds.

*2.2 Pythagoras experiments with weighted strings*

*"And having inured his hand and his hearing to the suspended weights and having established on their basis that ratio of their relations, he ingeniously transferred the bond, which fastened all the strings, from the diagonal stake to the bridge of the instrument which he called chordotonon or string-stretcher, and he transferred the amount of tension on the strings analogous to the weights, to the commensurate turning of the tuning pegs set in the upper part of the instrument. Using this as a standard and as it were an infallible pointer, he extended the test henceforward to various instruments, namely, to the percussion on plates, to auloi [an ancient double oboe] and panpipes, to monochords and triangular harps, and the like. And in all of these he found consistent and unchanging, the determination by number."* (Translation by Flora R. Levin)

Nichomachus wrote this about 600 years after Pythagoras lived. His account can hardly be relied upon for historical accuracy. In fact, there are important scientific errors: hammers of the varying weights described do not sound the intervals he refers to, nor do weighted strings operate in the way described; rather, divisions of the *length* of a string follow the proportions he outlined, while changes in tension follow the *square* of those ratios. (For more on this, see the discussion of the overtone series in chapter 9.) Nevertheless, even if the physical description is off, the legend does associate the correct numerical ratios with the given intervals.

A blacksmith shop could not have been the source of inspiration, and the initial experiments of discovery could not have been exactly what was described—these are merely dramatic touches of storytelling.

Rather, the story is designed to teach the numerical relationships (which do hold between the lengths of a divided string) in clear, simple terms. For instance, the weights of the hammers are contrived to use small round numbers for teaching purposes. This was not a matter of historical fact or of "divine guidance." The same ratios could be illustrated using larger numbers or fractions, but the simple ones were used from the outset, since otherwise the larger numbers would have to be reduced. Omitting the extra step gets to the pith of the lesson right away.

The story of Pythagoras is important not as a literal historical report, but for its overall meaning: the discovery that physically measurable principles of ratio operate in music; *music is mathematical.*

To some extent this observation formed a base for later science about music, but Pythagoras's discovery was also taken in another intellectual direction: it was not looked upon as a purely scientific matter describing natural facts. Rather, it became part of an overall philosophy which centered around a mystical worship of number as the essence of the universe.

The identification of numerically measurable ratios in the physical basis of music is crucial and true—even the actual ratios are correct, at least with regard to string lengths. But our identification of those facts, using numbers, takes place in the mind. The numerical ideas are derived from reality, but they are a human method of interrelating facts. Pythagoras started a strange philosophical error: he began treating the idea of number as something that existed intrinsically in the world, as though the idea were an invisible physical substance inhering in the things outside us in the world. Thus one sees in this viewpoint both an element of truth—facts in reality are measurable and laws can be expressed numerically—but confused in supernatural speculation.

This flight of fantasy came to have great influence in Western thought. It was fairly pervasive in Greek culture, and was taken up especially by Plato, who held that a world of Forms exists in a higher dimension where perfect Ideas are real objects. This was in contrast to the world we perceive around us which Plato thought was a degraded, imperfect reflection of that superior reality. Such was the basic pattern of religious metaphysics. This philosophy would come to have important consequences in music.

## CONSONANCE, DISSONANCE, & OTHER INTERVAL QUALITIES

Each of the musical intervals produces a unique sensory impression. The most obvious and basic distinction is between those intervals that blend versus those that clash.

The ancients spoke of this fact: Pythagoras was said to have observed that the octave (2:1), the fifth (3:2) and the fourth (4:3) were consonant, but that the major second (9:8) was an exception, that it was unlike the others. Thus inherent in even this early piece of lore is a distinction between those pairs of notes which blend versus those that clash. And more than that: there is a difference in mathematical complexity between the consonances and a dissonance.

Aristoxenus, too, used concepts of consonance and dissonance as integral to his summary of Greek music theory. The ancient Babylonians, we know from cuneiform tablets, used for their tuning method the difference between an "unclear" interval and a "clear" one. In the Hindu tradition, there is a concept of a note alien to the operative scale for a particular raag—such a note is "vivadi," meaning foreign and "cutting against the grain."

During the dark centuries after the submersion of the ancient Greek culture, men used intervals and their qualities, but left no record of being intellectually aware of them or consciously in control of them. The Roman Empire was not particularly interested in music, and the Dark Ages were, well, dark.

Around the year 800, Emperor Charlemagne unified Europe and, with his reforms of education and religion, ushered in a mini-Renaissance. During this period of greater literacy, greater artistic activity, and generally greater mental activeness, men began to experiment with simultaneous note combinations and to place their discoveries in writing.

In the process, they saw the necessity of a basic distinction between sonorities that blend versus others that clash. Notes sounding at once at the distance of a perfect fifth (for instance) blend together into a clear sound. In contrast, notes at the interval of a second or a diminished fifth clash against one another in a tense sound.

The notes of a fifth merge into a smooth sonority and create in the mind a stable, settled, and complete sensory impression. The brain is able to unify the tones and we experience the result in the form of an experience of this quality which men named *consonance*. The term comes from "con-" plus "sonare" meaning "to sound with."

Observe that two adjacent notes such as the step from C to D—the very relation that makes melodic connection possible—clash when the notes sound at once. The brain is, in effect, trying to fuse the notes into one sound, but is unable to do it because they both persist in sounding, which is a sort of auditory contradiction. The notes of a second would become united in melodic progression, but sounded as a simultaneity they create a disruptive, buzzingly nervous, unresolved sensation in the mind. The brain works to complete its processing of the sensations, but it fails, and we experience the result in the form of this sound-experience which men named *dissonance*. The term comes from "dis-" plus "sonare" meaning "to sound against."

Consonance is a sensory union of elements. Dissonance, outside of a musical context that makes sense of it, is a broken or fractured array of sense elements. Dissonances are very valuable and expressive in music when they are used in a way that integrates in context. We will learn about that in our study of counterpoint.

The identification of the sensory qualities of intervals did not end with the broad distinction between consonance and dissonance.

Among the consonances, men became conceptually aware of the difference between some intervals which blend completely and totally, as contrasted with others which also blend but not so fully. They formed the distinction between *perfect* and *imperfect* consonances. The perfect intervals—the fourth, fifth and octave—have a very pure, strong, stark sound to them; their notes fuse as completely as possible. The imperfect consonances—the third and sixth—make a richer, more euphonious sound. The perfect consonances are rather cold, while the imperfect ones are warmer and more sensuous.

The idea of larger or smaller versions of certain intervals also developed. There are major and minor 3rds and 6ths, which are consonant, and major and minor 2nds and 7ths, which are dissonant.

The perfect intervals, too, can be inflected in size. Make a fifth smaller and it becomes *diminished*, larger and it becomes *augmented*. All augmented and diminished intervals are dissonant. Most important in this category are the augmented fourth and diminished fifth; these are called the "tritone" which comes from "tri-" meaning three and "tone" in the sense of a whole step. A tritone is the span of three whole steps.

Perfect intervals made larger become augmented; made smaller, diminished. Major intervals made larger become augmented; made smaller, minor and smaller again, diminished.

### Relative Sizes of Interval Quality

|  | Larger ↔ Smaller |
| --- | --- |
| Intervals 4, 5, and 8: | A ↔ P ↔ d |
| Intervals 2, 3, 6 and 7: | A ↔ M ↔ m ↔ d |

Perfect intervals are never major or minor. Major/minor intervals are never perfect. Doubly augmented and doubly diminished intervals are possible, but they almost never make sense in the scale and are rarely used.

A complete interval name has two parts: a quantity and a quality. The quantity is the number of scale-steps, the quality is the particular size within that. From C up to A♭ is a minor 6th—it spans six scale steps but is the smaller size of 6th (compared to C up to A♮). From C up to F♯ is an augmented 4th—it spans four scale steps but is larger than the perfect 4th from C to F.

## ENHARMONIC EQUIVALENCE & INVERSION

Some intervals are equivalent in size. The distance from C up to D♯ is an augmented second; from C up to E♭ is a minor third. But D♯ and E♭ are the same key on the keyboard; outside of any musical context these intervals sound essentially the same; they seem interchangeable. We call such pairs *enharmonic* equivalents. The term comes from "en-" plus "harmonia," meaning "in tune." Enharmonic notes or intervals sound the same but are spelled differently.

These differences in spelling arise from different musical functions and therefore different mental impressions *in context*. The intervals C up to D♯ and C up to E♭ differ musically and psychologically because the underlying scale differs. C to D♯ occurs in the E harmonic minor scale. The interval is dissonant, giving an unsettled feeling and creating tension demanding resolution. Augmented intervals resolve outward: the D♯ would resolve up and press the C to move downward. On the other hand, E♭ is stable in relation to C and doesn't create such nervous tension; in the C minor scale this interval would be quite restful. This is why we have different spellings and different interval names even though in an absolute sense the intervals are equivalent.

Furthermore, we should not take for granted the equal temperament method of tuning used for keyboard instruments, which makes compromises so that the same keys can play notes in multiple scales. When instruments of non-fixed, adaptable intonation play or when people sing, the enharmonic versions of intervals are close but not identical. The natural intonation of the intervals C to D♯ and C to E♭ would not be exactly the same, but it is still so close that it is appropriate to consider them contextually different versions of the same pitch distance.

Interval sizes are best understood within the context of a particular scale, because it provides the measuring framework. It is the scale which makes C up to G♯ a 5th, but C up to A♭ a 6th, despite those intervals looking the same on the keyboard. There are five note names and five scale steps from C up to G, but six up to A. And psychologically, because of the framework provided by the scale, enharmonic equivalents create a very different sense of span. An augmented sixth feels expansive and large; a minor seventh feels tense and its notes pull inward toward one another. Thus two intervals which are enharmonically equivalent still create a very different mental effect because of their differing position and function in the scale.

There is another sense in which intervals can be equivalent: when they have the same notes, but relate by *inversion*. Just as to invert a fraction is to flip the numerator and denominator, to invert an interval is to flip which note is lower and which is higher. To invert an interval, move the lower note by octave so it is above, or move the upper note by octave so it is below. The inversion of E over C is C over E.

**Interval Inversion by Quantity**

$$1 \leftrightarrow 8$$
$$2 \leftrightarrow 7$$
$$3 \leftrightarrow 6$$
$$4 \leftrightarrow 5$$

It is a basic axiom of music that notes related by octave are equivalent. Identical pitches, sounding in unison, form a pitch ratio of 1:1. The next closest relationship is the octave, ratio 2:1. Pitches separated by an octave differ in register or range only, they are the same note and have the same function in the scale. This is why we give them the same letter name. Interval inversion is a result of octave equivalence.

The numbers of an interval and its inversion add up to 9. The inversion of a 5th is a 4th, of a 6th a 3rd, and so on.

They add up to 9, not 8, because although we have moved a note by 8 steps, one of the notes gets counted twice.

Interval Inversion by Quality

$M \leftrightarrow m$

$A \leftrightarrow d$

$P \leftrightarrow P$

There is a pattern to the qualities too: Perfect inverts to perfect. Major inverts to minor and vice versa. Augmented inverts to diminished and vice versa.

For example: C up to F is a perfect 4th; its inversion is F up to C, a perfect 5th. C up to D is a major 2nd; its inversion is from D up to C, a minor 7th. C up to G# is an augmented 5th; its inversion is G# up to C, a diminished 4th.

## DUELING WORLDVIEWS: "HARMONY OF THE SPHERES" VS. HUMANISTIC SCIENCE

Two opposite approaches to the theory of music originated in Greece. One school, flowing from Pythagorean number mysticism, spurned listening and studied ratios in and of themselves. The other school, expressing Aristoxenus's insistence that the ear is the judge of things musical, made concepts and rules follow from what we hear, not from self-contained mathematical deductions. The Pythagoreans cared about theory in a purely abstract way. Aristoxenus regarded theory as derivative from what we hear, and as a means to singing, playing, and enjoying music.

Wilhelm Windelband wrote in his *History of Philosophy*:

*"[The Pythagoreans'] theoretical investigations concerning music taught them that harmony was based upon simple numerical relations of the length of the strings... and their knowledge of astronomy, which was far advanced, led them to the view that the harmony prevailing in the motions in the heavenly bodies had, like the harmony in music, its ground in an order, in accordance with which the various spheres of the universe moved about a common centre at intervals fixed by numbers.... [The numbers are] eternal, without beginning, imperishable, unchangeable, and even immovable... Thus, then, the Pythagoreans found the abiding essence of the world in the mathematical relations, and in particular in numbers.... they regarded the heaven of the stars, on account of the sublime uniformity of its motions, as the realm of perfection; the world 'beneath the moon,' on the contrary... they regarded as that of imperfection."*

So we see the beginnings here in Western thought of the idea that a realm of perfect abstractions is separate from, and superior to, the shifting lower world of brute physical objects.

Henry Stewart Macran, in the introduction to his translation of Aristoxenus's "Elements of Harmony," elaborated on these contrasting approaches:

*"So busy were the Pythagoreans in establishing the mere physical and mathematical antecedents of sounds in general, that they never saw that the essence of musical sounds lies in their dynamical relation to one another. Thus they missed the true formal notion of music, which is ever present to Aristoxenus, that of a system or organic whole of sounds, each member of which is essentially what it does, and in which a sound cannot become a member because merely there is room for it, but only if there is a function which it can discharge.*

*"The conception, then, of a science of music which will accept its materials from the ear, and carry its analysis no further than the ear can follow; and the conception of a system of sound-functions, such and so many as the musical understanding may determine them to be, are the two great contributions of Aristoxenus to the philosophy of Music."*

The roots of these opposite approaches are as deep as you can go, in metaphysics, the study of the fundamental nature of reality.

Recall that Aristoxenus had been a leading pupil of Aristotle, the father of logic, the man who rejected the notion of any dimension of reality beyond this earth. Aristotle asserted that we do and should perceive the world around us, which is the one and only reality. As a consequence, Aristotle held that the good consists, in essence, of thinking about what we observe, and of pursuing values in life on Earth.

2.6 In his "School of Athens," Raphael encapsulated in gestures the contrasting worldviews of Plato and Aristotle.

In contrast, one of the major voices in the Pythagorean line was Plato, who held that a world of perfect Ideas exists in a higher dimension which represents true reality—and that the world around us is merely a shadowy reflection of the superior world, the World of the Forms. As a consequence Plato held that the good life consists of divorcing oneself from the concerns of earthly life in order to contemplate the Forms in heaven.

In his painting "The School of Athens," Raphael embodied these two worldviews: Plato, the older man, points upward; Aristotle, the younger man, spreads his palm down and outward toward the world around him.

Developments in the field of music followed the fundamental currents in philosophy. For centuries, the Pythagorean-Platonic view became dominant.

Plato's philosophy includes a doctrine of the Harmony of the Spheres, a theory of the heavens which describes perfect spheres with mathematical relations sounding silently among them in an ethereal music which is inaudible but which represents a supernatural principle of perfect order. (No, this does not make sense.)

The most philosophically crucial passage about music is from a discussion of Cosmic Harmony in the *Republic*. Plato gives a long and very detailed description of what he presents as the structure of the universe. He says there is a "line of light, straight as a column, extending right through the whole heaven and through the earth, in colour resembling the rainbow, only brighter and purer.... this light is the belt of heaven, and holds together the circle of the universe." There is a Spindle around which concentric spheres rotate. He tells us there are eight such spheres, he tells us their proportions and their color and brightness.

*"The spindle turns on the knees of Necessity; and on the upper surface of each circle is a siren, who goes round with them, humming a single tone or note. The eight together form one harmony; and round about, at equal intervals, there is another band, three in number, each sitting upon her throne; these are the Fates... who accompany with their voices the harmony of the sirens."*

The first thing to say about this is that Plato simply made it up, it is completely arbitrary and it makes no sense. But the importance of this description of the alleged structure of the universe is not in its narrow details. It did not take men long to forget the details of Plato's Cosmic Harmony, but they have always retained the essence. The essential is: there is a realm that is higher than this earth and above you—a realm of gleaming, perfect order, a realm of clean mathematical precision, a realm with coordinated, smoothly functioning interlocking parts in a grand metaphysical structure, a realm with voices singing notes that do not clash but blend together into beautiful harmony. That is the glorious superior dimension.

Plato despised this earth and the pursuit of pleasure as a corrupt indulgence. From *Protagoras*:

*"Second-rate and commonplace people, being too uneducated to entertain themselves as they drink by using their own voices and conversational resources, put up the price of female musicians, paying well for the hire of an extraneous voice—that of the pipe—and find their entertainment in its warblings. But where the drinkers are men of worth and culture, you will find no girls piping or dancing or harping. They are quite capable of enjoying their own company without such frivolous nonsense, using their own voices in sober discussion and each taking his turn to speak or listen— even if the drinking is really heavy."*

So Plato is in favor of the intellect, of order, of sobriety, and he looks down on people for their pleasure pursuits and for being mindless and uneducated, and he is opposed to the sensual, the physically pleasurable.

So what is the ideal for music that falls out of this philosophical viewpoint? Well, the message is: no pleasure, certainly no dancing, stay away from anything that appeals to a wide public, and instead orient yourself toward the superior dimension of mathematical perfection, harmonious order and beauty, and challenge the cognitive faculty to grasp the highest metaphysical forms and structures.

After the fall of the Greek world and of the Roman Empire it was the Pythagorean-Platonic school of thought that won out. Medieval thinkers continued in this tradition. For instance, Boethius, the famous theorist who transmitted Greek music theory to the Middle Ages, was an exponent of Plato's ideas. In his treatise on music, he gave great prominence to Plato's conception of the Harmony of the Spheres.

The Aristotelian approach embodied in the the work of such thinkers as Aristoxenus did not have much continuation until the Renaissance. Guido d'Arezzo, we shall see, was a rare thinker and artist who embodied the Aristotelian-Aristoxenian approach. He advanced our knowledge of the scale, created solfege and our modern form of musical notation.

But with regard to measurements of musical ratios which were both accurate and connected to human hearing, mankind had to wait for the 16th century scientific revolution.

In order for man to learn more about the science of music, he had to break from the worship of mystical floating abstractions and refocus on this world. He had to sweep aside rationalistic deductions detached from reality, and study the physical world. He had to drop the methods of the Pythagoreans and of Plato, and to rediscover the method of Aristotle.

The revival of the Aristotelian approach was the Renaissance. A central part of the revolution in thought was the scientific revolution, embodied in the work of such men as Galileo and Newton. They practiced a method of thinking which studied the real world and made measurements of it, and which derived laws of nature from systematically gathered evidence.

Using these new methods, after the long night of the Dark Ages, scientists were able to pick up where Pythagoras left off, but without floating off into the confusion of a mystical dimension. Sound was one of the things scientists began to investigate. And the body of scientific knowledge of sound came to a culmination in the work of a great German scientist of the 19th century—a scientist who is a preeminent example of Aristotle's kind of robust, blazingly clear, heroic, this-worldly rationality.

## HELMHOLTZ

In order to fully appreciate Helmholtz's synthesis and expansion of the science of music, we shall do well to understand some things about the man and how his mind worked. This question of thinking method and moral character lies behind the details of his discoveries, and helps us understand them in a more organic way.

Hermann von Helmholtz, born in 1821 in Potsdam, stated in an autobiographical essay that from childhood, and throughout life, he was troubled with a terrible memory for disconnected facts:

*"this showed itself in the difficulty which I still distinctly remember of distinguishing between right and left; later on, when I got to languages in my school-work, it was harder for me to learn the vocabularies, grammatical irregularities and idiomatical expressions, than for the others. History, in particular, as it was taught in those days, was quite beyond me. It was a real torture to learn prose extracts by heart. This defect has of course increased, and is a nuisance in my old age. I found no difficulty in learning the poems of the great masters, but the more laboured verses of second-rate poets were far less easy."*

Helmholtz's distinction lies not in this deficiency, but in his means of overcoming it. He figured out and practiced a fundamental solution, developing in his mind a tremendous capacity for *integration*—for bringing information together, for understanding the connections and relationships among facts. What Helmholtz lacked in the ability to memorize, he more than made up for in his ability to understand.

As his obituary stated, "In the study of science, 'the laws of phenomena' afforded the connecting link which his memory needed."

Helmholtz did not look upon the different fields of knowledge as separate, unrelated spheres; he regarded them as merely different facets of his basic interest: man and the world. And therefore his mind ranged freely through the disciplines, connecting and relating their contents.

He attended medical school, preparing to become a physician. He gained a thorough knowledge of the anatomy of living things, most especially human anatomy. This was practical knowledge, gained with a view toward what could be done with it to better man's life. He learned to perform surgery and to treat maladies.

He studied not only the static structure of the body, but its patterns of living action, its function and ways of moving. He did experiments on frogs to measure the speed of nerve impulses. He measured muscle contractions—the heat produced and even the frequency of sound emitted. He was especially interested in those points of connection between man and the outside world: the senses. He studied and measured light and the structure of the eye; he studied colorblindness.

His interests always pressed wider than medicine as well. He was especially interested in experimental and mathematical physics. Helmholtz was a brilliant mathematician, and like his knowledge of medicine, his mathematical approach was practically oriented. He did not look at numbers the way Pythagoras did, as ethereal properties imbued in the outside world. He looked at them as a human tool. He wanted to use math in the simplest, clearest way possible to capture important facts about the world. He was not concerned with theories of another dimension—only with rational knowledge of the real world around him.

Helmholtz is particularly known for discovering the law of conservation of energy. This law, which holds that the total amount of energy in an isolated system remains constant regardless of changes in forms of energy, is often thought of primarily in terms of the mechanics of inanimate matter. But Helmholtz got interested in the question from his study of living things. He knew that people tended to think of life as a sort of mysterious or supernatural extra force animating living things. But Helmholtz was secular, not religious, and was inclined to look at living things as wholly natural. He examined the various forms of energy both in living things and in mechanical systems, and proved mathematically that the sum remains constant. There is no divine energy input. Living things operate by means of the same natural forces and laws as the rest of the material world.

When Helmholtz died in 1894, an obituary in the *Proceedings of the Royal Society of London* stated: "It has been said that as each of seven cities contended for Homer, so seven sciences: mathematics, physics, chemistry, physiology, medicine, philosophy, and aesthetics claimed Helmholtz for their own, and it is interesting to note how early he took the comprehensive view of science."

Helmholtz also took an integrated view of art and science. He did not think in terms of a split between art, as emotional, and science, as rational. In all areas he was interested in both thinking and values. His mind ranged without hitch or reservation—without even so much as a question mark about whether it was normal—through the methods of experiment and measurement in the physical sciences, and through the sensitivities and philosophical meaning of art.

Biographer Leo Koenigsberger wrote that Helmholtz could repeat whole "books of the Odyssey, a considerable number of the odes of Horace, and large stores of German poetry." Helmholtz visited picture galleries to see the new paintings of the day, and wrote of his responses in his letters to his friends.

Helmholtz's approach reflects no trace of the disastrous split between the sciences and the humanities. He did not regard art and science as set against one another. He did not regard art as "subjective" and science as "objective." He regarded both the physical world and the expressions of man's consciousness as equally intelligible, equally real, equally legitimate, knowable, valuable and interesting. Both art and physics, he felt, were worthy of study and attention. He did not look at art as the province of a special elite who had access to exclusive insights; he regarded it as a part of life and a part of the world which could be understood by anyone just as the physical world could.

He had no inkling of the notion that the "cold, calculating" hand of reason would destroy expression and artistry. He looked at scientific study and reasoning as something that went hand-in-hand with art; he regarded the two as part of the same one world, as part of the same *secular* sphere that interested him. And he saw no conflict between science and artistic feeling. Quite the opposite, in fact: the means to artistic expression, he held, was *knowledge*. Reason did not kill expression, it served and enhanced it.

"He was filled with passionate enthusiasm for music and poetry, as well as for art and science." (Koenigsberger)

Helmholtz loved music. He played the piano proficiently. During his school days he wrote to his parents: "Any spare time I have during the day is devoted to music, and so far, even on the worst days, I have put in about an hour, and more on Friday, Saturday and Sunday. By myself I play sonatas of Mozart and Beethoven, and often with my chum the new things he gets hold of, which we run through at sight. In the evenings I have been reading Goethe and Byron, which K. borrowed for me, and sometimes for a change the integral calculus." How do you like that for a man of both art and science!

At the time of his work on the theory of the conservation of energy, he wrote a letter to his future wife about a concert he had attended: Beethoven's *Coriolanus* overture "is a jewel—so short, so convincing, so decided, and proud amid a host of restless and entangled motifs, while it dies off so sadly in melancholy strains… an unsurpassed masterpiece."

Helmholtz's mind was extremely careful and impeccably methodical. He took a holistic view of things. His was an active mind eager to understand the world in conceptual terms. He had a sweeping knowledge of the history of music and the source materials from the ancient world, and his writing is clear and eloquent.

No one was more perfectly suited to be the man who summarized, expanded, and systematized our scientific knowledge of music. The definitive tome on the subject, which has never been surpassed, is his treatise integrating facts of sound vibration and the nature of human hearing: *On The Sensations of Tone as a Physiological Basis for the Theory of Music*. It was published in 1863; he was 42 years old.

Helmholtz covered the basic physical facts in scrupulously careful progression giving the experimental and measurement-based proof of his conclusions. Sound is vibration of the air. A vibrating body, such as a string, transmits its quivering to the air around it, which transmits it to the ear drum, which passes it through the tiny bones of the middle ear to the cochlea, where an array of tiny hairs, each tuned to a unique frequency, picks up the vibration and converts it into nerve impulses. We thereby become aware of the sound, and the qualities we hear depend on the physical properties of the vibration.

Helmholtz stressed that there is a basic distinction between musical tones and noises. A tone is a clear, simple sensation—a sound with a definite, constant pitch. A noise, such as the sound of running water or the crumpling of paper, is a jumble of sound. A tone is the elementary type of sound. Noises are more complicated and can be compounded out of tones, as when you strike a bunch of adjacent keys on the piano. Tones have a simple uniformity that noises do not. Physically, a musical tone is a periodic motion whereas a noise is a non-periodic motion.

There are four, and only four, attributes of an individual musical tone: pitch, timbre, duration, and loudness.

Pitch depends on the speed or *frequency* of the vibration. When the vibration is faster, we hear it in the form of higher pitch. When slower, lower. With some forms of sound production we can observe an enlightening fact: at the very slowest frequencies of periodic vibration we sometimes perceive a series of separate, even clicks or taps. This regularity is the basis of rhythm. At a certain speed (around 20 vibrations per second), the cycles of vibration merge in our sound perception to create a new form of sensation, a continuous musical tone. This is the basis of pitch and its connections.

Timbre is the distinctive tone quality of a voice or instrument. It depends on the *form* of the vibration. If a vibrating body is used to trace the vibrating pattern on paper, we see that different timbres trace different shapes. If two tones have the same pitch but different timbres —as when the same note is played on a flute versus a violin—the period of vibration is the same, but the shape of the wave is different.

Duration depends simply on how long the vibrating body remains in motion.

Loudness depends on *amplitude*, the extent or strength of the vibration.

However, the meat, the essential substance of music comes not from the elementary properties of an isolated single tone, but from the *relationships* among tones.

This includes both time relationships (which we will cover later) and pitch relationships.

The siren, Helmholtz tells us, is one of the best instruments for studying the frequency ratios of music. (He was expert at creating and adapting devices to help him study and measure sound.) Here is a simplified diagram of the mechanism.

Using instruments like the siren, Helmholtz made comprehensive measurements of the ratios present among the tones of the various musical intervals, the various forms of the musical scale, and the various types

The rope turns the disc around the axle.

The tube propels a stream of air.

Each of the evenly spaced holes permits a single puff of air to pass through.

*2.7 Helmholtz's Simple Siren*

of chord. He integrated this information to a great extent, dealing with the increasingly complex network of relationships present when we use and combine the elements in musical composition.

\* \* \*

Let us summarize the qualities of the intervals together with Helmholtz's measurements of their frequency ratios.

The audible quality of a pair of notes depends on the ratio between the two frequencies. The frequencies of a *consonance* stand in a ratio made up of the smallest whole numbers, such as 1:2 (the octave) or 2:3 (the fifth), while the frequencies of a *dissonance* stand in a ratio made up of larger numbers, such as 8:9 (the whole step) or 8:15 (the Major seventh). The brain is able to integrate the simple ratio but not the more complicated one—unless, we shall see, it is placed in the proper musical context.

Some consonances are *perfect* in that their tones blend so completely and thoroughly that they produce a *clear, strong, stark* psychological impression. These are the octave (1:2), the fifth (2:3) and the fourth (3:4). Among these, the perfect fourth has a biting quality to it.

Other consonances are *imperfect* in that their tones are not so completely and thoroughly fused, such that they produce a *warm, rich, euphonious* sound. These are the thirds and sixths.

As you would expect, the imperfect consonances have ratios with numbers between those of the dissonances and the perfect consonances. All imperfect consonances are warm and rich, but the major third (4:5) and sixth (3:5) give a *bright and sunny* psychological impression while the minor third (5:6) and sixth (5:8) give a *dark and sultry* one.

Within the category of dissonances, there are two distinguishable qualities. The minor second (15:16) and major seventh (8:15) produce a more *harshly discordant*, more bitingly painful sensation in the mind. Their ratios are the most complex of all. In contrast, the major second (8:9) and the minor seventh (9:16) produce a *still clashing but much mellower and less painful* quality. The tritone (5:7) produces a very unusual, peculiar honking or pinching discord.

Pythagoras and Plato had made these ratios part of a philosophy of number mysticism, and postulated a supernatural dimension of the "Harmony of the Spheres." Scientists like Helmholtz dismissed such floating abstractions, and dealt with the subject by means of a properly secular, systematic, rational-empirical method. Helmholtz's study and summary of pitch relationships affirmed, clarified and fully grounded what had been indicated in the ancient story of Pythagoras and the blacksmith: an important basis of our perception of interval qualities lies in the physical pitch-ratios between the notes. Measurable quantitative relationships underlie and give rise to our affective, qualitative experience.

# 3

---

## SCALE

There is no question more crucial to music than the nature of the musical scale. It is the basis of all aspects of the notes used in music. It is the controlling factor, the starting point, the integrating framework of music, and a crucial determining factor of music's emotional content.

To fully cover the nature of the scale, this chapter proceeds in three stages.

First, we survey the information which teaches us what the diatonic scale is, and why it is timeless and universal. This includes a survey of the anthropological and historical evidence, as well as a survey of the underlying mathematics among the scale notes.

Second, we survey the different forms of scale—the different modes—to see the full variety of true human scales, and to distinguish them from certain scale-like constructs which do not have the same validity. Since the emotion of a piece of music depends in large part on the type of scale it uses, the various forms of scale will be analyzed to identify the unique emotional or psychological impression each produces.

Third, we learn of solfege and other similar systems of assigning symbols or signs to the notes for mnemonic purposes. These systems help us get a handle on the scale, and use it more easily.

(Certain further aspects of the scale will unfold in future chapters, especially the chapter on tonality, since tonality is the musical system which most consistently expresses the nature of the scale.)

### I - ANTHROPOLOGICAL AND HISTORICAL DATA ON THE SCALE

Anatomically modern humans first migrated from Africa into Europe and Asia around 40,000 years ago during the late Stone Age. Before this time Europe had been occupied by the Neanderthals, who did not leave evidence of advanced arts and culture. With the appearance of modern man, there was a quantum leap of culture and a profusion of signs of the start of a much greater scope of cognition. Men created and used stone tools, they buried their dead ceremonially (indicating personal feelings toward unique individuals), they wore personal ornaments, they created cave paintings and sculpture. And they made and played musical instruments.

A number of flutes dating from this time have been discovered in caves in southwest Germany; carbon dating showed them to be between 42,000 and 43,000 years old. A flute made of ivory and a tiny flute made from a bird's wing-bone were discovered in a mountain cave called Geissenkloesterle near the start of the Danube river. The bone flute, along with many others like it in the area, has cut marks on it which the maker used to measure the position of the holes. The spacing of the notes was not random or haphazard, but a result of conscious calculation.

Prehistoric music expert Friedrich Seeberger, one of the authors of reports on these discoveries, fashioned closely modeled replicas of the two flutes. Both of them sounded the notes of the major pentatonic scale, the pattern of the notes C-D-E-G-A-C. This scale is found throughout the world in folk music and primitive traditions. Two examples: African folk songs—familiar to many of us in the form of spirituals passed down from black slaves in America; and Chinese folk music.

About thirty-five millennia later, exactly the same flute technology was employed in China. A set of flutes dating from around 7000 BC was discovered in Jiahu near modern day Shanghai. These flutes share so much in common with the European ones that there is no question they come from the same tradition, despite the geographical separation: They are made from the ulna from a bird's wing; they have the same notches used by the maker to position the holes, and the same shape of the hole (smoothly indented to allow the pads of the fingers to make a perfect seal).

The Chinese flutes are in amazingly good condition and, astonishingly, one of them is still playable. It sounds a diatonic scale, the notes: A-B-C-D-E-F♯-G-A. There is also a tiny extra hole used to correct the pitch of the upper A to make it better in tune, further confirming the fact that the pattern of pitches was not random but a result of measured intention. (See "Prehistoric European and East Asian Flutes" in *Studies in Chinese Language and Culture - Festschrift in Honour of Christoph Harbsmeier*. Also the journal *Nature* vol. 401, 23 September 1999; vol 432, 23 December 2004, and vol. 460, 6 August 2009.)

Indian classical music is one of the oldest continuous traditions in the world. Because it is an oral tradition, handed down by gurus to their students generation after generation, we don't know exactly how old it is. But its roots are documented in some of the ancient writings that made the base of the Hindu culture, the Vedas, which date from the period from 1500 to 500 BC. Hindu culture, with its deferential devotion to tradition, was eminently suited to the maintenance and propagation of a musical system over millennia with minimal alteration, despite the fact that it was transmitted entirely by oral means without the aid of notation.

The *raag* is the form of Indian classical music. It is a set of musical parameters which serve as the basis for an improvised vocal and instrumental performance; a traditional rendition of a raag lasts 40 minutes or so. Different types of raag use different scale patterns to produce their effects. Many of them are standard types of diatonic scale or slight alterations of a diatonic pattern. The Hindu practices are another musical tradition—involving billions of people over millennia—in which the diatonic scale plays a central role.

Tablets with cuneiform writing from ancient Babylon, dated between the 18th century BC and the 3rd/4th, have been deciphered by scholars. Some of them contain language pertaining to music, and one of them is a set of instructions on how to tune the strings of a lyre. The instructions start with a given main note. The other strings are then tuned in relation to it using perfect fourths and fifths—by means of finding the tritone, which is called "unclear," and then correcting it up or down. In the finished scale there is only one "unclear" interval (tritone) left. The instructions thus produce the notes of the diatonic scale exactly as we know it today. (See the work of Anne Kilmer, including: "The Discovery of an Ancient Mesopotamian Theory of Music." *Proceedings of the American Philosophical Society,* 1971; "Old Babylonian Music Instruction Texts" in the *Journal of Cuneiform Studies,* 1996; and "Sounds from Silence" available at www.bellaromamusic.com.)

Musicians of ancient Greece also had a scale system based on perfect intervals, which were filled in with the diatonic pattern of steps. The very word "diatonic" is Greek in origin.

The Greeks conceived of music basically in terms of *tetrachords*, four-note groups bounded by the interval of the perfect fourth (frequency ratio 4:3). All the forms of tetrachord were bounded by the same outside notes, those of the perfect fourth, such as B to E. There were three types of tetrachord, which differed in the positioning of the two inside notes: enharmonic, chromatic, and diatonic.

The *enharmonic* type of tetrachord used micro-intervals, bunched together at the bottom of the fourth in the pattern B-B♯-C-E. (By B♯ I mean the quarter-tone between B and C.) The "enharmonic" was named from "same sound" meaning that the bottom tones were heard as a bending or fluctuation of pitch, without each individual note having a discrete, stable, unvarying position.

The enharmonic tetrachord is really a technique for pitch inflections, rather than a scale principle. With its slinky bending of pitches, it was thought to be lascivious—lewd, sexually wanton or lustful, erotic with a connotation of moral degradation. The voice would sort of slither across the micro-intervals, with a hypnotic or stuporous effect. The blue notes of jazz are a similar use of micro-intervals or bending of pitch—and the resulting sound impression has the same reputation for being sultry and sexual.

Similar micro-intervals are used in Hindu traditional music as a form of ornamentation or bending of ordinary scale notes. This is regarded as a means by which the singer demonstrates mastery and virtuosity. These micro-inflections of pitch are not regarded or perceived as fundamental structure, but as decoration. People intimately familiar with Hindu music, who grow up on it, learn to "filter out" the pitch-bending to grasp the structure of the underlying array of notes, the basic scale. They do not mentally process the micro-inflections as different notes, but as inflections of the underlying standard scale-notes.

Enharmonic inflections are used only in musical traditions that lack the kind of harmonic (chordal) and modulatory (key-change) richness of Western music. In music of the Islamic and Hindu traditions, for instance, great use is made of subtle pitch inflections including pitch-bending and quarter-tones. The same was true of some styles of music in ancient Greece. These traditions did not develop systems for organizing many notes at once. They did not develop chords or chord progressions or harmonic cadences or harmonic progression from one key to another. They are single-line, monophonic traditions and therefore all expression must be carried by the intonation of one pitch at a time.

The *chromatic* type of tetrachord, which gets its name from "chroma" meaning "color," used half-steps bunched together at the bottom of the fourth in the pattern B-C-D♭-E.

This type of structure is still used in Western music, but incorporated into the diatonic system. Chromatic notes in a diatonic context, we shall see, have functions which are subordinate to the basic structure provided by the diatonic notes. (For instance, a chromatic tone can be used to pass between two notes a whole step apart and thus provide a certain sultry intensity to the movement.)

Both the enharmonic and chromatic tetrachords contain gaps. The enharmonic (B-B♯- C-E) has a skip from C to E, the chromatic (B-C-D♭-E) from D♭ to E. Thus they are not truly scalar.

The *diatonic* type of tetrachord, however, spread the notes across the 4th in a more even way, using only stepwise motion with no gaps. The pattern was one half-step and two whole-steps, for example: B-C-D-E. The word "diatonic" comes from "dia" meaning "across" and "tonos" meaning "to stretch." Unlike the other types of tetrachord, the notes of the diatonic pattern fill out and stretch across the fourth.

Aristoxenus says of the three types of tetrachord, "the diatonic must be granted to be the first and oldest, inasmuch as mankind lights upon it before the others; the chromatic comes next. The enharmonic is the third and most recondite; and it is only at a late stage, and with great labour and difficulty, that the ear becomes accustomed to it."

Greece was a rational culture, and the diatonic form of tetrachord is the rational one, the one based in ratio and measure and proportion as opposed to slinky sensuality or coloring effect. The diatonic system, we shall see, is the only one with a simple underpinning in the mathematical relationships among the pitches.

Because of the proportions among its parts, because of its rational structure, the diatonic tetrachord alone can serve as a building block for constructing a scale system—which is what the Greeks did with it.

The full diatonic scale is simply a combination of diatonic tetrachords. For instance, above B-C-D-E a new tetrachord can be attached on E: E-F-G-A. This gives the complete scale (which includes the C major and A minor note-series). Or similarly, a new tetrachord can be attached at the bottom on B: F♯-G-A-B. This produces the same pattern of intervals, merely transposed to that scale including the G major and E minor note-series.

The Greeks called their complete diatonic scale the "Greater Perfect System." The pattern was the same sound as from the white keys on our modern keyboard (leaving aside the effect of the keyboard's equal temperament). The Greek system had a narrower compass than ours;

it included only the notes from A to A in two octaves. However it is not the boundaries of their musical universe that matter, but the basic pattern they established for the diatonic array, because that pattern can be duplicated in any octave.

The Greek scale system was bequeathed to the West through the Roman Empire and is the basis of the entire subsequent development of Western music from the Christian Middle Ages, through the Renaissance, the Enlightenment, and the Romantic Era.

The chromatic type of proportions are incorporated into the diatonic system we use, not as a primary or basic structure but as inflections of the diatonic notes.

Now we have seen empirically and from the broad array of facts in the anthropological record that the diatonic scale is a part of man's nature. The next question is: what is the underlying reason? What is it about the structure of the diatonic scale that makes it *the* crucial form of human musical cognition? What is special about its structure *mathematically*?

## SCALAR MATHEMATICS

It was Helmholtz who scientifically studied and systematically laid out the mathematical relationships underlying scales, just as he had done for intervals. He wrote:

*"The individual parts of a melody reach the ear in succession. We cannot perceive them all at once. We cannot observe backwards and forwards at pleasure [as we can in looking at a painting]. Hence for a clear and sure measurement of the change of pitch, no means was left but for progression by determinate degrees. This series of degrees is laid down in the musical scale. When the wind howls and its pitch rises or falls in insensible gradations without any break, we have nothing to measure the variations of pitch, nothing by which we can compare the later with the earlier sounds, and comprehend the extent of the change. The whole phenomenon produces a confused, unpleasant impression. The musical scale is as it were the divided rod, by which we measure progression in pitch, as rhythm measures progression in time."*

Let us look first at the scale in the way the Greeks did, using the building block of tetrachords. Only now we'll bring in the pitch measurements in terms of frequency ratio.

Let us compare these three types of tetrachord—diatonic, enharmonic, chromatic—using two facts about musical perception:

1. The basis of musical intelligibility is frequency relationships that are reducible to small whole-number ratios, which the brain is able to integrate.
2. To interrelate tones, a lowest common denominator must be found. We know this from measuring and explicitly calculating the frequency ratios of music; and in hearing music one's brain must perform some neurological equivalent of "finding the lowest common denominator" to interrelate and integrate the sensations.

## Diatonic

| B | C | D | E |
|---|---|---|---|
| 3/4 | 4/5 | 9/10 | 1 |
| 15: | 16: | 18: | 20 |

(interrelated by LCD 20)

## Enharmonic

| B | B♯ | C | E |
|---|---|---|---|
| 3/4 | 31/40 | 4/5 | 1 |
| 30: | 31: | 32: | 40 |

(interrelated by LCD 40)

## Chromatic

| B | C | D♭ | E |
|---|---|---|---|
| 3/4 | 4/5 | 5/6 | 1 |
| 45: | 48: | 50: | 60 |

(interrelated by LCD 60)

*3.1 The Three Types of Greek Tetrachord, showing the frequency ratios between the notes, and the lowest common denominators needed to interrelate the notes.*

There is no question that the diatonic form of tetrachord is mathematically the simplest, and that it provides the best basis for integrating sensations. Interrelating its notes requires the smallest "lowest common denominator," 20 for the diatonic, versus 40 for enharmonic and 60 for chromatic; and its reduced, simple-form ratio is made of the smallest numbers, 15:16:18:20, versus 30:31:32:40 for enharmonic and 45:48:50:60 for chromatic.

(It is worth pointing out that none of these numbers is my own stipulation. I took the ratio measurements from established scientific sources such as Helmholtz. Whenever there was an option as to how the ratio could be expressed, I chose the simpler form. But the LCDs of 20, 40 and 60 resulted out of those scientific measurements; they were not my own or anyone else's prior contrivance. They are simply a report of the facts.)

Next let's look at the mathematical patterns behind the complete diatonic octave. Remember that the 7-note diatonic scale was conceived by the Greeks as being constructed out of diatonic tetrachords. For instance, B-C-D-E can be extended by attaching another four-note group in the same pattern (half-step, whole-step, whole-step) to the top note: E-F-G-A. This combination gives all the notes of the C scale: C-D-E-F-G-A-B-C. This is a useful way of constructing the scale from a simpler uniform part (or conversely, breaking it down into simpler uniform parts).

It is interesting to consider the theory suggested by some historians, that the Greeks before the 5th century BC had only a 4-note scale, and that when they encountered the culture of Mesopotamia (which had the full scale since as early as 1500 BC), they expanded to the full 7 notes. The Greeks may have incorporated the larger scale into their own music by interpreting the 7-note series as a combination of their prior and familiar 4-note groups.

For simplicity we'll consider the major and minor modes here, with the knowledge that other scalar modes have similar underlying mathematical patterns.

**The Major Scale**

| Scale Degree | 1 | 2 | 3 | 4 | 5 | 6 | 7 | 1 |
|---|---|---|---|---|---|---|---|---|
| Note name | C | D | E | F | G | A | B | C |
| Frequency Ratio | 1: | 9/8: | 5/4: | 4/3: | 3/2: | 5/3: | 15/8: | 2 |

*3.2 Ratios for the major scale*

The frequency of the second step of the scale, D, is 9/8 of the starting frequency; the third step of the scale, E, is 5/4 times the starting frequency; and so on. If we express these same relationships in algebraic form, (as shown below) the amazing, beautiful simplicity of the major scale becomes readily apparent. (Below, the relationships are shown with the tonic note C at the center of the series, which makes the simple pattern more apparent.)

**The Major Scale,** frequency ratios expressed algebraically, tonic at the center

| Degree | 5 | 6 | 7 | 1 | 2 | 3 | 4 | 5 |
|---|---|---|---|---|---|---|---|---|
| Note | G | A | B | C | D | E | F | G |
| Ratio | $x-\frac{1}{2}x$: | $x-\frac{1}{3}x$: | $x-\frac{1}{8}x$: | $x$: | $x+\frac{1}{8}x$: | $x+\frac{1}{4}x$: | $x+\frac{1}{3}x$: | $x+\frac{1}{2}x$ |

*3.3 Algebraic ratios for the major scale with the tonic shown in the center*

All of the numbers in the denominators of these ratios are 2, 3 or small multiples of 2 (4 or 8). We know from hearing that the major scale is affectively the brightest and sunniest of all musical scales; this is because of the underlying mathematics which are so elegantly simple. The human brain is easily able to integrate tones using these proportions.

The minor scale differs from the major on steps 3, 6 and 7. (We employ the "natural" form of the minor for our illustration here.) This scale gets its dark affective quality from greater mathematical complexity of its distinctive scale notes.

**The Minor Scale** (natural form)

| Degree | 1 | 2 | 3 | 4 | 5 | 6 | 7 | 1 |
|---|---|---|---|---|---|---|---|---|
| Note | C | D | E♭ | F | G | A♭ | B♭ | C |
| Ratio | 1: | 9/8: | 6/5: | 4/3: | 3/2: | 8/5: | 9/5: | 2 |
| Ratio | $x$: | | $x+(1/5)x$: | | | $x+(3/5)x$: | $x+(4/5)x$: | $x+x$ |

*3.4 Ratios for the natural minor scale*

Observe that no interval of the major scale involves a frequency division into fifths (i.e., has 5 in its denominator), but *all three* of the distinctive tones of the minor scale do. Another common inflection of the minor scale, the augmented fourth/diminished fifth, which would be an F♯ or a G♭ here, has a ratio containing a division into fifths as well: 7/5 or, algebraically, $x+(2/5)x$. The fact that all the distinctive notes of the minor scale involve the same type of mathematical division is a testament to nature's consistency and intelligibility.

With regard to the underlying mathematics, there are other ways of looking at the diatonic scale as well. If you take any note (such as C) with the fifths above and below it (G and F), then build a major triad (ratio 4:5:6, or if you include duplications of octave 1:2:3:4:5:6) on each of those three notes, you get the total collection of the diatonic scale: C-E-G, G-B-D, and F-A-C — placed in order: C-D-E-F-G-A-B-C.

Another method is the so-called "Pythagorean" cycle. After the unison (1:1) and the octave (2:1), which duplicate the same note, the simplest musical interval is the perfect fifth (3:2). This is the simplest interval which gives a new note. It can be used to generate the entire scale. Simply roll out a stack of perfect fifths above a given note (F-C-G-D-A-E-B); the first seven notes, reshuffled into one octave, are those of the diatonic scale. This seems to be the same as the method described on the aforementioned cuneiform tablet from ancient Babylon.

Aristoxenus explains this method in his treatise on Harmonics, which proves that the method was known to the Greeks. He says that the stepwise intervals allow for a certain range of variation in pitch without changing the quality of the interval. Consonances—what we call the perfect intervals—on the other hand are precise and inflexible; their notes have no span of possible pitch alteration. "The ear is much more assured of the magnitudes of the concords than of the discords. It follows that the most accurate method of ascertaining a discord is by the principle of concordance." In other words, the pitch of discordant (stepwise) movements in the scale must be determined by the relations of perfect consonances (the perfect 4th and 5th). To find the steps, "one should take the Fourth above the given note, then descend a Fifth, then ascend a Fourth again, and finally descend another Fifth. Thus, the interval of two tones below the given note will have been ascertained. If it be required to ascertain the discord in the other direction, the concords must be taken in the other direction."

Earlier on in the cycle of fifths are the simpler notes; the first five notes make the pentatonic scale (C-D-E-G-A-C). Later in the cycle are more complex notes; the sixth and seventh notes of the cycle (F and B) bring in the intense, key-defining dissonance of the tritone.

Beyond these notes you begin to get the accidentals used to change from one key to another. A "key" is a central-note with its surrounding scale. From the cycle we already have the C Major scale. Adding more fifths carries us into new keys one note at a time: first F♯ which changes the scale to G Major, then C♯ which changes it to D Major, and so on. The cycle of fifths moving downward instead of upward generates the accidentals that propel you into the flat keys: first the note B♭ takes the key to F Major, then E♭ to the key of B♭ Major, and so on.

The Pythagorean method of tuning produces a small deviation of certain notes from the "just" tunings indicated above: scale-steps 3, 6 and 7 are a little more sharp than they would be using the proper ratios. However, these differences are so small as to be melodically/perceptually insignificant. We easily recognize a note as having the right position in the scale, and the note does not even strike us as being out of tune, if it is within a certain narrow range from the perfectly pure intonation. An additional related fact is that certain intervals can be expressed in ratios which are numerically different but close enough to sound the same to us. Both 9/8 and 10/9 are whole steps and are basically interchangeable since the difference in sound is so minimal. The limits of discrimination, and the question of what makes a significant musical or expressive difference must be taken into account.

With regard to the issue of understanding the basis and validity of the diatonic scale, beware of the fallacy of question-begging, of presupposing the conclusion in the argument. If we looked at the Pythagorean cycle from a purely deductive point of view, starting with the assumption that the scale has to be derived from simple numbers, there would be no basis for insisting that the scale have 7 notes. You can generate the whole chromatic scale, the entire series of 12 half-steps filling an octave, using the cycle of fifths. The notion of stopping at 7 notes presupposes that we are already familiar with the diatonic scale and know what we are leading to. (Nevertheless it is worth noting that scientists have identified the unit-capacity of working memory to be 7 plus or minus 2.)

No, the validation of the diatonic scale is not deductive. We don't have to generate it out of nothing, or out of some axiomatic postulates, to prove it. The proof is primarily *inductive*—it is drawn up from the wide range of data available to our experience and our collected observations. We have already seen the enormous array of evidence from anthropology. The mathematics help explain why certain note patterns can be successfully processed by man's auditory perception system, and indicate what underlies our musical nature. But we start with common-sense observation.

### DRAWING ON OUR ORDINARY EXPERIENCE; CONCLUSION

When young children sing, improvising a vocal melody, they sing patterns consistent with the diatonic scale. Think for instance of the "taunting tune" one hears so often on the playground, with the note pattern G-E-A-G-E. (The tune of "London Bridge is Falling Down" has a close resemblance to this pattern as well—and of course, like all children's songs, "London Bridge" is very plainly diatonic.)

When young children or untrained adults are asked to listen to a scale played they know immediately, without prior training, when a wrong note is played. They are also able to sound out the notes of the major scale on the piano on their own without prior music instruction, purely by trial and error from their innate human musical sense. Every music teacher knows from experience that the major scale, and melodies using the major scale, are the first thing to teach to children because they are able to grasp it; knowledge of more advanced things necessarily builds on that basis.

Today many people, on the premise that everything is subjective, discount this sort of behavior as mere cultural conditioning from an arbitrary tradition. On the contrary, these human abilities are not a result of prior exposure to certain scales. For one thing people today are exposed from birth to a vast array of different kinds of music; further, we have always been exposed from birth to all sorts of noises. But these exposures do not create any consistent intuition about exotically inflected scales or noises.

The teaching tool of solfege (do-re-mi-fa-so-la-ti-do) has been widely used for centuries up to the present day. Learning this diatonic series enables previously untrained singers, and even people who are downright untalented, to read and sing music at sight in a remarkably short time. No such corresponding tradition based on the chromatic or enharmonic note patterns has ever taken off. Attempts to do so fail because they work against the natural human musical sense. (Shortly, we will see one such attempt which led British teacher Sarah Glover to switch to a diatonic method.)

Another piece of evidence: the diatonic scale is the foundation of our music notation system. The lines and spaces of the musical staff give place to the diatonic notes; the diatonic array is built into the form of notation itself. Notes which depart from diatony—chromatic or enharmonic notes—require the addition of further symbols, such as sharp signs or flats. Once it had been devised, this notation system was rapidly disseminated to the whole of Europe and thence throughout the world, and has lasted for centuries up to the present day. Historically, no system of notation based on the enharmonic or chromatic series has ever grown from musical practice, spread, or lasted for a significant period of time.

Just as the diatonic scale is built into Western musical notation, it is built into the layout of the keyboard of the various keyboard instruments. The white notes are the diatonic ones; the notes outside the diatonic scale are separated—the keys are black, shorter, and set slightly higher than the white notes. There is an entire industry manufacturing and selling these instruments, which has been a successful business for centuries. Enormous, lasting institutions like that do not come about and thrive for nothing.

The diatonic scale came into existence when man came into existence, as the archaeological record shows. It is found in cultures throughout the ancient world from Asia to Africa to the Middle East to Europe. It is the scale of virtually all known folk music and all Western "popular songs." How could tunes become broadly popular unless they employed patterns consistent with what the human brain can integrate?

We should not expect that in order for a pattern to qualify as an inherent human cognitive requirement, every culture and every musician in the world should invariably use it. Man has free will and it is possible for him to go against his own nature.

To understand this point more widely: the fact that there are principles of thinking and communication does not automatically prevent a person from being illogical or ungrammatical. The fact that there are principles of what is morally right doesn't force you automatically to be honest or just.

And the fact that the human brain requires the basis of a diatonic scale in order to successfully process musical relationships does not mean that man is incapable of making incoherent sounds. Man is a being with volition, with the power of choice, and it is possible for him to go against nature and right, either by ignorance or by deliberate intention. The fact that people sometimes go wrong does not invalidate proper standards.

Given what has happened to music in modern times it needs to be said that the diatonic scale is far from being a "Western social construct." The evidence shows overwhelmingly that it is timeless and universal. It is an objective need of man's mind. It is a cognitive pattern inherent in and required by the nature of the human brain.

## II - MODE

In a certain sense we speak of *the* musical scale, of a single pattern of pitch division which is the one and only musical scale. This is true, and that pattern is the diatonic scale. But in another sense, there are many kinds of scale—what we call *modes*. These are the various segments or inflections of the diatonic scale. The term "mode" is of course closely related to "mood" and for good reason—the kind of scale employed by a piece of music is a crucial determinant of the emotion it arouses.

The diatonic scale can be thought of in modern terms as simply the array of white notes on the keyboard. This does not mean only the major scale, of course. The note series beginning on any given white note is a unique pattern—such as D-E-F-G-A-B-C-D—and these are also diatonic. These segments are called the "church modes" because they were used in the chants for services in the Roman Catholic church in the Middle Ages, before the development of the Western system of harmony. Likewise, transpositions of these patterns to other starting notes are also diatonic.

Medieval music was based on the received tradition from Greece (even though laws of music, like everything else, were attributed to God). Greek writers on music had named the different types of scale by the various city-states in the Greek alliance. Each "tribe" had its own distinctive style of music, there was a Dorian, a Phrygian, a Lydian and so on. These names referred to "modes" in the broad sense of "styles"—including not only the scale but all the other aspects of music as well including the rhythm, kinds of instruments, methods of ornamentation, vocal qualities and so on. Later thinkers began using the names to refer to the scales alone, and usage of the names was fairly inconsistent and ambiguous.

The Medievals inherited the Greek names, but in the confusion of the fall of the Roman empire, and in the church's campaigns to eliminate pagan sources, and the subsequent age of ignorance, the continuity of the tradition was broken. When Heinrich Glarean, a Swiss music theorist, cataloged the various modes—which he did in his treatise *Dodecachordon*, published in 1547—he used a naming system which adapted Greek terminology. Some of the names are his own invention based on his readings about Greece (Ionian, Aeolian, and Locrian). Other modes he designates with traditional Greek names, but in a way that doesn't correspond with the already confused ancient usage. The result is, the Western tradition ever since has used Glarean's naming scheme which has practically no connection to the earlier Greek conceptions. Glarean's naming system has become standard, but it leads to enormous confusion when we try to relate these modes to the statements by the Greek philosophers about "Dorian" music, "Phrygian" music and so on.

For clarity's sake today it is wise to identify the modes using the starting note of the pattern on the white keys of the keyboard. The C-mode (Glarean's Ionian) means the pattern of whole and half steps using the white notes of the keyboard beginning on C; the D-mode (Glarean's Dorian) means the pattern using the white notes beginning on D; and so on.

To memorize the series of modes starting from C-mode using Glarean's names, a mnemonic will help you remember the first letters, such as: "I don't play loud music at lunch." (Ionian, Dorian, Phrygian, Lydian, Mixolydian, Aeolian, Locrian)

The modes are not unique to Western Christendom. They are also found, for instance, in the oldest and most developed musical tradition outside of the West: the Hindustani tradition, the ancient tradition of India. On the surface, ancient Hindustani music and modern Western harmonic music could not be more different. The Hindu tradition is single-line while the Western employs a full system of harmony. The Hindu tradition is entirely oral and improvisational, the Western sets fixed compositions in the form of notation. The Hindu tradition employs pitch-bending and micro-intervals as an ornamentation of the main notes, the Western does not. Yet the underlying scalar commonalities are profound and pervasive.

The northern Indian classical system organizes raags into categories by musical mode. Each category or *thaat* is named after a common raag which exemplifies the category. This classificatory system was settled by early 20th century musicologist Vishnu Narayan Bhatkhande, born in Bombay and educated in the institutions of the British Empire. He drew upon ancient texts, upon the Carnatic melakarta classification (from the South Indian tradition) devised around 1640 AD, as well as what he could learn first-hand in visiting various schools of music. He brought British-style rational order to the bewildering variety of raags in the oral tradition.

Six of Bhatkhande's ten categories match literally the Western modes on C, D, E, F, G, and A. The others are very closely related as well.

The following chart gives a one-page summary of various modes. This is not a totally exhaustive list of possible scales, but an indication of the principal scale-types while showing the range of variety.

The chart is followed by an explanation of the emotional impact of the various forms of scale. There are two fundamental categories: those which are built around a major triad and are basically bright in feeling, and those that are built around a minor triad and are basically dark in feeling.

## Modes, Forms of Minor, Inflected Scales

A name in italics indicates a mode based around a *major* triad.
A name in bold face indicates a mode based around a **minor** triad.

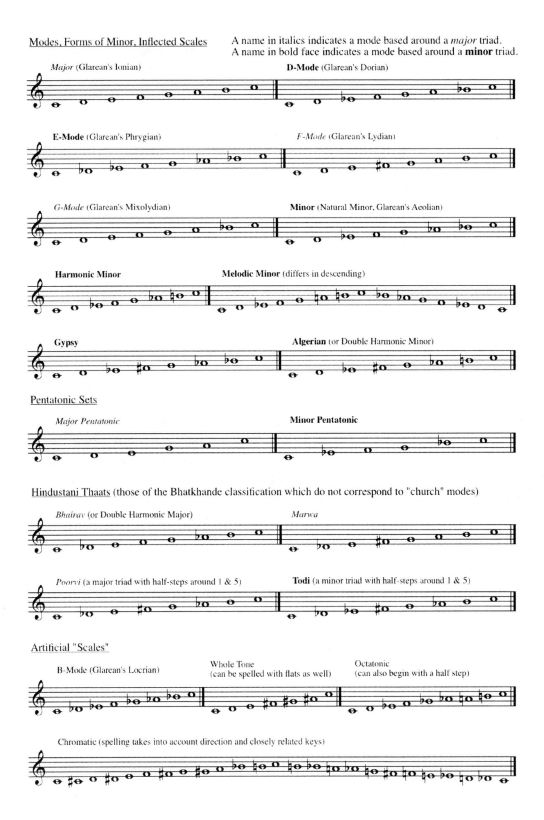

## Pentatonic Sets

## Hindustani Thaats (those of the Bhatkhande classification which do not correspond to "church" modes)

## Artificial "Scales"

## MAJOR MODES

Modes with a major triad (ratio 4:5:6) at their core are emotionally brighter and sunnier. Different inflections create different slants on the basic clarity and brightness, depending on which minor notes are introduced—on how much of a darker hue is mixed in, and where. Each scale is defined by its pattern of intervals: W=Whole, h=half, A=augmented, m3=skip of a minor third.

### Major (C-mode, Glarean's Ionian): W-W-h-W-W-W-h

The major mode is of course the simplest and brightest of all modes. All the notes make perfect or major intervals above the tonic.

In the music of India, the raags of the *Bilawal* thaat employ this scale. Just as in the West, this scale is the most basic and considered the default, natural form of scale. Ironically, though, raags based on this scale are rare—nearly all Indian classical music is dark, which is an expression of the basic worldview of the Hindu religion. A variation called Alahaiya Bilawal is common though; it is a morning time raag.

### Major Pentatonic: W-W-m3-W-m3

Another important scale, used as the basis of simple music including many children's songs and a huge amount of folk music from Ireland to China, is the *pentatonic* scale (called "penta" because it has only five notes). It is the pattern C-D-E-G-A-C.

Notice that this is a subset of the notes of the diatonic scale; compared to the 7-note major scale, it is missing steps 4 and 7 which form the dissonant tritone. It is also missing the half steps between degrees 3-4, and between 7-1. The pentatonic scale contains no tritone and no half steps—in this respect it is "dissonance-free" and therefore has a very serene, quiet, relaxed feeling. It is incapable of producing effects of intense direction or mental pull.

The major pentatonic scale is used in the music of India, in the *Bhoop* raag which is about the morning time, and is serene and simple, even a little bland. It is a rare instance in Indian music of a clear, bright, optimistic feeling.

The pentatonic scale is also embodied in the series of black keys on the keyboard. In this sense, out of the twelve possible notes, it can be looked at as the inverse of the diatonic set, which is embodied in the white notes.

### F-mode (Glarean's *Lydian*): W-W-W-h-W-W-h

The major scale with an augmented fourth scale degree. The character of the raised fourth step gives the scale an extra "sparkle" or bit of brightness, but also some tension and a slightly more wistful quality. The tritone between 1 and 4 introduces a mystical, unsettled hue.

Raags of the Hindustani *Kalyan* thaat employ this scale. The Kalyan (a.k.a. Yaman) raag is one of the most common, one of the most ancient, and one of the first learned by students. It evokes a feeling of a serene love touched by sadness of separation from the lover.

**G-mode** (Glarean's *Mixolydian*): W-W-h-W-W-h-W

This is essentially the major scale with a lowered 7th, giving the scale a distinctive cool and mellow feeling.

In Hindu tradition, raags of the *Khamaj* thaat employ this scale. The Khamaj raag is thought to be romantic, sensual or flirtatious.

**Bhairav:** h-A-h-W-h-A-h (a.k.a. double harmonic major)

Hindustani thaat *Bhairav* uses the major scale with lowered 2 and 6—in other words, a half-step above each note of the major triad. (This is related to *Bhairavi*, which uses the E-mode.)

The half-steps above 1 and 5 give a tinge of pain ornamenting the bright major 1-3-5. The augmented seconds create pulling tension and a husky, exotic flavor.

"Bhairav" means "terrible" or "frightful," and is the angry, destructive form of the Hindu god Shiva. Music of the *Bhairav* thaat "is extremely vast and allows a huge number of note combinations and a great range of emotional qualities from valor to peace. This raag is usually performed in a devotional mood in the early morning hours. The vibrations of the notes in Bhairav is said to clear one's whole mind." (SwarGanga Music Foundation)

Notice that Bhairav has the same pattern of notes as the Algerian (double harmonic minor) scale, only starting on its fifth. For this reason it is sometimes called "double harmonic major." It has a major triad as its base sonority rather than a minor one—but the scale still has two augmented seconds in it!

**Marwa:** h-A-W-h-W-W-h

Hindustani thaat *Marwa* uses the major scale with raised 4 and lowered 2, a different way of ornamenting the root and fifth.

Like in the Lydian mode, the augmented 4th step creates an unsettled, mystical wistfulness. Like in the Bhairav thaat, the half-step above the main note creates a tinge of pain, and the augmented second between 2 and 3 gives an exotic flavor. Other than those factors, however, the scale retains the bright clarity of the major 1-3-5, as well as the major form of steps 6 and 7.

"The overall mood of this raag is of sunset where the night approaches much faster than in northern latitudes. The onrushing darkness awakens in many observers, a feeling of anxiety and solemn expectation." (SwarGanga)

**Poorvi:** h-A-W-h-h-A-h

Hindustani thaat *Poorvi* is essentially a major triad with half-steps surrounding the root and fifth. The half-steps create a sort of dreary, pained motion ornamenting the very stable and strong notes of the major triad.

It is "deeply serious, quiet and mysterious in character and is performed at the time of sunset." (SwarGanga)

## MINOR MODES

Modes based around the more complex minor triad (ratio 10:12:15) are darker in sound-feeling compared to major. Each minor mode gives its own unique slant to the basic brooding, somber quality of the central minor triad. There are more variations of minor scale than of major.

### Minor (natural minor, A-mode, Glarean's Aeolian): W-h-W-W-h-W-W

The natural minor is the prototypical somber mode, though the major 2nd step makes it a little stronger and less anguished than the E-mode (Phrygian).

In Hindu tradition, raags of the *Asavari* thaat employ this scale. The Asavari raag evokes a mood of renunciation, sacrifice and pathos.

### Minor Pentatonic: m3-W-W-m3-W

This is the same series of notes as the major pentatonic, but beginning on A: A-C-D-E-G-A.

Notice that the common form of minor pentatonic is *not* A-B-C-E-F-A, which would take the major pentatonic and lower the third and sixth. Instead, it is the same array of notes as major (C-D-E-G-A), but starting on a different note.

The major pentatonic was "missing" steps 4 and 7; the minor pentatonic is "missing" steps 2 and 6—which has the same effect of eliminating dissonance from the scale. Only now the minor triad is the core of the scale instead of the major.

Therefore the minor pentatonic is still clear and simple, but with an overcast, almost sinister darkness. In certain uses it can have quite a primitive, menacing sound; in others it is tranquil yet melancholy.

### D-mode (Glarean's Dorian): W-h-W-W-W-h-W

This is essentially the natural minor scale, but with a raised 6th degree. Thus it has the dark somberness of minor but with the slightly piercing brightness of the major sixth. (The piercing aspect comes from the tritone between 3 and 6.)

In the music of India, raags of the *Kafi* thaat use this scale. The Kafi raag, which is very old, is said to evoke a romantic dynamic between lovers in which the woman lovingly complains about the heartache her lover causes her.

### E-mode (Glarean's Phrygian): h-W-W-W-h-W-W

The anguished half-step above the tonic, the distinctive feature of this scale, lends it a unique flavor of despairing melancholy. This scale is even more minor than the minor scale: the natural minor scale has a major second, but the E-mode has minor intervals up from the tonic to every note (aside from the P4 and P5).

(As a curiosity, observe that the E-mode has the same pattern of whole- and half-steps as the major scale, but in reverse.)

In the music of India, the raags of the *Bhairavi* thaat use this scale (not to be confused with Bhairav which is major-based). The Bhairavi raag, which is used to end concerts (like a little encore), is said to evoke feelings of romantic love but with a touch of sadness. It is the most complex raag, which is based on the E-mode but in which singers use all 12 chromatic inflections. According to the SwarGanga Music Foundation: "Bhairavi is a powerful raag filled with devotion and compassion. Bhairavi is actually performed early in the morning in a peaceful, serious and occasionally sad mood. Traditionally it is rendered as the last item of a program, for its unique fullness of sentiments as well as its wide scope of the tonal combinations."

**Harmonic Minor**: W-h-W-W-h-A-h

This is the same as natural minor but for the raised step 7 which leads or pulls upward to the tonic. It is used for chordal harmony, which is where the name comes from. The inflection of scale-step 7 is essential to maintaining the feeling of the key-note as central, as raised 7 creates a tritone between 7 and 4. A distinctive property of this scale is the augmented second between steps 6 and 7, which gives a strangeness and disturbing nature to the dark sound when that interval is heard melodically.

**Melodic Minor**: upward W-h-W-W-W-W-h, downward the same as natural minor

The rising form of the melodic minor is the same as natural minor but with steps 6 and 7 raised on the way up. The raised steps eliminate the A2 in the harmonic minor and make a smooth melodic motion up to the tonic—which is where this scale gets its name. On the way down, steps 6 and 7 return to the natural form since the notes lead away from the tonic and not toward it.

A distinctive property of this scale is the series of 4 adjacent whole steps on the way up. This is also the only standard scale which differs in rise and fall.

Notice how important the strong pointer of the leading tone (raised step 7) is to defining the tonic note. Improvise for a while using only the notes of the natural minor scale (in, for instance, A minor) and you will soon find yourself hearing the notes oriented to the tonic note of the relative major (in this case, C). Without the definition provided by the leading tone—and the tritone between it and the fourth step—the ear does not continue to perceive the notes as oriented to the minor. This is why the use of the harmonic and melodic inflections of the scale are so important to keeping the dark minor sound.

Melodically, the changing versions of 6 and 7 in rising versus falling can create a kaleidoscopic, shifting element, almost a feeling of wild darkness.

**Gypsy**: W-h-A-h-h-W-W

This is the same as the natural minor, but with a raised step 4.

This scale has the strangeness of an A2 interval between steps 3 and 4. It has the darkness of the minor triad, the pain of half-steps above and below 5, and the mellowness of lowered 7. It has the mystical augmented 4th. In the characteristic "gypsy" usage this scale creates a brooding melancholy but also a sense of danger and foreboding—a feeling sultry and ominous, sometimes smoldering and sometimes frenzied. It is a scale with a peculiar capacity to be evocative of evil.

(The same name, "Gypsy," is also sometimes given to the "Algerian" scale below.)

**Algerian**: W-h-A-h-h-A-h (a.k.a. double harmonic minor)

This is natural minor but with the raised form of steps 4 and 7.

The distinctive element of this scale is the presence of two augmented seconds—which is why this scale is sometimes called the "double harmonic minor." The notes of this scale pierce the soul with a dark and furious quality. It is the spiciest and most exotic scale.

**Todi**: h-W-A-h-h-A-h

The *Todi* thaat in Hindu tradition is essentially a minor triad with half-steps surrounding the root and fifth. Thus it has a very pained hue to it.

According to the SwarGanga Music Foundation, "Todi pictures nearly always show a petite, beautiful woman, holding a veena [a plucked stringed instrument], with deer around her, standing in a lovely, lush green forest. Todi represents the mood of delighted adoration with a gentle, loving sentiment and is traditionally performed in the late morning."

[**B-mode** (Glarean's Locrian): h-W-W-h-W-W-W; This "mode" is not a part of musical practice, and in fact should not be considered an independent form of scale. It is listed here, as in other expositions, only for theoretical completeness. Because it is based around a diminished triad, not a major or minor one, this mode's supposed main note, B, cannot hold as a cognitive center. Even in India, this array is not considered a real scale, nor does it form a category in the thaat classification system.]

**Blues Scale**

The "Blues Scale" is not a scale in the same sense as the others. It is not a definite series of notes, but a technique of inflecting certain notes of the major or minor scales. You can look at it as being a major scale in which the third, fifth and seventh are often lowered, or a minor scale in which the same steps are frequently raised.

The essence of the blues feeling is not a stable series of notes but the mixture of the dark and bright. As musician Joe Craig put it, the blue quality is a musical color "that sits 'on the fence' between major and minor tonalities simultaneously, wobbling back and forth."

The ambiguity and fluctuation between major and minor notes is the essence of the "blue" feeling. Thus, a singer or guitarist often bends the pitch of steps 3, 5 and 7. A pianist switches back and forth between the major and minor thirds, often using one as a grace note to the other in attempt to get at the pitch "between the keys" or "in the cracks." The major and minor thirds might even be played simultaneously as part of a chord that is major and minor at once.

The blues arose from the attempts of black slaves in America to get the sounds they knew from African tradition, but using Western instruments which are not constructed or tuned for that practice.

## SYMMETRICAL "SCALES"

Aristoxenus repudiated the idea asserted by some of the Greek musical thinkers that the musical scale should be made up of equal intervals of the smallest possible size. He insisted that the scale is judged by ear, and there is no predetermined rule that the scale should be made up of equal intervals. Nor, for that matter, is there any rule set in advance that the scale should consist of *un*equal intervals—the ear must be the judge.

In modern times there have also been some artificial "scales" which do not arise from human musical practice or by ear, but are constructs from speculative theoretical deduction. These are helpful to know as a contrast to the true scales.

❄ **Chromatic** - a series of half-steps (12 notes per octave)
❄ **Whole-tone** - a series of whole-steps (6 notes per octave)
❄ **Octatonic** - a series of alternating whole and half steps (8 notes per octave)

These "scales" are symmetrical in that every note has the same pattern of intervals above (or below) it. This is in contrast to the diatonic scale, in which each note has a unique array of intervals above and below.

The diatonic scale has a distinctive structure giving each note a unique and recognizable position, thus helping orient the ear and mind. The "symmetrical" scales do not provide such a framework, and their effect is disorienting; their sound produces an experience of bewilderment or uncertainty—in harsher or more frenzied cases, of actual chaos.

The characteristic emotion of sounds based in chromatic and octatonic patterns is bitterly acerbic, malevolently and pervasively painful.

The chromatic series gets its name, of course, from the Greek tetrachord used for "color" effect. Indeed such notes can be used for coloring within the context of the diatonic scale. But then the fundamental is the diatonic array, and the chromatic tones are a temporary ornament. If and when the chromatic scale becomes the fundamental structure, if and when its notes are used freely of any connection to diatony, the organizational framework is lost, intelligibility is sacrificed, and the emotion degenerates into pervasive bitterness.

The whole-tone series is mellower and gives a hazy, mystical effect, as one hears in many passages by Debussy. Here is the opening of "Voiles" (Veils) from his first book of Preludes:

*3.6 Debussy's Prelude "Voiles" uses the whole-tone series*

## UNIQUE NUMBERS OF INTERVALS IN THE SCALE

Here is another perspective on the specialness of the diatonic scale.

Take a diatonic scale and count the number of each kind of interval: How many half steps are there from any note to any other note in the collection? How many whole steps? Minor thirds? etc. For instance, counting thirds: above C there is a M3, above D a m3, above E another m3, and so on. By this method, tabulate the numbers of each size of interval. Since the question of which note is higher doesn't matter in this context, the inversions of intervals should be counted as the same as their smaller forms—a P5 is equivalent here to a P4, a m6 is equivalent to a M3, etc.

You will find that in the diatonic 7-note collection there is a *unique number of each type of interval*. Among the notes of the scale there are:

1 tritone
2 half steps
3 major thirds
4 minor thirds
5 whole steps
6 perfect fourths

This property of a unique number of each type of musical interval was discovered by Princeton academic and modernist Milton Babbitt. Babbitt had a background in mathematics and applied mathematical concepts such as "set" to musical structures.

The property is extremely rare and unique. Pitch sets—a "pitch set" is any collection of notes with a unique pattern of intervals—have been studied comprehensively, and out of the entire universe of possibilities this property belongs to only two. One of them is the diatonic scale, the other happens to be a stack of six half-steps—in other words, half of the chromatic scale. (I set aside subsets of these collections which have the same property.)

Comparing these two, notice that the diatonic set has a maximal number of perfect consonances; the largest presence is the perfect fourth (3:4) or perfect fifth (2:3). The stack of six half-steps, in contrast, has a maximal number of complex dissonances; there are more minor seconds (15:16) than any other interval; the minor second is a particularly piercing dissonance. In the diatonic set the simple consonances predominate and make the fundamental structure. In the six-note chromatic set, the complex dissonances predominate and make the fundamental structure. This makes it obvious why the diatonic set provides the kind of simple framework the brain needs to organize sensations. Because of its structure based on simple relationships, the diatonic scale is uniquely able to provide an orienting context for the mind, a framework with an unmistakable, unambiguous structure.

A stack of six half-steps happens to have the property because it is just the total universe of possible notes using standard musical intervals—the chromatic scale—but cut off in such a way that there are 6 half steps, 5 whole steps, 4 minor thirds, etc. This is merely a schematic format, like a list of the possibilities. Such a summary we can understand conceptually, in an abstract way, but it does not serve as the auditory system's framework for perceptual orientation.

As a disruptive member of the "avant-garde," Babbitt did not take the diatonic scale for granted, but considered it just one among many possible combinations of notes. This gave him a broadened perspective, a perspective which led him to apply mathematical set theory to analyze any combination of notes. In systematically examining all possible note collections, properties such as this one, which he and his followers called "unique multiplicity of interval class," revealed themselves.

Babbitt was part of a modernist movement which rejected any diatonic basis of music as mere outmoded tradition. This led him to compare the diatonic scale on an equal footing to other possible note collections.

Ironically, that comparison revealed a significant reason that the diatonic scale *is* natural, special, unique, and cognitively necessary.

## THE TENDENCY OF CORRECTING INFLECTIONS

Temporary inflections of notes of the scale in the course of melody are quite common. For instance, a minor note is often used in an otherwise major context to create a poignant tinge of sadness, or a raised fourth step to create a pointed, pulling sensation.

If you improvise a bit using these sorts of alterations, you will find your ear drawn to notes that correct the inflection sometime after it happens, to restore the scale to its normal form. This form of compensation or correction is fairly consistent in musical compositions. Consider this example from Mozart's *The Magic Flute*, in which Tamino sings of the powers of the titular instrument.

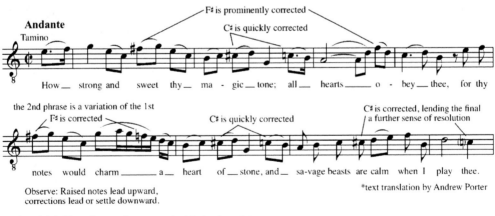

3.7 *This melody by Mozart illustrates diatonic correction following chromatic tones.*

Knowing this tendency provides us with a useful tool for expression, and confirms our knowledge that the diatonic scale is the fundamental basis of human musical cognition.

## III - Solfege

The common method for learning the steps of the scale is through solmisation or solfege. You are probably familiar with the series from *The Sound of Music*: Do-Re-Mi-Fa-So-La-Ti-Do.

These syllables are a standard way of teaching singing. Each syllable is a mnemonic for a single step of the major scale, and they are arranged in memorized series. The sound of each syllable fuses in mind with the sound quality of its scale-step.

In the song "Do-Re-Mi," Maria teaches the children to sing. Each phrase of the melody of her song begins on a note one step up in the scale from the start of the previous phrase. The melody, which is unforgettable, thereby serves as a basis for recalling and using the various notes of the scale. This, we shall see, was precisely the method by which solfege syllables arose in the first place.

The theatrical situation of Maria simultaneously teaching the children to sing and cheering them up, engaging them with an unforgettable, lively and sunny tune, adds further to the vividness of the impression. The nonsense syllables in the melody are temporarily (and amusingly) made into real English words for teaching purposes: "Do" becomes "Doe, a deer, a female deer"—"Re" becomes "Ray, a drop of golden sun" and so on. The peppy rhythm of the song and the rhymes ("sun" and "run," "thread" and "bread" etc.) add to its memorability.

Speaking between the iterations of the melody, Maria summarizes: "Do, Re, Mi, Fa, So, and so on are only the tools you use to build a song. Once you have these notes in your head you can sing a million different tunes by mixing them up…. When you know the notes to sing, you can sing 'most anything."

This Rodgers & Hammerstein musical, which first appeared on stage in 1959, and on screen 1965, made this teaching device very famous. But where does this method come from? Like with any human practice, in order to understand, accept and use it, we need to know where it came from. We need to know what facts gave rise to it in the first place.

The song "Do-Re-Mi" took its "gimmick" from the man who 1000 years earlier had originated the system. Solfege was part of a package of innovations made by a genius in Italy around the year 1000.

## Guido d'Arezzo

Guido d'Arezzo, born around 991 AD in Italy, began his career as a Benedictine monk at the monastery of Pomposa. At the monastery he trained the choir and became frustrated by the slowness with which singers learned music. The old method was nothing more than rote imitation and memorization, which left a singer totally dependent on his teacher. In Guido's own words, the prior practice meant that one needed "to have constant recourse to the voice of a singer or to the sound of some instrument to become acquainted with an unknown melody, so that as if blind we should seem never to go forward without a leader." (from Guido's "Letter Concerning an Unknown Chant," quoted in Strunk's *Source Readings in Music History*)

Early on, Guido began to challenge the existing methods, devising new, more efficient approaches and techniques—all of which related to the nature and use of the musical scale.

One of Guido's new devices was a more precise and more easily readable form of music notation.

The ancient Greeks' form of notation—which used letter-names for notes written above the syllables of the text sung—had long-since been lost to the world.

The earliest notation after the Greeks appeared during the 9th century as part of Charlemagne's standardization and dissemination of cultural products from the Roman Church. It simply used marks of rising or falling pitch above the words, as an approximate reminder to the singer of the motion of a tune he already had memorized by rote. These squiggles are called "neumes" from the ancient Greek "pneuma" meaning breath or spirit; the method is called neumatic notation.

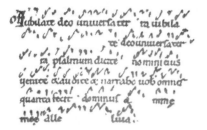

3.8 Neumatic notation's contour-squiggles above the text help the singer recall the shape of the tune he previously memorized.

It is easy for us to take for granted that "high" and "low" mean the same thing for pitch and for position on a page; pitch and page position have become a virtual identity to the Western mind. But this was actually quite a revolutionary means of notation; it was the first time in history that height of pitch was shown *positionally* on the page. Even the Greeks had never done that; they had used only letter names written for the notes— all in the same horizontal position above the words. Neumatic notation is the first form of music notation to fully embody a conceptual distinction between the words expressed in written language, versus the pitches expressed in musical notation.

Later on in the Carolingian period, pitch relationships were made more definite using a single horizontal line among the neumes so that there was a baseline of comparison for when the same note recurred, and for approximately how large each interval was.

Then, in the *Musica Enchiriadis* (Handbook of Music), also from the 9th-century Carolingian Renaissance but still before the time of Guido, a more comprehensively exact form of notation appears. It used rows marked off by horizontal lines. Each horizontal space or row was the notational place for one note of the scale; the row was defined by a note-name on the left. The syllable sung would be written inside the row for that pitch. (Notice, the example in figure 3.9 shows two melodies sounding at once in parallel motion.)

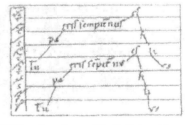

3.9 "Tu patris sempiternus est filius," in Dasian notation, from the 9th century text Musica Enchiriadis

This form of notation is called "Dasian" (or "Daseian") notation; the word comes from the Greek "daseia," which means "rough breathing" at the start of a spoken word.

Dasian notation became the first fully objective form of music notation since ancient Greece: the notes could be read from the page with no ambiguity as to their relative distances or intonation. The notation communicated the intervals of the melody completely and exactly—and independently of whether a singer had ever heard the tune before. The same notation meant the same thing to everyone from place to place or from the 9th century to the 21st.

Like neumatic notation, and like written words, Dasian notation showed time, the order of sounds, from left to right. Also like neumatic notation, it showed pitch by position on the page, low or high. But Dasian notation did not use special marks notating pitch; it *did not make separate notation of text and pitch.* It placed the words inside the various spatial positions for the notes.

Guido's innovation was to combine the marks from neumatic notation with the defined lines from Dasian notation, thus gaining the advantages of each: the separation of text-markings from pitch-markings from neumatic notation, plus the precision of the horizontal lines from Dasian notation. Further, Guido used not only the horizontal spaces as positions for pitch-marks, but also the lines. A neume could be on a line or in a space; this made the notation much more compact.

Guido's comprehensively exact and compact form of music notation has been in use ever since. (See figure 3.11 for the Guidonian form of notation.)

His original notation contained only four lines; it was expanded to five lines when music expanded its boundaries in the Renaissance. Guido had also used color-differentiation: red lines were used to mark the places for half-steps, while black lines were used to mark the ordinary whole-steps. This practice fell away, however, as it was not essential to the notation—it already specified where the whole and half-steps were by defining one line with a letter name.

The resulting form of notation is, in essence, a *scientific graph.* The vertical axis shows pitch measured in mathematically defined increments, the horizontal axis shows time, also in mathematically defined increments. (The exact notation of rhythm took longer to work out than that of pitch, and Guido took important steps to make rhythm notation more exact.) Thus, music notation in this format shows information in the same way as a chart of the stock market or of population growth.

Using this improved notation, Guido, along with his brother Michael, began to compile a new collection of church songs, called an *Antiphoner.* In the prologue to the *Antiphoner,* Guido described the new notation:

*"The notes are so arranged, then, that each sound, however often it may be repeated in a melody, is found always in its own row. And in order that you may better distinguish these rows, lines are drawn close together, and some rows of sounds occur on the lines themselves, others in the intervening intervals or spaces. All the sounds on one line or in one space sound alike. And in order that you may understand to which lines or spaces each sound belongs, certain letters… are written at the beginning of the lines or spaces."* (quoted in Strunk's *Source Readings*)

Of course, these lines became the modern musical staff, and the letters at the beginning became our G, F, and C clefs.

Where had the idea for this format come from? Guido's written methods arose from his in-person, oral and gestural methods. As Stuart Lyons has suggested, the four horizontal lines were the on-paper version of Guido holding up his hand with four fingers pointed horizontally. Guido would point to a particular finger or the space between fingers to indicate a certain note of the scale. This system was itself an ingenious method of communicating pitches in real-time without the need to stop and explain, and without the need of notation.

(Later Medieval authors illustrated the "Guidonian Hand" held upright, accommodating many more notes, each assigned to one of the various finger joints.)

Innovations like this raised the ire and envy of the monks at the monastery. They were set in their ways. They were devoted to age-old traditions accepted unquestioningly and practiced as familiar routine. They resisted and resented anything that upset these routines, and here was Guido asking questions, seeking out and implementing new and better ways of working.

As Stuart Lyons wrote in *Horace's Odes and the Mystery of Do-Re-Mi,*

*"Guido d'Arezzo was a young music scholar of exceptional talent, who clashed with the established monks because of his insistence on new methods of music-teaching. The older monks held that musical harmony was given by God. To tamper with the time-honoured methods of teaching Gregorian chant was sacrilegious and to persist in changing them put individual pride above community commitment. They accused Guido of heterodoxy and pride. Guido felt the atmosphere 'so choked by the snares of the envious, that you can scarcely breathe.'"*

The monks threw him out.

Guido moved to Arezzo, where he became the leader of the cathedral choir, and where he continued to innovate. The Bishop of Arezzo commissioned Guido to write a book about music, and around 1026 he penned *Micrologus* (the title was a standard one in the church, meaning "manual," "synopsis" or "short explanation"). This book became one of the most influential texts on music for centuries, and came to be part of Guido's growing renown—which would later expand into a fame of legendary proportions.

Guido's *Micrologus* systematically covered the essentials of the subject. He laid out the notes of the scale, including how to tune the monochord to get them. The monochord was a very primitive instrument, a sounding box with a single stretched string; a bridge could be placed at various points along the string to divide it and produce different pitches.

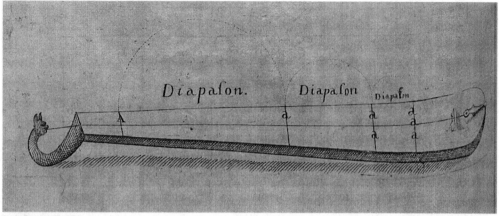

*3.10 Illustration from 1624 of a Monochord, showing the "diapasons" (octaves) from A up; each time the string is divided in half, it gives a higher octave of the same note.*

Guido explained the traditional method of deriving the notes and placing the bridge, by measuring the proportions, and he also explained his own new method which required fewer steps. (Incidentally, it is thought that the letter names we use for notes of the scale came originally from points on the monochord which were marked "point A," "point B," etc. just as in geometry. When the string was divided at that point, it sounded the corresponding note of the scale.)

Guido designated intervals by the number of scale-notes they span across—a unison, second, third, etc. He classified the various modes or types of scale used in the church. He explained "What note should hold the chief place in a chant and why." He explains when to use B♮ (natural), which is described as "hard" and when to use B♭ (flat), which is described as "soft."

Harkening back to a Greek concept that music has influence over the soul, Guido wrote of musical character types which appeal to a person depending upon his inner nature. One person is attracted to the "lame hops" of one style, another to the "joyfulness" of a different style. Or one to the "volubility" of a certain style, another to the "sweetness" of another. A crucial element of these character-styles was the mode, or type of scale, employed by the music.

He gives instruction on how to compose new melodies. (This was not something done in the church which held that its traditional music, having come directly from God, was the eternal, unchanging, one and only proper music!) He spoke of grouping notes together into phrases which closed at a suitable place to breathe.

Music was traditionally sung with unmeasured time values, flowing with the cadence of the words; Guido wrote that "it is good to beat time to a song as though by metrical feet." (A foot is a beat in poetry.) And he measured the time-values of notes. He used many concepts of poetic rhythm, and stressed the connection between musical and poetic rhythm. He suggested parallel melodic phrases, which would balance one another, as lines of verse do. So he was one of the earliest thinkers to deal with rhythm by measured conceptual control, rather than the traditional unmeasured practice of flowing with the approximate rhythm of the words.

Guido's *Micrologus* was one of the first sources to deal with the new art of polyphonic singing—of singing multiple notes at once. He gives some of the first rules of counterpoint, rules for creating a second voice accompanying a given melody, so that the two voices make a sound that is not "hard" [*durus*] but "smooth" [*mollis*].

Guido's achievements made him famous, in large part because he could do something people found astonishing: he could give a singer the ability to know and sing a tune he had *never heard before*. To people of his time, this seemed like sideshow magic. They were in awe of it as a stunning spectacle.

How did he do it? He invented *solfege*.

Singers in the past had learned music by rote imitation of a teacher, or by the cumbersome use of the monochord to get correct pitches. But Guido found the monochord to be a childish method—he thought it was, in effect, an unprofessional and inefficient crutch. He knew that in practical reality a singer needed an *internal* and *independent* means of knowing what note to sing.

He started out by giving his singers a formulaic way of composing a melody for any text. He simply assigned each vowel to a particular note, and whatever vowel a syllable used, that determined what pitch to sing. The vowels were: Ah—ey—ee—oh—ooh. Any syllable with "Ah" was to be sung on scale-step 1, any syllable with "ey" was to be sung on scale-step 2, and so on.

Assume the C Major scale. If the singers needed to sing the words "Christe eleyson" (Christ have mercy) but didn't have a known melody for it, they automatically knew to sing "Chris-" on E, "-te e-ley" on D, "-son" on F. It was a sort of predetermined mechanism of choosing the melody notes, a system to simplify the creative process and enable the singers to do it instantly.

Guido had gleaned this method from noticing patterns in the way church songs typically used certain notes for certain vowel sounds, and this was a surprisingly effective formula. Using this formula, his singers were able to improvise, on the spot, a melody for any religious text—and without need for planning time spent in advance.

But the ultimate importance of this trick was not in the melodies that resulted. It was in the fact that it *gave Guido the idea of assigning a unique verbal sound to each step of the scale*. It gave him the important new idea of assigning a meaningless syllable to a note, of using a linguistic sound not to denote things in the world, but as a mnemonic for the characteristic sound and relative position of a particular note of the scale. It was imperative that the syllables were nonsense syllables; they could not be concepts referring to things in the world, or that meaning would predominate and get in the way. The syllables had to be associated purely and exclusively with the sonority and audible musical character of each scale-step.

Once he had that idea it was a short step to the creation of a solmisation system. Guido wrote a letter to his friend Michael explaining the new method:

*"We need to implant deeply in memory the different qualities of the individual sounds and of all their descents and ascents. You will then have an altogether easy and thoroughly tested method of finding an unknown melody…. If, therefore, you wish to commit any note… to memory so that it will promptly recur to you whenever you wish in any known or unknown chant, and so that you will be able to sound it at once and with full confidence, you must concentrate upon that note… at the beginning of some especially familiar melody. And to retain in your memory any note, you must have at ready command a melody of this description which begins with that note."*

According to the letter, Guido used a melody familiar to all his singers, the melody of a "Hymn to St. John" in which each line of verse, each phrase of the melody, began on a unique note of the scale: the first phrase began on the first step, the second on the second, the third on the third, and so on. He took the starting syllable of each line, and adopted it as the mnemonic for that step of the scale: Ut-Re-Mi-Fa-Sol-La.

<u>Ut</u> queant laxis          So that your servants may,
<u>re</u>sonare fibris,          with full voices,
<u>Mi</u>ra gestorum         resound the wonders
<u>fa</u>muli tuorum,         of your deeds,
<u>Sol</u>ve polluti           absolve the sin
<u>la</u>bii reatum,           from our stained lips,
<u>S</u>ancte <u>I</u>oannes.         O Saint John.

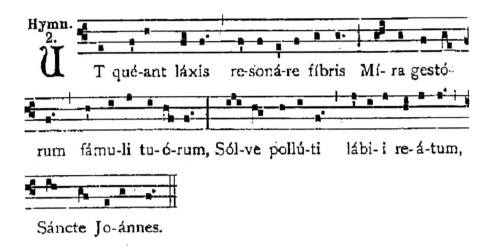

Hymn. 2.

UT qué-ant láxis re-so-ná-re fíbris Mí- ra gestó-
rum fámu-li tu-ó-rum, Sól-ve pollú-ti lábi- i re-á-tum,
Sáncte Jo-ánnes.

*3.11 "Ut Queant Laxis," the source of solfege, in Guidonian Notation*

Guido's singers came to know the sound of each scale degree by recalling the appropriate phrase of that melody. Thus the first syllable of each line became the name of its own step of the major scale. The name of the scale-step served to help the singer call to mind the sound of the pitch; it developed his ability to find the right note in his mind's ear before he sang it aloud.

Guido reported to Michael that after learning his method choirboys "were able before the third day to sing an unknown melody with ease, which by other methods would not have been possible in many weeks." And as for training a singer, with the older methods singers "have succeeded in gaining only an imperfect knowledge of singing in ten years of study" but his methods "produce a perfect singer in the space of one year, or at the most in two."

Guido's methods not only enabled singers to read and sing the notes, it also enabled them to accurately transcribe melodies immediately upon hearing them.

Guido became so acclaimed for his innovations that the Pope invited him to a visit in Rome, and on his visit the Pope "did not give up or leave the place where he sat until he had satisfied his desire to learn a verse himself without having heard it beforehand, thus quickly finding in his own true case what he could hardly believe of others." (Guido's *Letter*, in Strunk)

All prior musical theory, throughout the ancient world including Greece and the later practices of the Christian Church, had been oriented primarily around the darker sound of the various minor modes. This is why our notes are lettered beginning with A on the first note of the natural minor scale. But Guido used for his system the first six notes of the *major* scale. This was a profound shift in approach and reflected progress toward greater enlightenment. The major scale is cognitively simpler and emotionally sunnier. This reflected a fundamental change in mindset: turning away from the somber mysteries of the Dark Ages, and turning optimistically toward a bright, clearly intelligible future.

There is more to the Guidonian story than most history books tell, and it turns on just this issue of the backward dogmas of the Dark Ages versus the life of innovation and progress entailed in the active mind of a man like Guido.

Scholar Stuart Lyons, in preparing a translation of the Odes of Horace (published in 2007), came across an obscure reference suggesting that Guido had borrowed the melody of his teaching tune from a song by Roman/Greek poet Horace. This led Lyons to a Medieval manuscript ("M425") which included the "Ut queant laxis" melody—precisely, note for note —but as a setting of of a poem by Horace. This manuscript is known to have originated in the area of northern Italy in which Guido was active, and it is known by means of handwriting style that it was created prior to Guido, during the 10th century. The new words of the Hymn to St. John ("Ut queant laxis") were written by Paul the Deacon—a Benedictine monk and historian who wrote Latin verse as a hobby—in the 8th century, and there is no record of them being connected with the melody before Guido's letter.

Guido had hidden the true source of the melody he used to teach the scale-steps. The actual melody was a worldly tune, a setting of a love-poem by the Roman poet Horace. The poem was "Ode to Phyllis." It has a decidedly pagan content. It ends:

> Come to me now, my own last love,—
> No other girl will keep me warm,—
> Learn, learn the music! come along,
> And with your lovely voice perform!
> Dark cares will become less with song.

Here is the first stanza in English and Latin.

| | |
|---|---|
| Est mihi nonum superantis annum<br>    plenus Albani cadus; est in horto,<br>Phylli, nectendis apium coronis;<br>    est hederae vis | I've a full flask of Alban wine,<br>    Phyllis, that's nine years old and no more;<br>My garden has parsley you can twine<br>    For garlands, and a mighty store. |

So if Guido had used the original ode by Horace, the first six solfege syllables would have been: est-su-ple-ca-fi(phy)-ap—very different from the ones we know, but just as plausible!

(The true source of the melody, from the song of Horace, was proved by scholar Stuart Lyons, who is also the translator of the verse above, in the book *Horace's Odes and the Mystery of Do-Re-Mi*.)

Guido knew he could never reveal his pagan source. Even in a letter to his best friend, in which he explained the system, he sticks completely to the story that he used the Hymn to St. John.

In his lifetime the entire world known to Guido was ruled with an iron fist by the Christian (Catholic) Church. Horace's works were pagan, and freely expressed issues of love and sex, and treated God irreverently. His work had been banned in Rome and in France.

Guido knew from experience how worldly innovation would upset the dogmas of the church and result in envious antagonism from the clergy. His brothers, resenting his inventiveness, had driven him out of the abbey of Pomposa. More seriously than that, Guido knew that defiance of church doctrine would get him *killed:*

*"As a young boy at Pomposa, Guido will have been aware of the fate of Wilgard, a well-known grammarian in Ravenna, thirty miles away. Wilgard attempted to revive classical literature and declared that there was as much truth in the Latin poets as in the revelations of the Holy Scriptures. He paid for his belief by being burned at the stake."* (Lyons)

Guido's writing style followed the standard forms of religious deference of the day. Every personal accomplishment is humbled by the insertion of "with God's help" and by the addition of such sentiments as "our actions are truly good only when we ascribe to the Creator all that we are able to accomplish." These were obligatory forms of communication under the dominion of the Church and like everyone, Guido would have been brainwashed into incorporating such self-abnegation into his thinking; to whatever extent he was able to free himself of these ideas, he would have known he could only publish his work by presenting it with the strictly enforced Christian meekness.

When Guido visited the Pope, he was offered a position in the Papal service in Rome. Guido declined the offer, citing the heat in Rome as too much for his health. Should we take that excuse at face value? It may be plausible that a person at this time would have had health difficulties even in his thirties—but does it really make sense that he would turn down the security of the most prestigious, sought-after, and admired position in his field because of the *weather?*

And is the weather so dramatically different less than 150 miles to the north where Guido settled? During July and August, the hottest months of the year, Rome is in an average temperature range of 70-90 degrees Fahrenheit (at least, those are the numbers today), while Arezzo is in a range of 62-84 degrees—a difference of roughly 7 degrees. This may make Arezzo more comfortable during a couple of hot months, but is it enough to give up a great career over? Guido did not ask for vacation time during the hot months of summer, he refused the position altogether. So the more apt question is: did Guido even want such a position, even if the weather had been perfect?

The consistent and logical explanation is that Guido made a safe, formally polite excuse instead of expressing his true feelings. He knew from hard experience that his inquisitive mind and innovative spirit would raise the ire of the Church rulers. Logic suggests that despairing of "the heat in Rome" was the one acceptable way Guido had to avoid a life under the watchful eye and unlimited power of the Pope.

And if, as is likely, Horace's song was a popular one known throughout Rome, Guido and his choristers would have been knowingly singing false religious words to a "sinful" worldly tune—an act of coordinated, though veiled, rebellion. Just because people of this time went through the motions of paying homage to the church doesn't mean that they sincerely felt that way—not when the penalty for deviation was being burned at the stake. The Church had an enforced monopoly on matters of intellect and spirit; there was at this time no alternative but to operate under its auspices. Yet for all we know, Guido may have despised the Church —and he may not have been alone.

In seeking advice on his future course, Guido was warned by the Abbot of Pomposa that nearly all the city Bishops were accused of simony—of buying and selling church powers— and told he should avoid living under their dominion.

On that advice, Guido retired to a private life in a quiet monastery near Arezzo (declining another invitation, this one from the Abbot).

What were Guido's true feelings about the passive religious mindset versus his own active, thoughtful pursuit of practicality in the world? Like so many of his time, he was forced to hold his tongue. Such are the perils of censorship in any age.

Despite the tragic aspect of the world Guido lived in, we can be grateful that he navigated his course as deftly as he did. He gave music a new foundation, a new life, and a new capacity to grow. For everything we love in music—for all the centuries of subsequent development which his work made possible—we have him to thank for his intelligence and courage.

## The Transition to Modern Solfege

In one of those fluctuations that are lost in the sands of time, the first solfege syllable "ut" was transformed to "do." The open "o" rather than the closed "u" was easier to sing; and placing the consonant at the front of the syllable rather than the end made it consistent with the others. One possible explanation for the origin of "do" is the French contraction "d'ut." For instance you would say that A minor is the "ton relatif d'ut," the relative minor key of "ut." This is just a hypothesis as to where the sound could have come from.

The high Renaissance brought important advances. Around 1440, just a little before the time of Michelangelo and Leonardo da Vinci, Gutenberg invented the printing press with movable type, enabling for the first time the mass production and dissemination of written ideas. The prior method of propagating written work was by hand-copying; monks would copy manuscripts, often rephrasing or elaborating, interweaving multiple sources, and so on —with a resulting variation from copy to copy. The printing press, however, put texts in a unvarying, standardized form, giving a stable identity to an author's work.

Once the printing process was established and more common, one of the most common items printed, in addition to the Bible, were church hymnals. Church psalm books printed in the later 1500's began to include the starting letters of the solfege syllables near the notes written on the staff. This facilitated sight-singing by singers with less ability to interpret music notation. Thus the notation gave not just the absolute pitch but the sound of the scale-step in the key. The inclusion of letters to indicate the solfege syllable in printed music continued for hundreds of years and became quite common. In the nineteenth century, the letters were included in sheet music for popular songs, enabling people without much musical training to sing them at home.

For centuries, singers had contended with only the six-note solfege series Guido had originated: Ut-re-mi-fa-sol-la. In order to accommodate any notes above or below those six, the series had to be shifted in a complicated overlapping way. Only around 1550 did such thinkers as Zarlino begin to suggest the addition of a seventh syllable as a means of completing a one-octave series. "Si" was the chosen sound, derived from the last line of the Hymn to St. John (*"Ut queant laxis"*), which begins "Sancte Iohannes." (It was chosen despite the fact that the last line of the Hymn does not begin on scale degree seven—and of course in ignorance of the secular source in the song of Horace).

### GLOVER & CURWEN

Around 1800, after the development of chordal harmonic theory and practice, an English music teacher named Sarah Anne Glover revived and adapted Guido's solfege method. (English practice at the time had used an incomplete form of solfege with fewer syllables). Like Guido, Miss Glover was the leader of a church choir and like Guido, she became a teacher of teachers, so her approach became widely used.

In about 1812 Miss Glover was asked to teach a young schoolmaster to sing. She tried to help him plunk out the notes on the piano by assigning a letter from the end of the alphabet to each of the 12 notes of the chromatic scale, the notes we know as: C-C♯-D-D♯-E-F-etc. She marked these on the piano keyboard for him, but her student made little progress and she concluded the method was inadequate. She changed her approach to use the sound of the diatonic scale, specifically the major scale. She adopted Guido's solfege system which taught the student an association between the syllable sound and the audible note-quality of its unique step of the scale. Using this method, in which the syllables are verbal cues for the unique mental impression and relative position of each step of the scale, her student made progress. She saw the same improved results as Guido had 800 years earlier.

Miss Glover subsequently made some lasting changes to the syllables. In order for each syllable to have a unique starting letter, she changed the seventh scale-step from "Si" to "Ti." The shorthand became: D-R-M-F-S-L-T-D.

She dropped the "l" from "Sol" to make the sound open, and thus better suited to singing.

(She also re-spelled the syllables to make them more consistent with English spelling and pronunciation: Doh-Ray-Me-Fah-Soh-Lah-Te. These new phonetic spellings never caught on universally, however; people did not need the spelling to be anglicized because they already understood the Italian-style pronunciation.)

The term "solfege" had come from conjoining the syllables "sol-fa;" to recite a line using solfege was to "sol-fa" it. (The same origin is true of the Italian word "solfeggio." The similar term "solmisation" comes from conjoining "sol-mi.") Miss Glover's followers came to call her system "Tonic Sol-fa" meaning that the tonic, the keynote, was always treated as the central point of reference.

John Curwen, an English minister and a student of Miss Glover, became an enthusiastic promoter of her ideas. He built an empire on the teaching system. He started the Tonic Sol-Fa Association in 1853. He published a number of books on the subject, founded his own music publishing house to disseminate materials, and produced the journal *Tonic Sol-fa Reporter*. In 1863 he founded the Tonic Sol-Fa College.

Curwen stressed the importance of making the ear's *sense of key relationship* into the main starting point of music teaching. "Key relationship" means the relation of each note of the scale to the gravitational center that is the tonic or key-note. He wrote in *Account of the Tonic Sol-fa Method*:

*"There are many sources of the effect produced on and in the mind by a musical sound, but the principal one is its relative pitch or its key-relationship. We should naturally expect from this fact, that both in the writing and teaching of music the key-relationship of sounds would be the thing first taught, first seen, and most prominent."*

Curwen's most important and lasting contribution was a system of hand signals that are derived from the mental impression of each step of the scale. Using these signals, one sees, and in fact feels kinesthetically in the hand, the emotional effect of each scale-note.

 Do - The strong or *firm* tone

 Ti - The piercing or *sensitive* tone

 La - The sad or *weeping* tone

 So - The grand or *bright* tone

 Fa - The desolate or *awe-inspiring* tone

 Mi - The steady or *calm* tone

 Re - The rousing or *hopeful* tone

 Do - The strong or *firm* tone

*3.12 Curwen's "Manual Signs of Tone in Key" with descriptions of scale-step quality*

In one version of the presentation, Curwen notes that "These proximate verbal descriptions of mental effect are only true of the tones of the scale when sung slowly—when the ear is filled with the key, and when the effect is not modified by harmony."

In an elaboration on the value of the hand signs, Mr. J Proudman, a teacher using Curwen's methods, wrote that

*"I have used the manual signs with uniform success and believe them to be a great and useful adjunct to the Tonic Sol-fa system. I find that they teach mental effect in a large degree, and support the 'characteristics' of the various tones materially. Thus not only does the clenched fist bespeak 'strength,' the extended hand 'brightness,' and the hand held as in benediction, 'calmness' and 'peace,' (thus giving Doh, Soh, and Me); but the upraised palm well expresses the joyousness of Ray, and the finger sternly pointed down is a suitable action for Fah; while the drooping hand expresses Lah like a weeping willow, and the upward pointed fore-finger is a perfect picture of the penetrating Te. These signs are well in accord with the natural action of an elocutionist, and must, therefore, illustrate mental effect."* (Letter published in "The Tonic Sol-fa Reporter," 1870; quoted in Curwen's *The Teacher's Manual of the Tonic Sol-Fa Method*, 1875)

Some of Curwen's students traveled to America where they taught using his method—which spread the method into the U.S. educational system and eventually into the minds of Richard Rodgers and Oscar Hammerstein.

The practice of solmisation seems to be universal. The Islamic world uses the same solfege as the West, which it received during cultural trades at some point after Guido's time. Ancient Greece used syllables to sing the notes of the tetrachord, what we would sing as la-sol-fa-mi, using syllables such as ta and te. Hindu traditional music uses the syllables sa-re-ga-ma-pa-dha-ni; their pitch is adjusted to the pattern of notes for a particular raag. Byzantine music uses syllables derived from the greek alphabet: pa (alpha), vu (beta), ga (gamma), di (delta), ke (epsilon), zo (zeta), ni (eta). Related methods exist in Japanese tradition as well.

## NOTE NAMES IN THE ROMANCE LANGUAGES

Innovations in instrument construction during the Renaissance made keyboard instruments—the organ, clavichord, and especially the harpsichord—much more common. The visual-tactile sense is very dominant in man; it is sight and touch which give an awareness of entities, and the information received by these means tends to feel more definite and real than sounds we hear or feelings they arouse in the mind. So with the keyboard in view and under hand, people started to develop a more fixed conception of the musical notes. Instead of thinking of notes purely in relational terms, as men had done throughout history, they began to conceive of absolute, unchanging pitches fixed in one place.

Some languages, such as German and English, took note names from the positions for the bridge on the monochord, which were marked with letters for each note (thus, A-B-C-etc.).

In the Romance languages, those derived from Rome's Latin (as well other languages in Eastern Europe which picked up the practice), Guido's solfege syllables became the names of the fixed notes. Just as in English we refer to C, D, and E, so in French and Italian (Spanish, etc.) the names of the notes are Do, Re, and Mi. "D Major" in French is "Re Majeur."

This gave rise to the difference between absolute and relational designations—what we now call *fixed-* versus *movable-*do solfege.

❋ In the fixed system of the Romance languages, "Do" always refers to "C" regardless of the scale or key in which the note occurs. "Re" refers absolutely to "D;" and so on.

❋ In the movable system, "Do" always means the sound of the tonic note of the key; "Re" means the second step of the scale; and so on. Movable-Do was Guido's original system, and the system propagated by Miss Glover and John Curwen.

| | C Major | | | | | | | | G Major | | | | | | | |
|---|---|---|---|---|---|---|---|---|---|---|---|---|---|---|---|---|
| Solfege syllable: | Do | Re | Mi | Fa | So | La | Ti | Do | Do | Re | Mi | Fa | So | La | Ti | Do |
| Romance name: | Do | Re | Mi | Fa | *Sol* | La | *Si* | Do | *Sol* | *La* | *Si* | *Do* | *Re* | *Mi* | *Fa* | *Sol* |
| Letter name: | C | D | E | F | G | A | B | C | G | A | B | C | D | E | F# | G |
| Scale step: | 1 | 2 | 3 | 4 | 5 | 6 | 7 | 8 | 1 | 2 | 3 | 4 | 5 | 6 | 7 | 8 |

*3.13 Comparison of movable- versus fixed-do solfege*

There has been heated and seemingly irreconcilable debate among music teachers as to which system ought to be taught. There is no question that each step of the scale has a unique character to it, and that melody is properly understood using the unique sound-quality of each step of the scale.

However, the use of fixed solfege note-names in the Romance languages is a historical fact that grew up naturally in human musical practice, and it should be respected as such. The practice is not arbitrary or destructive; it is only the discrepancy between it and the relative system which causes confusion or disagreement.

Furthermore, French and Italian teaching methods, which are preeminent in their ability to produce good musicians, were disseminated to Russia, Japan, China, Korea and other places throughout the world including such conservatories as the Mannes College in America. Fixed solfege names are inherent in these methods; movable-do cannot practically be substituted without disrupting the overall character of the methods.

These systems include most especially training and methods in the tradition of Nadia Boulanger, the great pedagogue and teacher of so many renowned composers, as well as the overall methods of the Paris Conservatoire. The Bel canto singing tradition in Italy is another important Romance-language, "fixed-do" system.

Therefore, in order to learn the scale-degree sounds in a fixed-do frame of reference, scale degree numbers can be used in place of movable solfege syllables. "One" in place of "do," "two" in place of "re," etc. (Seven must be shortened to "seb.") This, too, is a method commonly used by music teachers. It gives the student familiarity with the sounds of the various scale degrees while reserving the solfege syllables for the fixed note-names. Whatever is lost from this setup is more than made up for in the total package of value provided by the important French and Italian pedagogical systems.

One of the crucial elements of training in the French system is the exercise of reading note names in rhythm, speaking them aloud, which helps the student automatize the interpretation of notational symbols while separating this skill from other issues such as instrumental or singing technique. It is a form of mental training, which improves the student's ability to process the visual inputs of notation and translate them mentally into the stage preceding performance: note identification. It is a superlative method of training students in reading music proficiently.

But this method doesn't work well using the English letter-names for the notes for reasons of pronunciation. C, D, E and so on are all closed vowels, which don't roll off the tongue in speech very smoothly, particularly in faster exercises. E and A have no consonant and therefore are not good for articulating rhythm. F has the consonant at the end which causes a final closing of the lips which impedes continuity. And almost all the vowel sounds of the letters are "ee" making them less differentiated than those of the solfege syllables.

There is a further respect in which fixed solfege is in fact superior for advanced musical training: the handling, in real-time, of notes that do not belong to the major scale. With very simple music, using only notes of a single major scale with no modulation, movable solfege works fine. But for anything more advanced, movable-do becomes impossible to implement in real-time.

A musician playing or singing must contend with the fact of rhythm and continuity. The music doesn't stop because his mind is behind where it needs to be. He does not have the luxury of stopping to contemplate, he does not have time to pause and plan without concern for doing the next action at the right time. He must keep going. Therefore it is impractical to create a system which requires too much analysis preceding the output of the right sound; the musician must be able to rely on his automatized knowledge of what the notes are.

Movable-do can handle notes outside the scale only by means which require too much thought to complete before implementation. For a change to a new key, one must analyze the music in advance, use transitional syllables (such as "fi" for #4, the raised form of scale-step 4) and change to the syllables of a new scale at the right time. This is particularly difficult since the same accidentals can transition to multiple keys depending on the underlying harmony. For that matter, a note *within* the scale can be part of a new key if the underlying accompaniment brings in an accidental—which means the melodic line contains no visual cue for the key-change. There are also ambiguities in minor; some schools use a "la"-based minor which requires new syllables for the raised forms of steps 6 and 7. Others use a "do"-based minor in which steps 3, 6, and 7 are altered to "may," "lay" and "tay." The use of such convolutions is totally impractical in any real-time musical performance, which is the realistic paradigm that training must adhere to. In real-time, it is impossible to read the pitch, analyze the key and the harmony, retrieve the correct syllable from memory and coordinate the voice to sing. By the time the singer has gone through that whole process, his chance to sing the note has long-since passed. It is more than a brain can do.

However, a serious difficulty arises for the student taught movable solfege first (or who simply picked it up from the *Sound of Music*), and who later is asked to read musical exercises using fixed-do note-names. The fact that the note names do not correspond to the scale-step sound he automatized inevitably throws him off and becomes a source of confusion and para-lysis. In order to read notes using fixed-do, he has to break apart a mental integration; he has to learn to separate the note-name (do) from the scale-degree sound (step #1). This requires a lot of effort and concentration, but it can be done; and this student will eventually be able to flip effortlessly between systems, increasing not only his mastery but also his versatility.

## Summary

We have seen the anthropological and historical data about the scale. We have examined its mathematical base, including the unique properties of the diatonic scale. We have sur-veyed the range of variety in human scales, and differentiated those from certain artificial con-structs which do not arise from human musical practice (such as the octatonic scale). We have learned the way in which the emotional character of music flows in large part from the form of scale it employs, and that the basic distinction is between those modes based around a major triad versus a minor one. We have learned some of the tools, such as solfege and Curwen's hand signs, which both show the nature of, and help us make more facile use of, the scale.

The essential of the overall picture here is the cognitive role the scale serves. The scale is the measuring framework of pitch, which makes note relationships intelligible. It is the brain's fundamental integrating core, the central nexus for its processing of music. It is the basic form of musical context.

Since the scale—the diatonic scale—serves such a crucial role in making music compre-hensible, it is important to state its formal definition.

A simple way to encapsulate the diatonic scale in our modern context is: the pattern of white notes on the keyboard. The major scale is not the only scale available in this array. The various "church" modes, such as Dorian and Phrygian, are as well. And of course transposi-tions of these same patterns to other starting notes are also diatonic. (For instance, a major scale could be started on A or C or any other note; it just has to have the correct pattern of intervals.)

Various inflections of the diatonic scale are legitimate as well. Notice that the melodic minor changes the pattern for steps 5-6-7-8 on the way up versus down, but both motions use the diatonic tetrachord: W-W-h on the way up, and W-W-h on the way down.

Now, what about scales with augmented seconds? These are inflections of the same under-lying pattern, and have actually been used in non-academic music—for instance, in Klezmer, Hindustani, and Gypsy music. The augmented second can still serve as a melodic interval, and counts as a part of the scale in an extended sense—provided it is integrated into an otherwise diatonic framework. This means that the third scale-step (whether major or minor) and the fifth (always perfect) must be in place as the basis of order for these exotic inflections. Notice that the Hindustani thaats of the Bhatkhande classification which use augmented seconds conform to that pattern. Notice also that the one cut of the diatonic array which cannot serve (and never has served) as a functional musical scale, the B-mode, is the one with a diminished fifth above the main note. The fifth of the scale *must* be perfect.

In contrast, certain patterns are decidedly *not* diatonic. The symmetrical divisions of the octave are the leading examples of this type of artificial construct. The chromatic scale is not a scale but a schematic layout of all the possible pitches and intervals in equal temperament tuning. The whole-tone scale is the closest to being intelligible, but it is still amorphous; its cloudy mirage of sound is not too offensive, but there are no whole-tone melodies and there cannot be—go ahead and try to write one and see what you come up with. The chromatic and octatonic "scales" annihilate the comprehension of line. If you attempt to use them as the basis for a bit of music, they will destroy its coherence and intelligibility. They are totally contrary to the needs of the brain.

Because the cognitive validity of music depends on its diatonic basis, it is important that the definition of "diatonic" be available in terms of scientific precision as well. This is what the Greeks gave us and scientists such as Helmholtz systematically verified. A scale is a division of the pitch spectrum into steps, whether whole or half. A diatonic scale is one built out of diatonic tetrachords—four-note stepwise units filling the span of the perfect fourth (3:4), containing two whole steps and one half-step, the most basic form of tetrachord making the ratio 15:16:18:20.

# 4

---

## TIME

### RHYTHM & LIFE

Billions of years ago in evolutionary history the first single-celled organism, unlike the vast mass of inanimate matter, controlled its own motion. Natural selection shaped the cell over generations to maintain its own integrity by orchestrating an increasingly complex set of chemical processes. These processes were geared to make sure that the right material, such as food or waste, moved to the right place at the right time.

Later, more complex organisms, those with many cells, evolved more sophisticated systems for moving internal materials. Plants bring nutrients up from the soil and circulate the products of photosynthesis. Animals have a circulatory system which distributes resource materials throughout the body, carries away waste products, and carries chemical signals such as hormones.

Animals evolved another level of control, the capacity of locomotion. An animal controls the motion of its body in the world. The first and simplest form of locomotion seems to have been the flagellum, a hair protruding from a single-cell organism which it flapped around to propel itself. This means of motion was crude and rudimentary, but enabled some movement toward food and out of harm's way.

Animals are distinguished from plants by the fact that they have a whole system of senses and muscles to move themselves around in the world. To live, an animal needs to control when, how and where to move its body. The senses and motive powers work as one integrated system. The senses receive and integrate information from the world, and the brain then activates muscles to make use of that information. The animal sees and hears its prey and runs after it, or perceives a predator and hides.

Bodily motions involve an amazingly complex yet smoothly elegant coordination of the various muscles of the body. In order to execute a motion such as running, muscles throughout the body must work in concert with one another. The timing of each muscle contraction must be right in relation to all the others—and no wrong muscle contractions can occur—or the motion ceases up, it becomes constricted or bumbling, it doesn't flow and the animal fails to move in the way its life requires.

Regular, rhythmic pulses are nature's means of coordinating living action. Consider just how many biological actions employ regular, rhythmic pulses to keep muscle contractions coordinated: the heartbeat, breathing, walking, running, swimming, throwing, sex, speech, cleaning, cutting, typing. And notice the way man in his industrial production has used the principle that rhythmic action is more efficient and enables greater speed: assembly lines are rhythmic, as are machines in general. A machine must function rhythmically if its parts are to work together continuously and without interfering with one another. That is the same principle of action built into an animal's body by evolution.

There is a class of very serious disorders involving irregularity of heart rhythm. Effective movement is smoothly coordinated and regular; it is graceful and fluid, not bumpy, halting or irregular. When we speak of an athlete having excellent coordination, or of a youngster being awkward or gangling, we are referring fundamentally to rhythmic factors.

The motions of an animal's dynamic system are initiated, orchestrated, and controlled by the central nervous system, which has its own internal clock. This clock regulates such things as the cycle of sleep and wakefulness (circadian rhythm). But the brain's faculties control the timing on many levels from longer time cycles such as day and night to short ones such as the quick, almost reflexive action of seeing and catching a ball.

Some parts of the sensory-motor nervous system are evolutionarily older and relatively more primitive, such as the spinal chord and the lower structures of the brain. Other parts of the system, in man, are much more advanced and evolutionarily recent; these are the higher brain centers which enable more complex cognitive action and which enable fully human, self-aware, self-conscious conceptual intelligence.

Man, in Aristotle's definition, is the rational animal; he is in a biological category with other animals, yet is distinguished by his capacity to think, to know the world conceptually, to form abstractions. In his *Nicomachean Ethics* Aristotle stated, "The Good of man is the active exercise of his soul's faculties in conformity with excellence or virtue, or if there be several human excellences or virtues, in conformity with the best and most perfect among them."

It is the use of the distinctively human faculty that is enlightening, and makes man more civilized. When the functions of higher intelligence are used, they elevate all aspects of human life and action. However, when these functions—the ability to grasp meaning and moral values—go unused, actions become low, crude, vulgar, physicalistic, and animalistic. When man chooses not to use his rational faculty, he becomes a mere animal. That is fine for the lower animals who don't posses a rational capacity to begin with, but for man such an abdication represents a failure to live up to his own nature.

The faculty of reason brings a new dimension to all aspects of life including one's bodily movements. For man, there is not only the fact of physical motion, there is the question of his self-conception. A certain way of moving *means something* to a man. Movement can be inhibited and nervously tense—or confident and free. It can be an expression of slinky, slithering spinelessness—or of an unflappable upright posture. It can be loosely casual or more formal. It can be primal and physicalistic—or civilized and elegant. It can be crude and vulgar and reduce man to a mass of giggling flesh—or it can reflect the dignity of self-esteem. It can be visceral and from the gut—or it can be graceful and light. It can flail wildly out of control —or it can be expertly, masterfully controlled. It can be driven by base hormonal impulses, or led by the mind. For man, there is not only the mechanical fact of muscle motion, there is also the moral question in man's mind: *what kind of being am I?*

This is the expression of one's view of man's nature in bodily movement—and artistically in the form of dance.

Dance is generally much easier to talk about than the rhythm or motion of music, because you can see the moving body and grasp the motion both visually and kinesthetically by imitation. Sound, in contrast, cannot be seen or touched. But since music arouses motion—motion of the body and of the soul—the same issues are involved. The question just becomes: what kind of sounds arouse what kind of motion?

Dancers and their audience members know of the natural correspondence between the sound of music and the appropriate manifestations in dance. There are certain physical, one-to-one relationships: louder music stimulates larger movements; articulated, staccato music stimulates similarly articulated movement as opposed to more flowing, and so on. And of course the most important thing is that the overarching emotional content of the music be properly expressed. A joyous, ebullient music with a dragging, listless dance would be a mismatch.

Notice also the correspondence between the type of motion made by musicians to produce sounds, and the type of motion those sounds arouse in the listener. When a violinist sweeps down with the bow in a grand, strong motion, that produces a certain kind of sound, and that sound arouses an impulse in the listener to make some grand, strong motion. When a pianists fingers bounce lightly and quickly off the keys, this produces a delicately soft and detached series of notes, which in turn arouse the listener to move in a way that is delicate, light, and with some sort of pointed articulation to the movement. The listener's response is not created by any kind of inference or deduction or abstract conclusion, but by a basic connection of action creating stimulus and stimulus creating response. The musician and the moving listener are exploring and experiencing the same causal relationship, but in different directions.

With all of this in mind we are now prepared to answer the question: what is rhythm?

*Rhythm is an experiential time measurement enabling the integration of complex human action, both physical and mental.* This can mean the coordination of social action, as when people march together, dance together, or chant together. But the root sense is the process of integration inside the individual person, the process in which many little component actions are coordinated into one larger action. In physical movement this would be, for instance, coordinating many muscle contractions to produce the unified, overall action of running.

In mental action this would be for instance coordinating many steps and trains of thought into one cognitive project, a project of understanding a topic comprehensively—which must be done by coordinating the elements in time. Or: The timing and rhythmic flow of the words in a poem help you hold the poem in mind as a whole, and grasp and retain all the threads of its meaning in one unified bundle. Or: a logical argument is a steady progression marching you inevitably to a certain conclusion. If you introduce bumps or distractions— ideas that fail to contribute to the progression—the argument starts to fall apart and the momentum dissipates. The argument is less clear, less powerful and convincing, the arrival at the conclusion is awkward and stilted. The non sequitur is the most anti-rhythmic thing there is.

In all cases, rhythm is a means of bringing actions together into a package by controlling their timing, so that they fit together as a system directed to accomplish some larger purpose. Rhythm is therefore inherently and fundamentally connected with action that is *efficacious*. This is also why rhythmic action is pleasurable and a form of enjoyment. Life is action; rhythm is an expression of successful life.

### RHYTHM AS MEASUREMENT

Rhythm is something more for a man than it is for an animal. Men produce rhythm as an end in itself, for the sake of a certain pleasure in the regularity. The lower animals do not; they merely use rhythm in the mechanical nature of their bodies while they are taking action for food and other basic needs. Though animals undoubtedly experience some form of pleasure in flowing, smooth action versus discomfort in uncoordinated action, there is no evidence to suggest that they get the same powerful emotional charge from rhythmically coordinated action per se. Why?

Pleasure is nature's reward for successful action. The intensity of the pleasure is proportional to the scope of the action integrated.

Man is capable of integrating his action in a fashion much more complex and wide-ranging than for the lower animals. Man makes lifelong plans and coordinates his actions to work toward them. He trains himself to run better, swim faster, catch more consistently. He marches into battle. He chants at a political rally. He gives speeches. He creates, memorizes and recites poetry. He thinks through complex issues and problems and figures out what course to take to solve the problem or reach the goal. Lower animals do not and cannot do these things.

What is it that gives man such a great capacity of action? It is not his body, which doesn't differ that much from the other primates. It is the power of his *mind*. That is what enables him to coordinate a greater number of actions spread widely in space and time. Think first of an orangutan reaching over to the next tree;  then think of a man inventing a product, raising capital, devising means of manufacture, building a factory, executing a marketing plan, shipping the product to stores, offering sales and coupons and promotional incentives, calculating profit or loss, expanding or contracting the business according to all the relevant information. The difference is truly amazing.

And the difference in cognitive capacity shows up in how much pleasure can be gotten from coordinated action.

A central means by which the mind integrates action is *measurement*, whether implicit or explicit. There is a reason the name of man's distinctive faculty, "rationality," comes from the word "ratio." The mind uses quantitative relationships among sense inputs to learn, plan and act in a coordinated fashion.

Measurement requires a uniform unit that serves as the basis for interrelating quantities. When Galileo, sitting in the Cathedral of Pisa in 1583, first noticed a swinging chandelier and measured the period of its swing, it was his pulse that he used as the means of measurement. The pulse or beat is the uniform unit making up the measured action that is rhythm.

A beat is a regularly recurring pulse measuring human action. "Beat" and "pulse" are synonyms of course—these terms cannot be given verbal definition because they are names for a physical-perceptual primary. They are not complex abstractions but mere pointers to something we know by direct experience. A beat or pulse is a physical, kinesthetic unit, one which we feel in moving. If you tap your hand on your knee regularly, each point when your hand strikes your knee (and the sound it makes) marks a division of time. Or, if you drop your arm down in the air and then lift it again (like a conductor does), the point at which you change direction marks a beat.

There is a sense in which the beat means the instant of articulation separating one time unit from the next, and there is a sense in which it means the span of time between one articulation and another. Both senses are legitimate since they are part of the same process of division and just give a different emphasis.

Rhythm is an *experiential* measurement of time, not a scientific one. The purpose of rhythm is not to explicitly, numerically identify a quantity of time, although we use explicit numerical measurement to help us understand and deal with rhythm. Rather, its purpose is to *feel* the regularity *in one's own action*. And yet this experience is indeed quantitative: it is a measured-out kinesthetic and cognitive-emotional phenomenon, a matter of directing physical and mental action coordinated in time.

A basic principle of regularity is mandatory for rhythm; but absolutely unwavering, scientifically and mechanically precise regularity is not needed, and is in many cases contrary to nature. The body and mind have in their nature a certain flexibility, a dynamic ability to use and adjust to slight variations from perfect regularity; these variations in fact help keep the tissues fresh and free rather than monotonously worn—and this includes the feeling and state of one's muscles as well as one's nerves. Flexibility and fluctuation within a certain range of precision is natural to organic, dynamic action. A human being may use a metronome for practicing certain skills; but this does not mean that a man is a metronome or that he should be.

Nor does this mean that human nature is flawed or deficient—on the contrary it means that overly rigid ideas are flawed and deficient in their understanding of the reality of man's nature, which is measured and often astonishingly precise, but also organic and flexible.

Measurement of rhythm is hierarchical—there are *levels* of time division. Some divisions are very broad, others are finer; larger units subsume smaller ones and smaller ones combine to form larger. The pattern of division is exactly analogous to the hierarchy of length measurements.

Observe the nature common to time divisions of musical notes, and length divisions on a ruler:

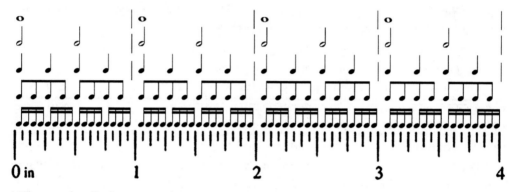

4.1 *The correspondence of length measurement and time measurement.*

Some beats are accented while others are not; in other words, some are strong and some are weak. *Meter* is a regularly recurring pattern of strong and weak beats. A *measure* (or bar) is one instance of a metrical pattern. On a higher level, there are also strong and weak bars.

There are two basic types of meter: duple and triple. In *duple* meter, the strong and weak beats alternate; every second beat is stressed. A march is a duple meter. In *triple* meter, each strong beat is followed by two weak ones; every third beat is stressed. A waltz is a triple meter.

The muscles of the human body are organized in opposing groups. The biceps contract to bring the forearm closer to the body, while the triceps contract to counteract that by pulling the arm away from the body. A related opposition on a higher level is the operation of the paired limbs, the legs and arms which alternate for walking and other actions. Duple meter activates muscles in alternation, in a binary back-and-forth, giving the music a certain angular, decisive feeling. The cleanly marked and sharply articulated left-right-left, military feel of a march exemplifies this.

A triple meter, on the other hand, uses the muscles in a more complex and flowing interaction, not a simple alternation of opposing muscle groups. Triple meter arouses more curved, arc-tracing motions of the body. Thus it has a smoother, "rotary" sort of feel. This is just the kind of motion of the flowing, graceful waltz.

There are also more complicated meters built out of these basic components and in which the effects are similarly derivative. A quadruple meter is basically a duple-duple. A quintuple meter reduces to a combination of either 2 beats plus 3, or 3 beats plus 2.

Rhythm and meter are not the same thing. Meter is an underlying, repeating pattern of strong and weak pulses, which remains constant. Rhythm is the timing and duration of the sounds in all their details, which timing may or may not coincide with the beats or the meter. A note can begin on the beat or between the beats. It can last one beat or several, or a fraction of a beat. The beat doesn't change but rhythm does. The meter is the background measuring framework; the rhythm of the music operates within that context and by conformity to it as the underlying structure.

It is a fundamental aspect of musicianship to maintain a *separation of meter and rhythm*. The rhythm means the timing of the musical sounds, which can change over time; the beat means the constant element, the unchanging measuring pulse which creates the framework the events fit into. A very common mistake, which is the basic problem of all people with poor rhythm, is adapting the beat to a particular rhythm one is implementing. Imagine, for instance, that a musician is keeping time by tapping his foot to the beat, while he speaks a rhythm that is more complex and varied. In the correct case, the foot keeps going without change regardless of the vicissitudes of the rhythm he speaks. In the erroneous case, the musician makes his foot move in exactly the same pattern as he speaks; he fails to maintain the constant measuring pulse and finds that his foot and his mouth are doing the same thing; he loses the separation of the time-keeper from the rhythm. This is the failure to separate pulse and rhythm, and once a musician has this problem it can only be overcome with great effort. He will acquire secure rhythm if and when he is able to maintain two mental/physical "tracks": one that unwaveringly measures out the pulse and another that has the flexibility of creating varied rhythms over that.

The beat divides time, measuring it out into regular intervals. The next question pertains to the *sub*division of the beat. This is the same issue, but on a smaller scale. There are two basic divisions: *duple* which subdivides the beat into two equal parts and *triple* which subdivides it into three. Just as before, the duple pattern tends to give a more angular feel, while the triple gives a more flowing one—except that on this quicker scale, the effect is less gross or pronounced. Rather, the feeling takes place within, and tempers, the larger-scale feeling established by the duple or triple emphasis of the beats themselves.

An architectural analogy is instructive here. The finer divisions are like the band of ornamental marks around the cornices of the temples of the Acropolis, while the columns are like the regular beats. The form of division in the finer increments contributes to the impression one gets, but in a subtler way than the enormous, evenly spaced columns.

4.2 & 4.3 *The Parthenon's rectilinear masculinity and march-like duple division suit a temple to Athena, goddess of wisdom and war. The Erechtheum's flowing, feminine grace uses more delicate divisions including circle quintuplets.*

The complete definition of a meter specifies the number of beats in one measure (one instance of the repeated pattern of strong and weak beats), and then the subdivision of the beat. Here are some examples of the various types of meter:

**Duple meter, duple subdivision:** J.P. Sousa's "Stars and Stripes Forever"

**Duple meter, triple subdivision:**
Beethoven's 6th Symphony, "Pastoral": "Shepherd's Song; cheerful and thankful feelings after the storm"
Allegretto (with contentment)

**Triple meter, duple subdivision:** Johann Strauss Jr.'s Waltz from *Die Fledermaus* ("The Bat")
Allegro grazioso (Gracefully cheerful)

**Triple meter, triple subdivision:** J.S. Bach's *Jesu Joy of Man's Desiring*

**Quadruple meter, duple subdivision:** Chopin's Nocturne in E Minor, Op. 72, No. 1
Andante (Walking pace)

Chopin's melody has duple subdivision, which sings over an accompaniment in triple subdivision.

**Quintuple meter, with a mixture of duple and triple subdivision:**
Tchaikovsky's 6th Symphony, "Pathetique," 2nd Movement
Allegro con grazia (cheerfully with grace)

Notice how Tchaikovsky's slurs indicate division of the measure into two beats plus three.

*4.4 Examples of melody in the various types of meter*

Swing rhythm is a different kind of subdivision of the beat. It subdivides not into two equal parts nor three but into a certain *un*equal pattern. The extent to which the later of the two notes making up a beat is "swung"—sounded later than it would in a standard or "square" duple division—is flexible; different kinds of music place the swung note differently to create a subtly different feel.

Often the beat is divided into two parts, the first of which lasts 4/7 of the beat and the second of which begins at 5/7. That said, the feeling is not a strict measurement or rule-conforming mathematical feeling, not even a division into a large prime number such as seven parts. Rather, the feel is of a movement in two parts with the second one coming a little late or "lazy" so that it "swings" into the next beat. (This is why we notate it in the same way as strict duple division, though there is an unwritten practice of making the subdivision unequal according to the swing feel.)

Notice the term "swing" names a kind of motion. To "swing" according to Merriam-Webster means "to cause to sway to and fro." The feeling of swing rhythm is the opposite of formal accuracy or the tension of strict conscious self-control or measurement. Its movement-feel is casual, relaxed, loose.

## Poetic Rhythm

Poetry of course shares with music the attribute of rhythm. And in both cases the rhythm serves to integrate mental and physical action. Poetry is a helpful way of considering the mental aspect because talking about the language of a poem is easier than talking about the abstract rhythmic patterns of music.

> A charm invests a face
> by Emily Dickinson
>
> A charm invests a face
> Imperfectly beheld.
> The lady dare not lift her veil
> For fear it be dispelled.
>
> But peers beyond her mesh,
> And wishes, and denies,
> Lest interview annul a want
> That image satisfies.

This poem, with the slow, leisurely if not melancholic pacing typical of Emily Dickinson, is in quadruple meter with triple subdivision. It gets a broad, steady feel from the alternating beats of the quadruple meter, but something of a more flowing, swinging or rolling feeling from the triple subdivision. How does this relate to the poem's theme of a lady who wishes to retain the mystique of being slightly obscured? The quadruple meter invests the poem with decisiveness and resolution, creating a feeling of the lady's determination not to dispel her veil of obscurity; the flowing triple subdivision softens that, making the feeling not sharp and decisive but somewhat rounded, gentle, more feminine. Thus the rhythm of the poem helps create the aura of both the lady's determination and her demureness.

The rhythm of the poem also serves a cognitive end. It helps you hold it in mind as one structure. The pacing of the sounds serves as a means of integrating the words into the single entity that is the poem. The first two lines, "A charm invests a face/Imperfectly beheld" are halting; each line has a beat of silence following it to keep the meter. The next two lines flow continuously, there is no beat of silence between them: "The lady dare not lift her veil/For fear it be dispelled." But then the line stops on "dispelled," landing decisively on a strong beat. This is the tight integration of the timing of the words with their meaning. The second stanza employs the same rhythmic structure, creating a parallel and reinforcing the pattern in the mind.

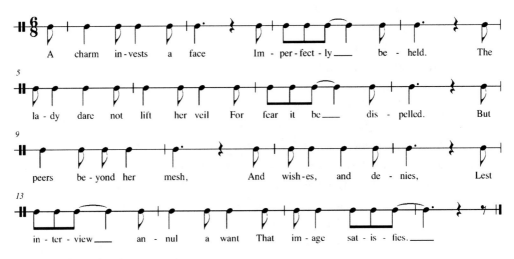

*4.5 The rhythm of Miss Dickinson's poem in musical notation*

A hallmark of poetry is its extreme concentration of meaning. The time values, which are a musical aspect of a poem, assist in building meaning densely into such a short literary minia-ture. A similar process takes place in music, even without words.

## THE METRONOME

The metronome came very late in history. Dietrich Nikolaus Winkel invented it in 1812—after Bach, Handel, Vivaldi and Mozart were long dead, Haydn had just died (1809) and more than half of Beethoven's career was already behind him. The name of the instrument is of Greek origin: *metron* = measure, *nomos* = regulating. Winkel began with Galileo's understanding of pendulums, and discovered through experimentation that a counterweight above the pivot point of the pendulum would regulate the motion to continue uniformly at the relatively slow range of paces used in the music he knew. He added a scale for positioning the upper weight to control the rate of beating. Winkel failed to file a patent, however, and four years later the invention was patented by Johann Nepomuk Maelzel, who is typically cited as the inventor.

The metronome is a helpful tool. A common problem in music is "stuttering" or permitting oneself a lot of stops and starts instead of a continuous regular flow, which is necessary in practicing as much as performing. The metronome can help a student stay on track.

However, the metronome also led to a more mechanistic way of thinking, as though men were to be judged by the standards of machines instead of the other way around. People began to prize precision and perfect, mechanical accuracy of rhythm—since it was thought to be scientifically measured and therefore rational, objective and proper. This of course fails to take into account the biological nature of man—which includes the fact that within an overall context of efficacious regularity living things are evolved to handle and use a certain range of flexibility and fluctuation from perfect mechanical precision.

One of the effects was a re-interpretation of tempo markings. For ages, composers had marked the heads of their scores with Italian terms indicating the character and pace of the work. "Andante" means a walking feeling. "Allegro" means "merry, cheerful, joyful, jolly, mirthful, light-hearted, jovial, sportive." "Vivo" means "alive, living; bright, lively." "Grave" means "heavy, weighty; serious, grievous; deep; grave, solemn."

These terms are evocative, multifaceted and *emotional*. But with the advent of improper obedience to the metronome, and with the modern attitude that emotion is "unscientific" and not to be mentioned, the terms were pared down and defined often exclusively in terms of pace measurements. Andante is defined as a range from 76–108 bpm, Allegro from 120–139 bpm, and so on. This loses the original meaning of the terms. The measurements can be helpful and need not be ignored, but they cannot replace and stand in for the *host* of measurements indicated by the full meaning of the character terms. Nor can the metronome numbers summarize where one has an appropriate range of interpretive options, or along what parameters (such as loudness, pace and pace variation, articulation, elongation of certain notes).

The character terms had communicated a feeling, an overall, holistic characterization of the composition including much more than pace. They helped the interpreter hold a broad standard in mind to fulfill the purpose of the piece: the communication of its emotional theme. Instead this broad conceptual approach was restricted down to a focus on one measurement of one parameter—an impoverished and unmusical approach to music.

## CONCLUDING SUMMARY

Let us summarize the key points on the nature of rhythm.

There is a profound connection between rhythm and life. The pleasure of rhythm is nature's reward for successfully coordinated action.

The efficacious regularity of rhythm is a form of measurement. Rhythmic events can be measured explicitly and numerically, but the essence of rhythm is the experience of action coordinated in beats. It is a unique phenomenon which one can only call an implicit, experiential sort of measurement.

Not only physical but also mental action is, or can be, coordinated in rhythm. Reciting a poem in your mind, for instance, is a rhythmical act. Cognitive acts take place in time and must be integrated with one another, just as physical motions must.

The *beat* is the unit of measurement. *Meter* is a recurring pattern of strong and weak beats. Metrical organization is *hierarchical* in that there are small subdivisions and larger spans organized in levels of measurement like marks of length on a ruler.

Different forms of experiential measurement, different forms of rhythm, arouse different shapes or qualities of action. Alternation of strong and weak beats—binary measurement, as in march tempo—produces more angular action. Triple groupings of beats, as in a waltz, produce more flowing, arc-tracing motion. These facts depend on the complementary muscle groups in the body, and on the analogous phenomenon of change of place in the mind.

Rhythm is a crucial part of the nature of dance, poetry and music. Dance and poetry can teach us much about music; because they involve visible material objects they are easier to talk about.

Rhythm is a phenomenon present in the entire animal kingdom, but it has a special emotional power for man, who is capable of integrating actions much more complex and wide-ranging than those of the lower animals. Therefore the corresponding pleasure reward is greater. Furthermore, man is self-aware. He lives by means of the action of his mind, so the rhythms of the mind are of great significance.

A moral question lies behind human action, both mental and physical. Action of one kind embodies and makes apparent certain basic assumptions about one's nature as a man; action of another kind, another. Action can embody such moral fundamentals as whether or not you are in control of yourself; whether you lead from the mind or are driven by your gut; and whether or not you, as a being in possession of a definite spine, stand with the dignity of an upright posture.

# 5

---

## POLYPHONY

The glory of Western Music, its distinctive achievement and the source of its great power, is the control of lines sounding together, blended in harmony. The birth of this practice of "polyphony" or "many voices" is one of history's most auspicious events.

In order to understand the full background and meaning of this innovation, we will do well to bear in mind the music which immediately preceded it. It is Gregorian chant which formed the starting point for the development of polyphony.

Even though it grew from the starting point of Medieval Gregorian chant, the full blossom of Renaissance polyphony contrasts starkly with it, and has a radically different impact and meaning. These two styles of music, we shall see, are manifestations of two opposite schools of philosophical metaphysics.

### PLATO & GREGORIAN CHANT

We have all heard of the idea of Platonic love—a love that is purely spiritual, without expression in physical acts of affection. This term is a cliché part of the language now, but it only became so because it perfectly encapsulates the practical meaning of Plato's abstract philosophy. Plato upheld a superior dimension of perfect Ideas such as the Form of the Good, and looked down on the earthly world around us as an imperfect reflection of the higher Reality. Higher ideals, he held, were not to be sullied by involvement with the physical world around us.

Plato's philosophy was a continuation of the Pythagoreans' number mysticism, which "reified" abstractions—which treated them as though they were real entities existing outside of our minds in the physical world.

Plato was against worldly concerns and all forms of self-indulgence. He advocated strict self-control, directing the mind away from the lowly pleasures of this world and toward the lofty sphere of ideals. He set up a conflict between rationalistic contemplation, which he held as an ideal, and the practical concerns of life in the world. The man who succeeded in practical life was not the ideal. The man who had no need to concern himself with practical life, who could spend his days in spiritual communion with the higher dimension, was the great man. Plato's theory of knowledge was the pattern of divine inspiration or revelation, available only to the select few who had access to insights into the higher reality.

Plato's philosophy became the foundation of the Christian religion. Plato's Forms became thoughts in the mind of God. The world of Forms, the resplendent perfect sphere superior to this world and the object of Plato's longing, became heaven. The pattern of knowledge was communion with the Ideal, contemplation of the divine, and access by the elite to divine revelation and insight.

Christian monks became the practitioners of Plato's ideal, turning away from this world, dropping the concerns of selfish pleasure and fulfillment and happiness, withdrawing from practical life to contemplate the divine—in devotion to the day of death when they would enter the gates of heaven.

A crucial figure in the transition between Plato and full Medieval Christianity was Augustine. He lived from 354 to 430 AD in a center of Christianity in northern Africa, where he was Bishop of Hippo Regius (present-day Annaba, Algeria). The area was part of the Roman Empire and Augustine wrote in Latin. His views had enormous influence on the development of the Christian Church.

Plato's thought had still contained elements of Greek secularism and worship of man and his life in this world. But according to one of his contemporaries, Augustine "established anew the ancient faith." His views were the purified essence of Plato's supernaturalism, combined with Christ's moral code of self-sacrifice. Augustine stripped away the elements of the Greeks' joyous love of life and man, and replaced it with the somber tone and self-abnegating meekness of Medieval Christianity.

With Saint Augustine we start to see the prominence of the concept of sin and the feeling of shame. In his *Confessions* he writes (around 400 AD) of the torment he experienced regarding the pleasures of music. Here he taught a lesson that the Church heeded for about a thousand years.

In hearing melodies "sung with a sweet and attuned voice," the saint regrets a tendency to give them "more honor than is seemly." He insists on spiritual chastity: "this contentment of the flesh, to which the soul must not be given over to be enervated, doth oft beguile me…. Thus in these things I unawares sin." At times the shame would make him "wish the whole melody of sweet music… banished from my ears, and the Church's too."

He concedes that clear and suitable singing has utility, "that so by the delight of the ears, the weaker minds may rise to the feeling of devotion." But he bemoans,

*"Thus I fluctuate between peril of pleasure and approved wholesomeness…. Yet when it befalls me to be more moved with the voice than the words sung, I confess to have sinned penally, and then [I would] rather not hear music. See now my state; weep with me, and weep for me, ye, who so regulate your feelings within, as that good action ensues. For you who do not act, these things touch not you. But, Thou, O Lord my God, hearken; behold, and see, and have mercy, and heal me, Thou,*

*in whose presence I have become a problem to myself; and that is my infirmity."* (*Confessions of S. Augustine*, J.M. Dent & Sons Ltd., 1907, trans. E.B. Pusey.)

These were the sort of ideals that shaped the Church's tone, its culture's emotions, and the kind of music it desired. The music that resulted is known as Gregorian chant. It is named after Pope Gregory the Great.

Gregory, who lived 540 to 604 AD, was a major figure who organized the Catholic Church and consolidated its leadership role in the chaos following the collapse of the Roman Empire. He set the character of the Church as a strict conservative body ruled from St. Peter's Basilica in Rome.

Under Gregory's rule, the Church was said to have definitively cataloged and standardized the "Cantus Romanus"—the songs of the Roman Catholic Church. The chants were collected together into a book that became known as the *Gregorian antiphonal*, and the music came to be known as Gregorian chant.

The antiphonal notated the words sung, with marks above them indicating hints about the pitch of the melody, such as lines suggesting rising or falling motion. These marks served to remind singers of a tune they had already learned by ear from a teacher. Over time this book was disseminated throughout Europe; it became the common basis and standard source for music in the Christian Church.

Gregory was said to have taken the music in dictation directly from God's inspiration. He is often portrayed seated at a writing desk, with a dove over his shoulder singing to him.

However, scholars have found it to be nearly impossible that Gregory would have penned or collected the chants. There is no positive evidence that he was musically able; Gregory's earliest biographers say nothing about the subject of chant; the founding of the Schola Cantorum, the Church's singing school, appears to have taken place several generations after Gregory lived; these and many other facts call the attribution into question.

In fact, much of the Church's music had probably been taken from the pagan world and adapted to its purposes. Just as with the content of its ideas, so with its music, the Church drew upon secular sources while refusing to acknowledge them.

Rather, the attribution of the chants to Gregory should be understood as a propaganda story that the Church used to make people accept its chants as the one and only music, coming directly from God. It was a means of establishing the legitimacy of the music and persuading people to adopt it. From that motivation, the attribution makes perfect sense.

It was indeed fitting that the chants were named after Gregory in the sense that they express the spirit he symbolized, embodied and preached. According to the Grove Dictionary, Gregory led "a life of spirituality and asceticism." Gregory wrote in the preface to his *Dialogues*:

*"My unhappy mind remembers what it was in the monastery; how it soared above the vicissitudes of fleeting things, because it thought only of things celestial; and, though retained in the body,*

*transcended through contemplation the enclosures of the flesh; while even of death, which to almost all men appears a penalty, it was enamoured as being the entrance into life, and the reward of its labour."* (quoted in James Barmby's *Gregory the Great*)

Gregorian chant fulfills the Platonic and Augustinian ideals. The music is a single line sung by men's voices merging anonymously in unison. The sound reverberates through the Church, washing away any sharp clarity or incisiveness, and creating an atmosphere around you together with the smell of incense and the shadows encroaching upon dim, dusky candle-light. The music's quiet darkness and uniform flow avoid any stark contrast, any stimulating drama, any sensual richness, any vigor of rhythm. It is music turned away from the passions and pleasures of this world. It flows in a cool, even stream, somber and haunting. The sound is spiritually pure, austere, giving a suggestion of mourning, vast mystery and of melancholy longing for the divine.

Gregorian Chant
Kyrie from the Mass for Septuagesima Sunday

Kyrie eleison.          Lord have mercy.
Christe eleison.        Christ have mercy.
Kyrie eleison.          Lord have mercy.

*5.1 Gregorian chant embodies the Platonic-Christian ideal of austere contemplation of the mysteries of heaven*

## THE BIRTH OF POLYPHONY

Just before 800 AD Charlemagne conquered and united the majority of mainland Europe, encompassing the areas that today make up France, Germany and Italy. Charlemagne had conquered by force, by ruthlessness, by mercilessly decimating his opponents. But he was more than a common brute. He was a leader and unifier who used his mind and who valued learning. In the Dark Ages, the age of ignorance and illiteracy—and in fact the age of scorn for literacy as impractical—Charlemagne learned to read and write. He spoke not only German but also Latin, and he understood Greek. He studied science.

The areas of his kingdom were extremely diverse. Among many small and isolated areas people spoke different languages, practiced different religions, had different cultures. Charlemagne sought to unify his kingdom by collecting, standardizing and disseminating products of the intellect. He had laws collected and written down, compiling the accumulated knowledge of the courts. He had ancient songs of heroes written down (such as Siegfried the dragonslayer). He established schools to increase the level of the public's knowledge.

Charlemagne saw a common religion, Christianity, as essential to the unity of his kingdom. (In fact, Charlemagne's perceived moral authority and legitimacy had come in large part from his being crowned Emperor by the Pope in the year 800.) Charlemagne regarded it as of the utmost importance that his empire be united by a common worldview, the doctrine of the Christian Church in Rome. And therefore, by deliberate, systematic intention, the content of culture flowed out from Rome to the whole of Europe.

In essence, Charlemagne singlehandedly created modern Europe.

The century following his reign reflected the fruits of his effort to unify diverse elements and to revive man's intelligence. As a result the period is known as the Carolingian Renaissance (from his Latin name, Carolus Magnus).

However, this Renaissance did not last. The devotion to Christian dogma Charlemagne enforced simultaneously re-entrenched the mindset of the Dark Ages. There would be a relapse of darkness for hundreds of years once again before the full flowering of the European Renaissance took root after the revival of Greek influences.

But Charlemagne's mini-Renaissance nevertheless had major consequences for the arts, especially music. His reign meant, among other things, that the music used in the church had to be written down, copied, disseminated and taught throughout Europe. It was a project of standardization and communication on an unheard-of scale, and it led to a completely new level of musical activity.

It should be borne in mind what musical life was like in Medieval times. Musical life allaround was much smaller, less developed, and more constrained than it had been in the vibrant culture of Greece, or even in the Roman Empire whose warrior culture had despised music as effeminate and frivolous. Most of the musical theory of Greece was unknown, the scale-system of Greece had continued but only with much confusion and incompleteness; the keyboard instruments had not yet been invented—the only reliable instrument was the primitive single stretched string (the monochord) which had marks at the nodes for various notes so that it could be stopped and plucked, thus giving a correct pitch. Other than that there was no objective means of establishing pitch.

Instead of any exact measurements or clear concepts of music, thought on the subject focused on vague metaphysical speculation about Plato's "Harmony of the Spheres"—the alleged mathematical harmony sounding silently among the perfect Forms in Heaven. Music was transmitted orally, if at all, and the process of learning new songs was laborious and slow. Compositions could not be fixed in a reliable permanent form, but were consigned to a perpetual game of "telephone" in which the fallible memory (or deliberate creativity) of one singer could cause a new version of some old standard melody to take the place of, or coexist with the prior version.

But it is during the brief period of the Carolingian Renaissance that we find not only the first definite record of music employing simultaneous sounding notes, but also the first attempt to systematically understand its rudiments. It was the birth, not yet of harmony, but of *polyphony*. "Poly-phony" means "many voices."

The practice of sounding multiple notes at once seems to have existed sporadically and informally, without record, without any systematic control or explicit conceptions, for millennia in various places in the world—in the form of primitive improvisations.

Although we don't know the details of exactly when and where, we know with certainty that during the 100 years after Charlemagne, European musicians began to explore the possibilities of singing more than one note at a time.

Around the year 900, one hundred years after Charlemagne's unification of Europe, a "Handbook on Music" (*Musica enchiriadis*) by an unknown author gave an account of musical practices, complete with examples written in an early form of music notation. This document was almost certainly a result of Charlemagne's campaign to standardize the Roman church's doctrine and music throughout Europe. Thus we see a connection between the advent of music notation and the requirement of standardization and accurate remote communication.

The first stage of this progression was simply to have two groups sing the same line at the same time, but starting on different notes. The voices would sing together strictly in parallel, with the added voice singing a fourth below the original line. Because of the clear yet biting discord of the fourth, the effect is rather piercing and primal sounding. Sometimes the new voice would be a fifth below, which is still rather primal sounding, but not as harsh.

Gradually, people came to explore the possibilities of using different combinations, combinations more complex and varied than a melody with a shadow following it up and down in lock-step.

First they confronted the issue that if they wanted to sing in parallel fourths, there was a problem because one of the fourths in the diatonic scale is augmented (from F up to B). The augmented fourth makes a noticeably different sound, a peculiarly intense honking discord which sticks out like a laser in a dark room. The A4 is a form of tritone, which the church fathers had called 'the Devil in music'—*diabolus in musica*. To avoid that sound, a rule was made that one voice should stay on the same note at certain times, and only move when the "diabolus in musica" was safely avoided. Here's an example from the "Handbook":

Tu humiles famuli modulis
venerando piis,
se iubeas flagitant variis
liberare malis.

Your humble servants,
worshiping piously,
beseech you, as you command, to free
Them from diverse ills.

Parallel fourths would have sounded the 'diabolus in musica' below the note B.

Tu   hu - mi - les    fa - mu - li    mo - du - lis    ve - ne - ran - do    pi - is.
se   iu - be - as    fla - gi - tant    va - ri - is    li - be - ra - re    ma - lis.

*5.2 The earliest rules for combining voices came about to avoid the dissonant tritone, the 'diabolus in musica.'*

It deserves to be stressed that the first idea for how to make a new line vary from the main line, the first rule of composition, was propelled by the need to avoid the harshness, the ugliness and the jarring nature of *dissonance that did not integrate into the flow of the music.*

In the post-Charlemagne period, three things began to develop hand-in-hand: polyphony, notation, and rules. The rich sound of multi-voiced music, the capacity of writing it down accurately, and the formulation of guidelines for coordinating lines into a beautiful fabric—these three things fed into, boosted, and reinforced one another in a continuous upward spiral. This is the combination that made Western music what it is. It is the three-pronged base of knowledge that enabled the entire future development of symphonic art.

Beyond a very simple level, polyphonic music requires notation as the means of coordinating the lines, so that the right notes happen together at the right time. It similarly demands the formulation of principles of order, rules by which one can coordinate the lines in such a way as to achieve a flowing, beautifully integrated sonority through time.

Notation in turn facilitates composition and performance. The composer need not rely on his memory of a new melody, he can write it down. He can try out different things on paper and evaluate them. He can see as well as hear how the notes fit together. Notation enables the composer to form general principles for how to coordinate the lines from experience. He can learn that one kind of progression sounds bumpy and awkward while another blends and flows beautifully, and he can use that information for all of his future work without the need first to hear the notes in a live performance. The composer notates the music and the performers don't have to face the impossible task of executing all the details in real time from memory—they can read the score. They know when they have deviated from the plan of the music because of the way in which the sounds they made deviated from the notation.

The rules for coordinating the lines in turn enable the composition of an ever-more complex fabric. The increased understanding men develop by identifying abstract rules stimulates a demand for greater precision and detail in the notation.

The fact that these developments took place within the church can make it seem as though religion was behind the new progress. But in fact quite the opposite is the case. The new dimension of music did not grow from the teachings of Christ, Augustine, or Gregory, but from compromise with pagan-style sensuality and secularism. It was Greek principles—the antithesis of Christian self-abnegation and self-doubt—which led to the new progress. And it was not Plato's philosophy that undergirded the progress—his had been and would continue to be the base of Christian other-worldliness and rejection of this world as low. Rather, it was the perspective of Aristoxenus's teacher, Aristotle, which in the Renaissance began to reassert itself. Aristotle's focus on this world, and the value he placed on worldly happiness, are what were finding expression in the post-Charlemagne rebirth of the mind. It was not the mental lockdown of faith or the suffering of self-sacrifice which began to find expression, but the richness, mental fulfillment, and aliveness of multiple threads of thought weaving together in integrated harmony.

Nevertheless, just as the Bible was held up as the final and absolute Word of God, Gregorian chant was held up as a final and absolute model of perfect music. In the future development of music, this meant that the starting point and frame of reference was Gregorian chant. Just as thinkers accepted that scripture and the doctrines of the Church were the primary concern and the source of all knowledge, they took Gregorian chant to be the self-evident basis and starting point for all music. The music of the church was, to a large extent, all that was known.

So the method became: take a chant as the given, have one group of people sing the chant in longer, drawn out notes, and then have another group sing different notes around it (or use an instrument to play different notes around it). The Chant thereby became a "cantus firmus," a "fixed voice" which did not change, but was the constant element which one worked around.

The line of long tones of the Gregorian chant came to be called the "tenor" and the group of singers the "tenors." "Tenore" in Latin meant "to hold." And the contrasting, more florid line written against it came to be called the "countertenor."

Very, very slowly, by a long process of experimentation, practice, notation, performance, and judgment, men accumulated observations about which combinations of notes have which sorts of effects. They built up, by slow induction over centuries, rules for how to combine tones in a way that flows and is smooth and pleasing to the ear. These were rules about what the intervals were and how they should be used, how the notes should progress, and about what combinations were harsh or interrupted the flow.

These rules were codified by such thinkers as Tinctoris (in the late 1400s) and Zarlino (in his treatise of 1558).

In the 1500s, the High Renaissance, polyphony reached a culmination, exemplified especially in the music of Giovanni Pierluigi da Palestrina.

He was born near Rome in 1525, and his most important position was at St. Peter's Basilica, what is today the Vatican.

Palestrina's music is remarkable for its sweet harmony, its beauty and smoothness of progression. He was able to weave lines together with a new level of clarity, richness and fluid motion. His music was soaring, powerful, passionate, bright, lively, energetic, and yet spiritually pure—meaning *integrated*. His use of modulation, change from one key to another, was masterfully smooth. He was particularly effective in creating passages that introduce one voice at a time, the sound growing and blossoming as the texture of the music became fully fleshed out.

The opening of Palestrina's *"Sicut cervus"* exemplifies the magnificent flowering of sound he mastered:

Palestrina's
setting of Psalm 42:1

Sicut cervus desiderat ad fontes aquarum,      As the deer yearns for flowing fountains,
Ita desiderat anima mea at te, Deus.          So my soul yearns for you, O God.

5.3 *Palestrina's music was a culmination of Renaissance polyphony.*

Thus the West progressed from the austerely haunting mystery of Gregorian chant to the sensual richness and integrated complexity of Renaissance polyphony. In these musics one hears the change from the sadness and dark serenity of a passive mind to the fulfillment of a stimulated, challenged, active one. The change in music was an exact reflection of the underlying change in metaphysics from a Platonic, otherworldly, impersonal asceticism to an Aristotelian, this-worldly acceptance of the value of pleasure, enjoyment and intensely personal expression governed by laws of harmonious synthesis.

# 6

## TONALITY

6.1 The face of Michelangelo's David shows man's power of self-determination

The face of Michelangelo's *David* shows the crucial principle animating Renaissance art: man's *volition*. David prepares to confront the giant Goliath. His healthy physique and relaxed posture convey the efficacy and confidence that will lead him to victory. His face shows an intimation of fear, but together with firmness and resoluteness—the courage that will overcome the fear. The sculpture is a hymn to the power of the human spirit to guide successful action in the world.

During the Renaissance, the conception of man as a self-determined being, guided by the power of his own psyche, his life-course steered by his own judgment and virtue, found expression in all the arts.

In drawing and painting the newly developed method of *perspective* enabled artists to show the world from man's own vantage point, spreading out before him and receding to a distant vanishing point.

Literature dramatized the way in which a character's choices determine the course of his life. Around 1470, for instance, Thomas Malory collected in *Le Morte d'Arthur* the old legends of King Arthur and the Knights of the Round Table. The Knights' deeds are a result not of divine determination but of their individual motivation and character. Lancelot and Queen Guinevere choose to act on their romantic passion; the stories dramatize the consequences, including Arthur's response. Literature, in other words, began to focus squarely on how choices shape one's life course.

The principle of volition found expression in music as well. The Renaissance turned away from the uniform, coldly haunting austerity of Gregorian chant, and developed the sensuality, richness and splendor of polyphony.

The motion of polyphonic music was highly *directional*. Unlike Gregorian chant, it did not establish a feeling of unwavering peace and tranquility for contemplating the mysteries of the divine. Unlike later Impressionism, it was not a wash of sound dissolving the mind in bleariness. Polyphonic music did not "vamp" or continually repeat a snippet of music to create a feeling of riding in place. Its sound was a flow of diverse voices playing against one another and progressing to convergence and resolution.

From the earliest days of sung poetry, melodic closure had been made to match the closure of the language sung. A pause in the words required an appropriate pause in the music, but also an appropriate ending note. A phrase ending with a comma required some appropriate resting note to stop on; a sentence ending with a period required a stronger form of closure; the complete end of the poem required the most complete closure. The music needed to match and contribute to the feeling of "wrapping up" that came with the closure of a unit of meaning expressed in language. However, with a single melodic line, the feeling of motion to closure even at its strongest is rather mild.

In a polyphonic fabric, on the other hand, a much stronger directionality is possible. The lines can play off of one another, build up the level of activity and finally come together at a phrase ending. Thus polyphony is able to create a feeling of a much longer arc or trajectory of motion. It is able to build up a greater tension, to heighten anticipation, and to increase the satisfaction of arrival at the point of resolution.

The moment of closure of a phrase or composition was called the *cadence* after the Latin "cadere" meaning "to fall." The cadence became the end, the goal of musical motion, and all the musical elements—melodic shape, the use of scale-steps, rhythm, the interplay of lines— were marshaled to lead to it.

The cadence is the vanishing-point of perspective painting, it is the resolution a story's conflict, it is the foreseen goal in David's eyes, it is the center of mass in Newtonian physics.

One of the traits of music of the mid-1400s was the so-called "drive to the cadence," the shaping of the fabric of lines to lead strongly to the moment of phrase closure. The Dutch or Franco-Flemish School, including such composers as Josquin des Prez and Jacob Obrecht, was known for this technique using changes of rhythm, piling up of the voices, and clear stepwise movement of melody to lead strongly and decisively into the cadence.

Marshaling all the musical elements to lead to the cadence gave the music a sense of "pull" and direction over substantial periods of time. It created a sort of psychological compass whose needle unwaveringly pointed the way during the ebb and flow of the music. The draw of the cadence provided a continuous means of psychological measurement of the distance from the goal in the form of a sense of harmonic "place"—at home or far afield, in transit or arriving, off course or on it. It created a feeling of the length of the journey ahead: the distant vision of a goal far off in the future but still perceptible, the feeling of progress toward it, the possibility of being thrown off course temporarily and of restoring the proper direction, and the completion of a long process of mental exertion leading to a climactic anticipation and satisfaction as you reach the destination.

One of the means of creating a feeling of goal-direction in polyphonic music is the introduction and resolution of dissonances between the voices. The strongest form of all is the accented dissonance, the pattern: a consonant note sounds, it is held over or suspended as the other voices change to make it dissonant, and then that dissonant note gives way—it resolves down by step to blend once again with the other tones. This creates a smooth lead-in, followed by the tension of an incomplete and unstable element with its nervous energy, and then a release and satisfaction as the line yields back to stability. This pattern is an important ingredient in the push and pull, the ebb and flow, the directionality of polyphonic music.

So some of the ingredients to express volitional purposefulness in music were, as it were, on the table. What remained was for someone to provide a recipe for a new concoction that made the most of these—in non-metaphoric words, for someone to formulate a new system and place everything under a new principle.

## ZARLINO

It was Gioseffo Zarlino who, based on the effects being created in the music of his time as well as his era's implicit ideal of the importance of volition, formulated the principle of *tonality*. Tonality was a revolutionary and comprehensive new system of unity in music, a system that most intensely expressed the feeling of goal-direction.

Zarlino's own music is a magnificent and beautiful expression of feelings of yearning, of growing, of striving; his music has both solemnity and the tension of purpose in it. The same principle he laid down in theory, he implemented in his own composition.

Zarlino, born in northern Italy in 1517, was a singer, organist, and composer in the service of the Church. In his thirties he traveled to Venice to study with composer Adrian Willaert, the master of music at St. Mark's Cathedral. Zarlino himself eventually became the "maestro di cappella" at that church. He would become the teacher of many important pupils, including Vincenzo Galilei, the father of Galileo.

Zarlino's revolutionary treatise *The Institution of Harmony* (*Le institutioni harmoniche*) was published in 1558. The work was disseminated throughout Europe and widely discussed and commented on; it came to have enormous influence—and rightfully so, since it provided profound insight into the nature of music, and a definition of revolutionary new principles of structure.

Zarlino began with the law that consonance comes first:

Music *"is made up primarily and principally of consonances, dissonances are used secondarily and incidentally for the sake of greater beauty and elegance. Taken by themselves they are not very acceptable to the ear; arranged as they regularly should be and in accordance with the precepts [of counterpoint], the ear tolerates them to such an extent that, far from being offended, it receives from them great pleasure and delight…. a dissonance causes the consonance which immediately follows it to seem more acceptable. Thus it is perceived and recognized with greater pleasure by the ear, just as after darkness light is more acceptable and delightful to the eye, and after the bitter the sweet is more luscious and palatable. And from everyday experience with sounds we learn that if a dissonance offends the ear for a certain length of time, the consonance which follows is made more acceptable and more sweet."*

*"Just as there are ingredients in medicines and other electuaries, bitter and even poisonous in themselves, but indubitably health-giving and less harsh when combined with other ingredients, so many things which in themselves are harsh and harmful become good and healthful when combined with others. Thus it is with these relationships of music. And there are other intervals which in themselves give little pleasure, but when combined with others make marvelous effects."*

Thus, properly used dissonances heighten and intensify the effect of consonance.

Zarlino also followed the implications, applying the pattern to longer time spans, and creating a fundamental new principle: just as dissonant notes are ornamentations of consonances, so are *all* the notes of a composition part of an elaborate ornamentation over time of the central sonority of the composition. He originates the definition of *tonality*—the principle that a composition is oriented around a single tone (and the scale built on it, and the triad built on it), and that all of the music moves in relation to that center. The piece is unified by its center on the keynote. As Zarlino states it: "The composition should be subjected to a prescribed and determined harmony, mode, or tone (call it as we will), and that it should not be disordered." —A fairly modest way of stating the principle behind four future centuries of magnificently powerful music!

Composers including Zarlino's teacher Willaert had been developing this idea in practice, as the art of polyphonic composition became increasingly refined. With Zarlino the principle of tonal unity became an explicit law and fundamental method of integration. It opened the possibility of a fully self-conscious and consistent adherence to the pattern of unity around a tonal center.

"Tonality" is one of several important musical terms deriving from the Greek "tonos" meaning "to stretch." The tonic note is the central point of reference, the orienting center of a major or minor scale. The term derives from this principle of gravitational center; the tonic is retained by the ear and held in mind continually, even when it is not literally sounding, such that all subsequent sounds are related back to it as consonant or dissonant with it. Thus the tonic note is "stretched" over time in the mind as the reference note even when it is not literally sounding.

(Zarlino did not use the word "tonality" but he was the first to state the principle. The first use of the term dates from 1810 when Alexandre-Etienne Choron, a director of the Paris Opera, wrote on the history of music.)

A main law of counterpoint, Zarlino taught, is that dissonances must resolve; consonances are primary and dissonance is to be introduced only in such a way as to integrate smoothly into the framework provided by consonances. Since composers at this time were routinely using rich sonorities or harmonies (and had been for some time), the question arose: what is the most complex sonority that is still consonant? What is a basic sonority, of more than two notes, which does not require resolution, but to which resolving notes return? Zarlino answered that question: it is the *triad*.

Zarlino defines the triad, the three-note chord stacked in thirds. The central triad of a scale consists of scale-steps 1-3-5. (Be careful not to confuse this tri*ad*, a consonance, with the dissonant tri*tone*, the interval spanning three whole-steps.)

Zarlino identifies the triad as the archetype of all harmony, "For in this combination occur all the different sounds that can form different harmonies." He is very brief about this idea, but gives the seed of some crucial identifications:

1. sonorities with less than a triadic combination are not as full or rich,
2. any other notes which are added (aside from doublings of the existing notes) introduce dissonances and are therefore not elementary, and
3. other sonorities can be reduced back to the triad, as inversions or elaborations.

(It was a theorist by the name of Johannes Lippius who, about 50 years later, would coin the term "triad" and lay out the patterns of chord inversion.)

Zarlino first establishes the essential contrast between a piece that is an elaboration of a major versus minor mode or triad. When the triad is major "the harmony is made joyful" and when it is minor "the harmony is made mournful." The ratio of a major triad is simpler, 4:5:6. The ratio of a minor triad is more complex, 10:12:15.

It is important to stress that Zarlino refers not to the emotional quality of an individual chord in isolation, but to that chord as the central structure of a complete musical context derived from it and oriented around it. This is important because a single major chord on its own does not necessarily have a sunny effect; for instance it could lead to the tonic in a minor key, in which case it simply feeds into and accentuates the dark feeling. Similarly, a minor chord in a major key won't necessarily make the music sad. Rather, the effect is a result of the total auditory "picture," the overall context of music built around a central harmony.

Zarlino wrote that to compose a polyphonic work around a line of Gregorian chant taken as the given voice, one must first examine the chant carefully and "see in what mode it is composed, so that he may make the appropriate cadences in their proper places and may know from these the nature of his composition. For if inadvertently he were to make these inappropriately and out of their places, mixing those of one mode with those of another, *the end of his composition would be dissonant with the beginning and middle*." (Italics added.) Thus Zarlino has injected into Western thought the idea of unity of mode, of the consistency of the central sonority, and central mood, of the composition.

Clearly, he does not think of consonance and dissonance merely in terms of two-note combinations or even small groups of intervals. He thinks of the entire piece as a single consonant structure, with dissonances moving against it over a long span of time, leading to the ultimate resolution, the time when all divergent elements settle back to the home sonority. A harmony can be consonant as a momentary sound, but dissonant against the previously established tonic—and that dissonant relationship is part of the psychological effect of that chord in context. Thus musical integrity does not involve only simultaneous relationships, but relationships between retained past sensations and presently sounding tones.

Zarlino started with the local rule of counterpoint that a dissonance must resolve by step to a consonance. He concluded with a grand-scale vision of musical coherence, a grand-scale principle based in the nature of human musical cognition.

This advance was expressive as well as cognitive: tonality means the use of musical materials in such a way as to emphasize and heighten the feeling of gravitational pull toward the goal-note, the tonic, the main tone of the scale, the keynote. It means the pattern of opening up unresolved elements, and then resolving them. It means the development and strengthening of a sense of psychological direction, purpose and aim.

Other, related advances accompanied this revolution. Recall that Guido d'Arezzo's system of solfege originally included only six syllables. In order to expand the range to an octave or more, the series had to be re-started and overlapped. This tells us something about the conception of music at that time. First, the expected range of music was fairly narrow. Second, the scale, in its basic conception, was devoid of the dissonant tritone.

The Renaissance saw the completion of the octave scale by the addition of the 7th note. Solfege gained a seventh syllable, "Si," to accommodate it. (Zarlino himself had been one of the thinkers who suggested the name for step 7.) The 7th step, recall, is the leading tone, the note that pulls strongly toward the tonic. This development coincided with the expansion of the musical staff from four lines, which had encompassed the interval of a sixth, to five lines, which encompass the interval of an octave.

As polyphony developed, and composers began using more dissonance to create a feeling of expressive forward motion—always according to the rule that dissonances must resolve by step—they also began to harness the most powerful dissonance of all: the *tritone* (ratio 5:7). The tritone occurs in the complete scale between steps 4 and 7. This is the interval missing in the basic 6-note series of Guido's solfege. Recall also that the Church had declared the tritone to be the "devil in music" (*diabolus in musica*), so it had been forbidden and, in effect, cursed. The tritone was not an accepted part of music in the Medieval Church.

But as composers shook off the artificial restrictions of religion and sought more powerfully to express the new feeling of individual volition, they sought to exploit this particularly unusual and unsettling dissonance to contribute to the sense of direction in the music. It is true that, used improperly, the tritone is capable of swiftly wrecking order and intelligibility in music. But used in its natural role in the scale, it has a special kind of effect that no other interval has: it is the interval that defines the key.

There is only one tritone in the major scale, between steps 7 and 4, and because of the way in which it resolves and creates tendency tones, it orients the mind uniquely to the central tonic. In minor, there is a tritone naturally between steps 2 and 6; left alone this causes the music to gravitate to the relative major. Therefore the device of the harmonic and melodic forms of the minor scale came into being; these inflections of minor introduce a leading-tone on scale-step 7, and a key-defining tritone between steps 7 and 4—just as in major.

Thus the unique and intense power of the tritone was harnessed, brought into a diatonic system which not only made it intelligible, but also used the interval to heighten the feeling of psychological aim.

## SCALE-STEP

Tonality is the system which most fully expresses the nature of the diatonic scale.

As we learned in chapter 3, each tone of the scale has a unique emotional character, a unique mental or affective impression. This is the fact implemented in solfege. Recall also John Curwen's system of hand signs for the scale notes.

The distinctive psychological imprint of each note is a result of the unique contextual relationship between that note and all the other ones in the scale; it is a result of the network of intervals between one note and all the others. As a result, each tone has a particular function or role in relation to the others.

The underlying mathematical relationships of the scale give rise to this experience. A quantitative relationship is the underlying factor; a qualitative one is the result. Each note's emotional character registers in the mind not as a measurement per se, but as a feeling, a quality of sensation unique to that scale-step.

There are two levels. The first factor determining the quality of a scale-note is the interval between that note and the tonic. For example, the fifth of the scale has a strong and powerful effect because of being a perfect fifth (3:2) from the main note; the third note of the scale has a warm and euphonious sound because of the interval between it and the tonic (5:4). Certain tones, because of their consonant relation to the tonic, are stable or restful notes. Others, because of their dissonant relation to it, are "tendency" tones, which create a psychological pull toward the nearest stable note.

The second factor determining the quality of a scale-note is the set of intervals between that note and the other, non-tonic notes in the scale. For example, the leading-tone (7th step) pulls upward toward the tonic as intensely as it does not only because of the half-step (15:16) between it and the tonic, but also because of the dissonant tritone (7:5) between it and step 4.

Summarizing these inputs, here is a characterization of each step of the musical scale, by the number of its step (and giving each note's standard technical name):

1. The *tonic* note is the most stable and settled note of the scale; it has the strongest possible sound and offers the greatest satisfaction as a note of arrival and resolution. (The term "tonic" derives from the Greek "tonos" meaning "to stretch"—the idea being that the tonic is held in mind, stretched over time, as the main underlying point of reference of the scale.)

2. The *supertonic* is an unstable tone with the buzzing energy of a tendency tone pulling downward toward 1; yet as a whole-step rather than a half-step above the tonic it is a mellower, gentler tendency tone. It takes a bit of strength from being a fifth above 5. (The term "supertonic" comes from "super" meaning "above," just as "superscript" means "above the text.")

3. The *mediant* is a stable, warm tone which does give repose but not the complete closure that a melody reaches on the tonic. This step is very important for any element of richness and tenderness in musical expression. (The name "mediant" comes from this note's position halfway between the tonic and fifth.) In the major mode, this tone is sunny and bright; in the minor it is dark and pained.

4. The *subdominant* has a strong sound to it because of the perfect interval between it and the tonic, but it is a tendency tone because of the biting quality of the fourth and because of the dissonant tritone between 4 and 7. Thus 4 pulls downward to 3. (The name "subdominant" can be looked at in two ways: the note is one step "under" the dominant, just as "subscript" means "below the text." It is also the fifth below the tonic.)

5. The *dominant* is the most stable and settled note after the tonic, and is the secondary central note of the scale. It serves as the antipode to the tonic, the primary alternative to it, and the only contender for the main spot in the competition for centricity. This is why it is called the "dominant"—it prevails over the other notes of the scale. If the tonic is the earth, the gravitational center which pulls all the other notes toward it, the dominant is the moon—it orbits the tonic, but still exerts a pull of its own.

6. The *submediant* is a warm, expressive tone which tends to move by step to 5 for repose or, in a more energized rising motion, up by scale through 7 to 1. In the major mode, this tone is warm, bright and expansive; the whole step between it and the dominant makes it feel soaring and broad. In the minor mode, this tone is dark and anguished; the half step between it and the dominant makes it pull downward and gives it a poignantly pained feeling. (In a mirror image of the mediant-dominant relation, the submediant is half the distance down to the subdominant.)

7. The *leading tone* forms the most piercingly dissonant interval with the tonic, and it therefore pulls as strongly as possible upward to 1. It is a note that demands resolution. It forms a very dissonant tritone with scale-step 4, which is essential to its unique instability. When the seventh step of the scale is lowered it is not called the leading tone because it no longer has the same pull upward; instead it is called the *subtonic*. In this form, the note's quality is mellow and subdued and draws mildly downward.

The following diagram (inspired by similar ones by Marianne Ploger) shows the qualities of the steps in a graphical manner. Even though we number the scale-steps from the tonic up, in musical perception the tonic is the center of the system. The stronger, more stable tones are shown in a larger size; the less stable ones in a smaller size. The clear perfect consonances are shown with a stark font. The warm and sensuously rich notes are shown with a more gracefully shaped font. The dissonant tendency tones are shown in a more ragged font to indicate their nervous, buzzing energy and instability.

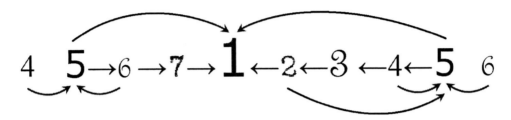

6.2 *The character and directional function of scale-steps in the system of tonality*

The diagram shows the fundamental gravitational structure of the scale. All notes are attracted to, and ultimately resolve to 1. The skip from 5 to 1 is a strong motion affirming 1 as the main note. Step 5 is the secondary main note of the scale; it exerts a pull of its own, attracting steps 4 and 6. The leap from 2 to 5 is analogous to the leap from 5 to 1, only pertaining to the secondary main note instead of the tonic itself.

In the course of music, many other motions will be heard. The notes do not invariably move in these directions. However these are the basic roles of the notes in creating an affirmation of the central status of the tonic.

The fact that certain notes have a certain function in the scale, and that each has a unique sound depending on its unique contextual position and role, was known by the Greeks. Aristoxenus explains that the names given to the notes in the Greek system (which were based on the position of the strings on the lyre), really meant the musical *function* of the notes. For instance, "lychanos" was the name for the step below the main note of the scale; since the main note was A, lychanos was our G. The name comes from "forefinger"—which one used to pluck that particular string on the lyre. But any form of G whether raised or lowered, according to the Greeks, still had the same function and should be called by the same name. So two different pitches could have the same scalar function. There is also the case of identical pitches having different functions; if two intervals were called by different names even though they were literally the same size, this was because their notes had different "jobs" in the scale. "The names," taught Aristoxenus, "have meaning only in their relation to one another." Thus the Greeks had the concept of scale-degree or contextual note function.

The Greeks had a conception that certain notes became central depending on the interval relations around them. When two notes were a fourth apart, the relation caused the upper note always to become the main note.

The concept *Mese* (the note we now call A) started out as the name for the note of the middle string of the lyre, but it came to have the connotation if not the exact meaning of the central note of the scale system. It came to mean, in effect, the tonic note.

In Porphyry's introduction to Aristotle's "Categories," he wrote that "It is from the Mese that we start to discern the functions of the other notes; for plainly it is in relation to the Mese that each of them is thus or thus."

Aristotle himself had spoken to this. From his *Problems*:

*"Why is it that if the Mese is altered, after the other chords [strings] have been tuned, the instrument is felt to be out of tune not only when the Mese is sounded, but through the whole of the music —whereas if the Lichanus [the step below the Mese] or any other note is out of tune, it seems to be perceived only when that note is struck? Is it to be explained on the ground that all good melodies often use the Mese, and all good composers resort to it frequently, and if they leave it soon return again, but do not make the same use of any other note? Just as language cannot be Greek if certain conjunctions are omitted... while others may be dispensed with, because the one class is necessary for language, but not the other; so with musical sounds the Mese is a kind of 'conjunction,' especially of beautiful sounds, since it is most often heard among these."* (quoted in Henry Stewart Macran's introduction to his translation of the *Harmonics* of Aristoxenus.)

The ancient traditions of Hindu music also contain conceptions of a scale having a main note and a secondary main note. The main note of a raag is called "vadi" and the secondary main note "samvadi."

The concept is present in Medieval Europe. Guido d'Arezzo wrote in *Micrologus* (from around 1026 AD): "The note that ends [a song] holds the chief place, for it sounds both longer and more lasting. The previous notes, as is evident to trained musicians only, are so adjusted to the last one that in an amazing way they seem to draw a certain semblance of color from it." He also adds that "carefully composed chants end their phrases chiefly on the final note"—in other words the main note of that particular mode. (translation by Warren Babb, 1978)

The modern Western harmonic system—with its use of the tritone in the context of the major and minor scales, its use of the fifth as the antipode to the main note of the scale, with its chords functioning based on the scale degree of the root, and with principles of counterpoint and rhythm directing to the cadence—is the system that has most exhaustively marshalled all resources to heighten the effect of the centrality of a main note. This is the most fully, thoroughly, and consistently developed system expressing the fact of centricity. It makes the tonic note have the strongest possible emotional pull, and gives the music a sense of course or plot, of a journey controlled fundamentally by a feeling of goal-directed forward progression.

## MODULATION

The sense of a journey in tonal music depends not only on progression from one note to another within the scale, but also on *progression from one scale to another.*

Music uses not only diatonic notes, but also chromatic ones—the "color" tones outside of the scale proper. Some chromatic tones are merely temporary ornamentations: for instance, in a C Major context, an F♯ could fill in a melodic motion from F up to G, in which case the F♯ is a chromatic passing tone. Or a motion from G to A♭ and back again would be a chromatic neighbor figure. These sorts of inflections are very local and do not fundamentally change the operative scale, they merely ornament its notes. Expressively, they introduce a tinge of feeling from another scale, which is why they are called "color" tones.

Other changes are more substantial. Think of the seven notes of the scale not in series sounding one after another, but as a context held by the brain, as a framework for comprehending the notes of melody. The passing and neighboring chromatic tones merely ornament, and reduce back to, the same scale. Other tones *replace* notes of the scale and thus shift the context, reorienting the mind to a *new* scale. This is called *modulation.*

The term "modulation" comes from *modulari,* meaning "regulate, measure off properly." Originally it meant alteration of pitch by measured degrees, but it came to name something more complicated: change from one scale to another by altering the pitches.

The seven tones of a key are a context held by the brain. To change one note in that collection is to change the total network of intervals, and therefore to change the main note of the scale, the note to which they all relate mathematically.

When the key changes, a single note changes its meaning and feeling because even though it stays the same in itself, the context around it changes. For example, the note C in the C-scale is the most stable possible note; but if the underlying scale shifts to the G-major collection, the same pitch obtains a totally different character: C becomes step 4, which is unstable and yearns to settle downward. So modulation—change of key—introduces a vast new dimension of expressive effect and nuance.

We have already learned about the Greek "Greater Perfect System," the Greek term for the diatonic scale in two octaves from A up which they bequeathed to the Western World. The Greeks also had a *Lesser* Perfect System. This system, like the other, was created by connecting together four-note scale units or tetrachords. But in the Lesser Perfect System, a change of scale was built into the system. The scale was basically the "white notes" of our keyboard, but because of the way in which the tetrachords were connected, the lower part of the scale contained a B♮ and the upper part contained the option of a B♭. Thus, that particular accidental, the flat applied to B, became the first and very important alteration. This can be thought of as the most elementary means of changing the scale.

The Greek system of music allowed for very flexible inflection of many notes of the scale, but this B♭ was incorporated in a much more definite way. It became part of a stable theoretical idea, not just an informal, occasional practice.

The use of B♭ is so ancient that the German language has actually incorporated the note into its letter-names. In German, B refers to our B♭; H is used for our B.

Medieval music, derived from the traditions of Greece, employed no sharp or flat other than B♭. In the D-mode, which Glarean called "Dorian," the B♮ was frequently changed to B♭. This took away the distinctive note of the D-mode pattern, the raised sixth; instead, the scale was transformed to be the same as the normal natural minor scale, but with the pattern of notes shifted to start on D. This was the start of the idea of differences in *key*. A key means a major or minor scale oriented around a particular main note. The keys of C major and G major are both major scales, but they are founded on different central tonics. The keys of C major and C minor have the same keynote, but different forms of scale built upon it.

In music of the mature Western system of tonality, when an established tone (such as B♮) is replaced by a new inflection (B♭), that changes the scale and therefore reorients the music to a new tonic note. In C major, the addition of B♭ changes the key—modulates the music—to a major scale based on F.

The addition of a flat was originally referred to using words related to "soft" indicating the way in which the flat usually gets rid of a tritone and therefore eliminates that interval's harshness.

The other form of accidental is of course the sharp (♯). The words for this related usually to "hard" because of the tritone that a new sharp creates. The sharp enters later than the first flat, and originally came to be for the purpose of *creating a leading tone*. Therefore a new sharp typically modulates the music into a scale with a tonic immediately above the sharped note.

When a note is altered without changing which pitch is the main scale tone, we generally do not consider that a "modulation" but merely a "modal borrowing" or some form of ornamentation: a change from C major to C minor is not a modulation exactly, but a change of mode. However, when the central note is thrown to another pitch by the change, this is definitely a modulation, and the very reason for the concept. A change from C major to A minor is a modulation in the sense of a change of tonic note. Observe that although a modulation means the main note changes, the *type* of scale may remain the same, as in a change from C major to F major.

Observe the patterns of modal borrowing, chromatic ornamentation, and modulation in this invented melody, especially with regard to the emotional impression each produces:

## Cognition of Modulations

6.3 *Demonstrating the expressive effects of changes of key in a tonal melody*

Obviously, it is not necessary for a person to know, or think explicitly of, the collection of notes in order to be influenced by the changes. The integration, holding and updating of scale context is handled automatically by the hearing system as it receives the notes. (This is another example of musical mathematics giving rise to feeling.)

Notice the various emotional effects of the modulations. The bright opening sound of the major scale and the snappy rhythm make the piece rather festive; the early chromatic lower neighbor gives a tinge of burgundy coloring. The D♭ is part of another unusual tinge, and creates an ominous psychological impression preparing the mind for F minor; this is followed by a satisfaction of the desire for the key of F, but with the surprise of A♮ making the scale a sunny F major. The cadence on F gives an intermediate place at which the tune settles, but this barely registers as the melody drops us down into the dark sound of D minor, which continues with a version of the opening theme translated into a more solemnly somber feeling. The march up by scale to D—the highest note of the melody and the correction of the strange early D♭—has power and majesty. This continues with a repose on the tonic of the G scale. Another turn to the relative minor—this time E minor—brings back the dark sound but keeps the majestic strength. The slow stripping away of the sharps with the rise through C-D-E-F cleanses the palette and provides a respite of fairly gentle movement. A sudden tinge of chromaticism is swept away by a quick scale reasserting the home key of C, and the melody uses a transposition of an earlier turn to close itself, settling finally and with complete closure on the goal that had been set from the beginning.

Zarlino had defined the concept of *tonality*, a principle of unity which set a particular note (and the triad built on it) as the center of a composition, the center around which all of the music moves. The basic pattern of tonal music is: first, establish the sound of the main harmony and the main key, then depart from it, and then return to it. This principle is "scalable" (to borrow a term from computer science). It can be implemented on a very small scale or a very large one; it can be the pattern of a few chords in a short sequence, or the scheme of modulation spanning an entire symphony.

The unified progression of music using the tonal system creates a strong sense of gravity or pull toward the tonic. As the music moves away from the tonic, the listener experiences an impression of exploration or opening out into the unknown. When the music pulls together all the threads of exploration and concentrates forces to return to the tonic, the listener experiences a strong feeling of purposeful tension and anticipation, and then of the satisfaction of resolution.

A cognitively sane and controlled treatment of key-changes, and a smoothly integrated use of chromatic tones in general, is a hallmark of the great composer. Bungled, awkward, bumpy, crude and erratic treatment of chromaticism and modulation is the hallmark of the ignorant hack. The great composer is aware of the cognitive and emotional effects of chromatic tones and of modulations, and controls them accordingly, down to the smallest detail. The hack is unaware and therefore incapable of handling them properly. The hack, in effect, slaps the listener in the face by ignoring his brain. The genius pays the listener a great compliment by respecting and calling upon his integrative capacity according to its nature. The fact that the hack doesn't actually listen and doesn't actually care, shows up especially in this aspect of music. On the other hand, the great man's sensitivity, carefulness, intelligent awareness, and respect for man's consciousness is apparent. Instead of frustration he delivers beauty, sense, attractiveness, and pleasure.

### KEY RELATION

All of the changes of scale in the example above are smooth—the context shifts by only one note at a time. Modulations to *closely related* keys, keys that differ by only one accidental, create a very even, yet sparkling or scintillating subtlety. The effect is nuanced. Modulations to *distant* keys, on the other hand—such as an abrupt change from C-Major to B-Minor—are bold, dramatic, and shocking. Distant keys have few notes in common. The cognitive disruption caused by a sudden lurch of context gives a mental dislocation, it unsettles the soul and raises questions in the mind about the stability of the future course. Modulation to closely related keys is gentle and subtle; modulation to distant keys is boldly dramatic.

One important key relationship to know is the relation of relative major and minor. These are scales which, in their natural form, share all the same notes (and have the same key signature), but differ as to what is set as the tonic. In a major scale (such as C), tonicizing step 6 puts you into the relative minor (A); this is done using the leading tone of A (G♯). In a minor scale, tonicizing step 3 puts you into the relative major; this is done by stripping away the minor key leading tone (replacing G♯ with G).

Since it can be tricky to remember these relations, I've written a poem, some of the phrases of which may come in handy as mnemonic devices.

> Tip for the Traveling Musician
>
> On your quest I shall guide you with brevity and ease
>    By lending you the map between two relative keys:
> If you seek, I will wager, all the bright pep of major,
>    You'll find nothing finer than the third step in minor.
> If you hunger much the more for that remote, darker fix—
>    Simply march in the major up to note number six.
>
> Caution on your journey, now.
>    Don't lose your way.
> You've got to make a solemn vow,
>    Or none of your work will pay.
> In following the charted course between our two paired keys,
>    Take pains to never, ever forget your accidentals, please!

Relative major and minor share a key signature but have a different tonic note. On the other hand, when a major and minor key *differ* in key signature but have the *same* tonic note (as with A major and A minor), they are called *parallel* keys.

## THE RISE AND FALL OF TONAL INTEGRITY

Zarlino defined the law of unity around a central note and its major or minor triad, the law of tonality. This enabled composers to consciously and systematically control the musical elements to enhance the effect of unity of mode and of progression toward the goal of resolution.

An enormous body of techniques grew up, fleshing out the concept Zarlino defined. To recapitulate them briefly:

❋ The drive toward the cadence, using rhythm as well as the melodic shape to create a sense of momentum to the resolution.

❋ The introduction and resolution of dissonances, including the powerful, key-defining dissonance of the tritone.

❋ The use of the notes of the scale, including the tendency tones such as the leading tone, according to their contextual function ultimately leading toward the tonic.

❋ The use of modal borrowing and changes of key—to close keys or distant ones, reached smoothly or abruptly, with the concomitant reinterpretation of common tones—to create expressive effects including especially the feeling of departure, journey, and return to the main key.

❋ As we will see shortly, the use of chords according to the function of the chord in the scale also contributed to the sense of direction.

All this was part of the growing expression in music of man's volition, his power of integrity of mind and highly focused, single-minded purpose, his power to set a goal, keep it in mind, work toward it, and reach the satisfaction of achieving it.

This knowledge underlies a long future development of musical art. Renaissance masters such as Palestrina created a beautiful effect of voices flowing forward together and converging to resolution. Baroque masters such as Vivaldi created intensely propulsive progressions—think for instance of the vibrant energy of his *Four Seasons*. His kind of rushing crescendo was imitated by the composers of the Mannheim school who became known, among other things, for the "Mannheim steamroller"—a powerful, swelling crescendo. (Notice the musical phenomenon coincides historically with its namesake, the invention of commercially viable steam motive power.)

The large-scale classical forms, such as sonata and rondo form, developed on the basis of tonality and use it as the principle for organizing progression. Haydn used these forms to playfully toy with and humorously disrupt the expected formulaic progressions. Mozart filled the forms with elegant and tasteful, intense yet fairly reserved forward progression. Beethoven imbued them with great, titanic power and mighty, fist-shaking determination. Romantics such as Brahms, Dvořák and Tchaikovsky used them for their soul-searching passion and profundity, and for their amazing buildups and climaxes.

Heroism in music is impossible without tonality.

During the rise of philosophical Subjectivism in the late 19th century and especially in the 20th century, people lost interest in, diluted, or actively rebelled against the principle of volition and the corresponding principle of tonality. The fact of man's self-determination, his ability to guide the course of his life, was no longer the sole integrating basis of musical expression. People no longer felt defined by the efficacious process of working to achieve positive goals. They no longer held to a law unifying one's actions over time, and their emotions changed as a result.

Certain remnants of the tonal system remained and continued to be used in many styles of music but men no longer stuck to the essence, the feeling of integrity and self-determination. Instead, they wanted: to pursue an endless journey without fulfillment (as in Wagner), to have a haze or trance created in the mind (as with an Impressionistic wash of sonority, or later with psychedelic music), to explore the mental illness of a fractured, splintered psyche (as in Schoenberg and Berg). The principle of heroic mental/moral purposefulness and integrity was also radically diminished or dropped with the advent of more physicalistic feelings in America, as jazz swept people away with its loose, freewheeling physicality, as rock 'n' roll flung feelings of rowdy rebellion at the world, as people settled into the reassuring non-ambition and the laid-back, homely feelings of folk style.

People of the era of volition, from the Renaissance into Romanticism, found the face of the *David* in music to be a profound expression of their own power of self-control and self-determination. Today, the mainstream culture is not only uninterested in such feelings, it is actually antagonistic toward them. The typical person of modern times finds "classical" symphonic feelings to be at best alien, at worst annoying; he gives the impression of finding them ridiculous or abnormal. Expressions of the feeling of volitional integrity grate on his nerves— as you can tell from people's reactions, and confirm from the rates of record sales.

Unfortunately today the Renaissance feeling of the power of man's volition, and Zarlino's law expressing that in music, are long gone culturally. The great achievement of Western music has had its sunset, and the question lingers: will the future hold a new dawn?

# 7

## COUNTERPOINT

Polyphonic composition was made possible by the conceptualization of *how* to coordinate the voices. That body of knowledge is the science or art of counterpoint. The term comes from *"punctus contra punctum"* or "point against point," emphasizing the interplay of lines and the contrasting character of these melodic strands which grow together in harmony but dart against each other.

As we learned, experiments with polyphony were first notated during the Carolingian Renaissance of the 9th century, and right away in the record from this period, *Musica Enchiriadis*, we see thinkers grappling with the problem of dissonance that does not integrate into the flow of the music. The first rules of counterpoint came about to prevent dissonances from causing disruption or jarring ugliness—and to instead create note combinations of smooth, expressive beauty.

This tradition was continued by such important thinkers as Guido d'Arezzo, who also dealt (in *Micrologus* of 1026 AD) with how to combine lines so that they flow together beautifully. Over the next centuries, a very slow development took place in which men gradually figured out how to grow the combination of voices into an ever more complex fabric—culminating in the music of the 16th century Renaissance, as exemplified in the florid richness, passionate power, spiritual integrity, and beautiful harmony of such masters as Palestrina.

A number of thinkers along the way worked to codify the rules and generalizations accumulated on the art of counterpoint. These included Zarlino and, earlier, Flemish composer and music theorist Johannes Tinctoris. Their instructions for combining voices were part of the early stages of forming the science of counterpoint, and they necessarily formed the rules in a comparatively clumsy way. Often they were too concretely specific and narrowly prescriptive, because they could not yet boil down their observations into essentialized rules with wide applicability. They also fell short of seeing the rules in the form of a clear, comprehensive system.

Many principles of line shape and line combination remained implicit in the practice of composers such as Palestrina. Rules remained scattered, poorly formulated, and incomplete.

To a large extent it was a process of trial and error, with observations passed on orally by teachers to their students as a sort specialized skill or trade secret.

The knowledge was not brought together into a definitive system, essentialized and made both simple and comprehensive, and published in a form digestible by anyone.

Until Johann Josef Fux.

## FUX

Fux, born in 1660, was a contemporary of J.S. Bach. Both were exemplars of the late Baroque period and the early Enlightenment. Fux lived and taught in Vienna, which was the capital city of the Austro-Hungarian Empire and the center of cultural life at the time. The center of the center was the Emperor's court. Fux was the court composer and music master under three Emperors of the Habsburg dynasty. He was also the music master at the principal church of the Empire, St. Stephen's.

Fux was a prolific composer and an active conductor and teacher. He was well acquainted with the music of the past, and thoroughly familiar with developments on the leading edge of original work in his own time. He had an enormous breadth of knowledge, a rich and varied base of data, and a lifetime of experience to draw upon.

At age 65 Fux consolidated this knowledge into a book for the teaching of musical composition, a book which created a newly systematic, step-by-step method. It was written in Latin and titled *Gradus ad Parnassum* which means "Steps to Parnassus." In Greek mythology, Parnassus was the mountain home of the nine Muses, the goddesses of the arts.

As Fux wrote in his introduction: "I began... many years ago, to work out a method similar to that by which children learn first letters, then syllables, then combinations of syllables, and finally how to read and write. And it has not been in vain. When I used this method in teaching I observed that the pupils made amazing progress within a short time."

Fux was a great admirer of Palestrina and sought to create a method modeled on Palestrina's compositions. In fact, Fux wrote his treatise in the form of a dialogue between a teacher and student and in the introduction Fux tells us that he intended the teacher to be a personification of Palestrina. "By Aloysius, the master, I refer to Palestrina, the celebrated light of music... to whom I owe everything that I know of this art, and whose memory I shall never cease to cherish with a feeling of deepest reverence."

Fux took in the entire history of music and music theory before him and created a new summary, a new concentrated and essentialized system that clarified and integrated the theoretical elements that had existed before, and that prepared the student for future original work. He formulated fundamental, basic principles and created a step by step method for composition in its most elementary form. He thereby opened up a future that would draw upon, and bear the fruits of, a powerful new synthesis.

When Fux's *Gradus* was published in 1725, it represented the condensation of the entire Western musical achievement over millennia, as summarized by its leading and most knowledgeable practitioner, coming from the central cultural capital of the Western World. It was published at the Emperor's expense and disseminated to the entire European world where it was eagerly devoured by musicians hungry for the best knowledge they could find. The work was translated from the original Latin into German, Italian, English and French. It was cited and paraphrased in the major European theoretical treatises that followed.

The supreme importance of Fux's theoretical achievement may be known by considering the list of practitioners whose achievements his theory made possible.

The coy humor and light playfulness of Haydn's music? The intensity of his "Sturm und Drang" ("storm and stress") period? Haydn, the father of the Symphony? According to Alfred Mann, translator of Fux: "Haydn took infinite pains to assimilate the theory of Fux; he went through the whole work laboriously, writing out the exercises, then laying them aside for a few weeks, to look them over again later and polish them until he was satisfied he had done everything right."

The fluid beauty and elegance of Mozart's piano concertos? The dramatic power and psychological subtlety of his *Marriage of Figaro* or *Don Giovanni*? Mozart had been taught Fux by his father, who carefully annotated his copy of *Gradus*. Son Wolfgang used the book himself when teaching to the next generation.

The power and the glory of Beethoven's Symphonies? The sheer force of Will, the propulsive energy, the sense of irresistible and inevitable progression in his piano sonatas? The joy and the triumph of his *Consecration of the House* overture? An ambitious young Beethoven, hungry for mastery of the materials of music, had moved to Vienna and sought instruction from three teachers: Haydn, Schenk and Albrechtsberger. All three used Fux as the basis of musical study.

The sensuous beauty, the sensitivity and strength of Chopin's incomparable piano music? Chopin was one of the many subscribers in Paris to the newly published studies by Beethoven —which consolidated Beethoven's counterpoint exercises in the Fux method.

The tuneful mirth and mischief of Rossini's *Barber of Seville*? Rossini, too, was a subscriber to that publication—along with Cherubini, Berlioz, Meyerbeer, Auber, Paganini, Moscheles, Hummel, and Liszt.

The vocal melodies of Schubert? The bittersweet yearning and titanic power of Brahms' Symphonies? The sparkling orchestration and churning tumult of Richard Strauss's *Electra*? All three of these men stand in a direct line from Fux; they knew and honored his name and his methods.

Nearly all—or perhaps all—of the great music of the late 18th through the late 19th centuries has Fux's *Gradus ad Parnassum* behind it. He was the theoretician who opened up the field to these enormous achievements. It was he who gave these composers the conceptual grasp of how to systematically integrate musical lines into a harmonious fabric. It was he who taught them how to coordinate and control the musical motion, to build to a climax and taper away, to elaborate into a full musical texture, to shape a composition to grow outward from its beginnings and to blossom into its full complexity and elaboration and then to pull the strands together for the full power of direction to closure and resolution. He taught how to create and resolve conflicts both in pitch progression and in rhythm.

It was he who gave Mozart, Beethoven and Brahms the technical means to implement their passionate inspiration. It was he who gave them the control of the materials, to give coherence to the material of inspiration, the ability to plan rationally for the right expressive effect, the ability to harness the potential of the art form and make the most of it. These composers brought their passion and inspiration, their brilliant raw intelligence and ability, their eagerness to understand and use the elements of music to say what they were driven from within to say; Fux provided them with the intellectual framework and the systematic method that enabled them to do it.

It was no small achievement and no floating 'theoretical' impracticality. It was theory enabling practice: reason giving direction to passion.

Fux was wise enough to create a deliberately simplified, basic method that would teach universal principles, not details of any particular style. He created a method that was not a dogmatic attempt to make composers conform to a preferred style, but a basic framework and elementary base like arithmetic. This enabled the student to go on to employ the basics in his own way in whatever complexities of higher mathematics he chose to explore. Thus Haydn could still be the stiff yet quirky and humorous Haydn, Mozart could still be the tastefully and reservedly charming Mozart, and Beethoven could still be the heroic and mighty Beethoven —even though all three were drawing upon a common body of basic principles codified by Fux. He created a universal, style-independent system of basics.

Fux's system teaches not just details of note-construction, but also the process of constructive self-criticism, the process of honing one's discrimination and judgment. It inculcates a certain method of approach and leads the student to conceptualize the facts of what he hears, and to use that information for creating artistic effects.

The great composers learned basic patterns and became fluent in them so they could use them naturally and easily in their expression and as the basis for creating more complex structures.

I should mention that Fux's own music is, in my opinion, generic courtly fluff. There are some exceptions, but in general his music is cleanly and smartly done but doesn't have any enticing melody or any important emotional substance. It uses a lot of very standardized formulas of melody and orchestral effect and is very repetitive, with a minimal element of drama. Perhaps this is why Fux was able so effectively to summarize standardized, basic compositional patterns, and to remain style-neutral.

Remember that Fux's job was to churn out pleasantly simple background music for the events at a superficially elegant royal court, a court which looked at music as an easy diversion, not a mental challenge or anything of philosophical importance or deep emotional meaning. The idea that a composition was an important form of individual self-expression—a vehicle which made a serious statement that ought to be attentively listened to and contemplated—did not exist at the time. A household composer had the same social status as a maid or a cook: he was a servant.

Fux was not an independent, original, passionate creator with his own artistic vision to express and his own message to assert. That sort of personal artistry would only come into being later, and would depend on and make use of Fux's pedagogical achievement.

We proceed to learn what Fux learned from the Western World, and what the Western World learned from Fux—and we proceed to learn it in a way that, this author hopes, is even more clearly conceptualized, more effectively and concisely presented.

Fux organized the teaching of counterpoint into broad categories (genera) covering counterpoint in two parts or voices, then three voices, then four.

Each genus is divided into five species (and the five species are the same within each genus). The first species gives the assignment of writing the simplest possible counter-line to a given voice. Each subsequent species introduces further ornamentation or complexity, culminating in the fifth species which combines all the prior ones, teaching organic melody.

Once the first (two-part) genus is complete, the same progression is applied to three-part writing. Thus there is a spiral progression in which the student first learns each species with few voices, then loops back to cover the same five species on a higher level of complexity, with a greater number of voices to coordinate. The knowledge gained from covering the two-part genus is leveraged to handle the greater complexities of writing in three parts, then in four.

We shall limit our exposition here to cover the five species in two parts, and first species in three parts. This is enough to give the student a basic mastery of elements and to prepare him to study chord progressions in four-part harmony.

For coverage of all the permutations, the reader may refer to Fux's original treatise, *Gradus ad Parnassum* (translated by Alfred Mann as *The Study of Counterpoint*) which is written in dialogue form and is quite readable—or to the superlative *Counterpoint in Composition* by Felix Salzer and Carl Schachter.

The method of composing the "fixed voice" or *cantus firmus* we have already learned in Chapter 1 on "Melodic Shape." We now build upon such a single line in whole notes, using it as the base and the given element. The same principles of line shape we learned continue to be applicable to the new counter-lines.

The art of counterpoint builds upon all we have learned up to now, and necessarily involves more complexities and technical ideas, including the need of notating music. Learning counterpoint, even on a rudimentary level or in a preliminary way, is of enormous value; it teaches the way in which multiple streams of musical thought flow together. It teaches, in other words, the core of the symphonic principle.

I encourage you to get as much as you can from the remainder of this chapter, which can only be done by trying out the exercises yourself. If that is not possible for you, I suggest you skim the following to get the broad overall concepts and patterns and methods; you can always return to it later to flesh out your understanding.

## TYPES OF RELATIVE MOTION

In learning to combine lines we will need to use concepts of how the voices move in relation to one another. Between two lines there are four possible types of relative motion. (This diagram uses half notes, so that the stem directions will distinguish the upper and lower lines.)

Four Types of Relative Motion

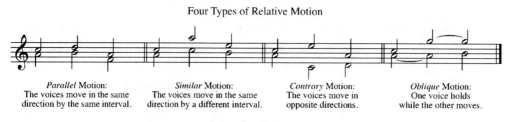

*Parallel* Motion:
The voices move in the same direction by the same interval.

*Similar* Motion:
The voices move in the same direction by a different interval.

*Contrary* Motion:
The voices move in opposite directions.

*Oblique* Motion:
One voice holds while the other moves.

*7.1 The various permutations of two voices moving in relation to one another*

## 1ST SPECIES: CONSONANCE

The first species of counterpoint study consists of writing a new counter-line against a fixed voice, with the counter-line being the most basic. We use only the simplest relationships. In the time values we use only whole notes—the fixed voice and the new counter-line make a time ratio of 1:1. They are literally note-against-note, or *punctus-contra-punctum*. This homogeneous rhythm creates a relatively strong, stable effect. In the pitch relations we use only consonances, for a simple, blended clarity between the two lines.

For our fixed voice, we'll take the first example from Chapter 1 (figure 1.1). In the following example here the counter-line is composed above the fixed voice. It could also be written below.

The new line may begin on any member of the tonic triad.

Approach fifths and octaves by contrary motion.

Write the number of the interval between the staves.

| 5 | 10 | 8 | 6 | 8 | 5 | 8 | 10 | 6 | 8 |

In this little composition, the fixed voice is in lower pitches, on the bass staff. The new line is composed above it.

*7.2 First Species studies consonance by adding a new line in whole notes.*

We are aiming here to create two different lines that fit well together. Each line must be independent and unique in the sense of having its own shape and character, but at the same time the lines must harmonize with one another. Therefore we want to avoid a situation in which the lines fuse together to become essentially the same line. This happens when the lines move in parallel fifths or octaves. These perfect consonances are so strong and cause such a total fusion of sound that the lines act as one; they merge. Since we are looking for unity in variety, not just unity, *avoid parallel fifths and octaves*. Even similar motion into a fifth or octave should be avoided; in our very simple texture, their strong sound results in a hard "bump" in the line, almost as though it should be the end, the last note.

To combine these points and state them in positive terms: *approach octaves and fifths by contrary motion.* That, in fact, was the way Beethoven summarized it.

In order to keep sufficient variety and independence of the lines, *no more than three consecutive instances of the same parallel interval* should be used. For instance, there is no objection to three parallel thirds in a row, but more than that makes one line into the mere shadow of the other.

The same principles of shape apply to the new counter-line as to the fixed voice: have one clear climax, use mostly steps with a few skips, fill in the gaps, etc. However, even though the new line must end on the tonic, it does not have to begin on it; it may begin on any member of the tonic triad: the tonic, third, or fifth of the scale. We wouldn't use a sixth even though it is consonant because it would start the music with a sound that doesn't establish the key.

The counter-line can be written below the cantus as well; this should also be practiced. A lower line, composed beneath the cantus, must never begin on scale-step five, because this creates a discordant fourth with the upper note. (In the course of the study of intervals, one of the refinements of classification was that even though the 4th is an elementary perfect consonance, when it sounds as a simultaneity above the lowest pitch of a sonority, it has the bite of a discord and thus in that one circumstance requires resolution.)

We want the two lines to fit together, but be different; their climactic points should not happen at the same time.

As you can see, we now begin to contend with the need to coordinate the *relationship between two lines.* In order to keep track of the intervals, *write the number of the interval between the staves.* Be sure to correct the interval if you change a note!

Consonance is a blended, harmonious quality between two notes sounding at the same time. Dissonance is a clashing, discordant quality between two notes. As you can hear if you play the various intervals, the unison and octave, the perfect fifth, and the thirds and sixths are consonant. The other intervals are dissonant. So the simultaneous intervals available for first species counterpoint are:

P1 (& P8)   P5   3rds   6ths

Be careful of diminished fifths, they are dissonant. There is one above the leading tone, and in natural minor, one above scale-step 2.

The perfect unison and fifth make a strong, stark sound. The thirds and sixths are richer and warmer. Using perfect consonances at the beginning and end of the exercise and thirds and sixths in the middle makes a progression with both definition and flow.

At this stage we don't use repeated notes so oblique motion is not an option, but it will enter in soon. All the other types of relative motion are available. Generally, a mixture of different types of motion, with plenty of contrary motion, makes for a beautiful combination of lines. Contrary motion is especially good for giving the lines separate direction and character.

## ITERATIVE METHOD

It is important to address the issue not only of *what* we are composing, but of *how* to do it. We should pay attention to both substance and method.

A common problem with creating things goes like this: let's say you have the task of writing an essay. You put it off because the project seems overwhelming and you don't know how to begin. Finally you force yourself to sit down and write. You put down the first sentence, but then you think twice, erase it, and write a new one. You continue, finish your first paragraph, and are on to the second. While you are working on the second paragraph you see some problems in the first one, so you go back and edit. This process continues until your first two paragraphs are very polished. You write a few more paragraphs but then you have to go to sleep. The next day, you come back to your essay and work on it some more. Your deadline is approaching and you are not done, so with increasing anxiety you race to put something, anything in to fill the pages. At this point you don't really care very much what you put down, you just want it to be done.

The end result of this process is an end product that is not very good. It is of uneven quality—the essay's first two paragraphs are flawlessly polished, the middle is rougher, and the ending is downright sloppy. The essay is not very coherent and doesn't make a convincing argument that leads from the first idea to an inevitable conclusion. It is probably missing some crucial elements of your argument.

And on top of all that, there was an enormous amount of stress involved in meeting the deadline, which maybe you didn't even meet after all. One of the many problems with this approach is that it treats time as though it is infinite. But in reality, everything is limited and for everything you create, you have only so much time. Your project has to be done when it has to be done.

The same problems arise in other areas, including with composing music. Where can we find a solution to this problem of how to effectively create something?

The field of computer programming has a good solution which applies to many creative projects, not just writing software. It is called "Iterative Development."

To "iterate" means to "do again, repeat." The Iterative Method consists, in essence, of repeatedly creating versions of your product, each of which has all the essentials required for completeness. The process of creating versions enables you to refine and expand your product, but while having a complete thing at each stage. Think for instance of a theater troupe preparing a play: there is a read-through, a walk-through, a dress rehearsal, then a performance. It starts out rough, but each time through is a complete version of the play, and with each iteration it becomes further refined, developed and polished.

Returning to our essay example for a moment: according to this method, to begin with, you create a rough but complete version, an outline—then another, a first draft. Then you go over it to refine it. The process of refinement continues, you cycle over it and revise to make it better and better. This enables you much more accurately to be ready on time for a deadline. Even if things are not up to the level of perfection you had hoped, if you run out of time, you can simply draw a line and say to yourself, "okay, now the whole thing is there, and I have been able to increase its level of perfection, and it is time to turn it in." And that's it.

The Iterative Method takes stress out of creating things because from the earliest stage in the process you have the whole thing finished in some way. What you are doing after that is just refining. The presence of all the parts is absolutely crucial, and they must be in place from the very beginning. The total picture, the complete entity, must be brought into existence—even in this rough way—as the first step. After that the refinement is not hard because you already have something to work on. And you can cycle over your product as much as is necessary to bring it up to the necessary quality level; but at any point, you are able to stop and let the thing be done. The level of refinement is not, after all, as important as having the big picture be complete. The big structure matters more than the little details.

Part of the reason the Iterative Method takes the stress and pressure out of the process is by helping you accept that it is okay for the first version of the product to be bare-bones, very rough, even crude *as long as it is complete* in the sense of having all the main parts the finished product has to have. In order to get the first draft down, the first working version, you must completely drop the idea that you "should" be able to create a perfect, pristine thing immediately—that's an assumption many people unfortunately have with regard to artistic creation. The process is messy, and that's okay. The perfection comes in increasing stages over time, and there is no such thing as ultimate, total, final perfection. There is just the choice of the level of refinement that is necessary and possible given the time limit.

Now let us apply this to our counterpoint exercises.

We want to make the big picture first, starting with what is given. You have the fixed voice, that is a given. There are certain things about the new counter-line which are also given. Fill in the last note and the second-to-last note since they are predetermined (but leave open the question of which octave they will be in). Then plan the overall shape of your line and write it down as a scrawl above or below the staff. This is just a tentative plan with a lot of flexibility, not one that has to be adhered to strictly. Place your climactic point: choose when it will happen and what note it will be (again, this is preliminary and can change later if necessary). But with these elements you have your total picture. All of the indispensable elements are in place.

Now flesh out the rest of the line by working out from these two points—the end note and the climax. Experiment with different ways of leading to the last note which are consistent with the shape you outlined. Experiment with different ways of leading into and out of your climactic note. And when you get close to the beginning, experiment with what pitches to start with. If you need to change the climactic note, that's fine.

This process of "working backwards," of deriving the details from the main points—the climax and the ending—is absolutely crucial if the line is going to hold together and have a sense of structure and logic, of flow and inevitable progression and resolution.

You'll want to know which consonant notes are available for each measure (or for the most important measures). Lightly mark the notes available above a given note: the 3rd, 5th, 6th, and octave. Allow for using these notes in a higher or lower octave. Eliminate the ones that won't work and continue from there.

You must control the intervals between the staves and unless you are quite advanced this means you must always *write the interval between the two staves,* and circle the dissonances. Use these written numbers to help you control the relation between the lines. For instance, this will help you spot fifths and octaves that are not approached by contrary motion. The study of counterpoint is the study of the *interrelation* of the two lines, and the intervals between the staves are the means of keeping track of the relationships.

You will find that the little composition you are creating is an interrelated whole. When you change one note, it can cause problems around it. One correction can lead to another and to another. Sometimes, in the most extreme cases, solving one little problem leads little by little to re-writing the whole thing. This is a natural part of the process because music is an organic whole. Dealing with the interrelationships and the network of dependencies is just what we are learning to handle in writing these highly constrained exercises. It is a messy process and that is okay. We shouldn't expect a perfect creation right off the bat, we should expect to shape it and sculpt it to make it better and better. That process and skill is what we are trying to learn.

## 2nd Species: Passing & Neighboring Tones

7.3 *Second species studies passing and neighboring tones by adding a second line in half notes.*

In the second stage of species counterpoint, we compose against the fixed voice a new line of half notes. The two lines have a ratio of time values of 2:1. The use of neighboring tones and especially passing tones makes the music more fluid rhythmically.

The new line follows the same principles of shape as we have followed up to now.

The downbeat of each measure will still use exclusively consonances (1, 3, 5, 6, 8). However, we now have the opportunity of introducing dissonances (2, 4, 7 & d or A) on the *second half of the measure.*

Consonances form the basic structure of music, the main framework which makes it intelligible. Dissonance, the clashing element, is secondary. Dissonant tones are subordinate and derivative; they must fit in around the consonances as a kind of ornamentation. A line must enter and leave a dissonance smoothly. *Stepwise approach into, and stepwise departure from the dissonant tone* makes it integrate into the overall harmonious structure. Instead of disrupting and jarring the mind, the dissonance becomes part of a smooth, natural flow. To leap into or out of a dissonance is to violate the ear's need for integrity of the sound; it causes the dissonance to be jarring, ugly, a blemish rather than an elaboration of the consonances.

The two types of dissonant tone here are the *passing* tone and the *neighboring* tone. Both occur on the weak part of the measure, not on a strong beat.

A **passing tone** fills in the space between two notes a third apart. It is the middle note of a three-note scale motion. See bars 3-4 above.

A **neighboring tone** is the middle note of this pattern: an initial consonant tone moves up (or down) a step and then returns to the original note. See bars 4-5 above.

Write the number of the interval between the staves and circle the dissonances.

A good method is to look for consonances on the downbeats, and then to lead into them with stepwise motion. As much as possible use leaps in the middle of the measure but *avoid leaps over the barline*. This will make the line smoother.

Octave leaps in the counter-line can be useful, but be sure to fill them in.

In this species, the counterpoint line may begin with a half note rest, which helps set the lines apart.

Use only notes that are diatonic to the scale, and no chromatic motion. In minor keys, be careful which form of the minor scale you use. If the line leads down from the tonic, the natural/descending melodic is best; if it leads up to the tonic, the rising melodic form is best.

### RATIONAL VS. IRRATIONAL CREATIVITY

In studying counterpoint, a crucial question arises: what is the status of rules?

There are, fundamentally, three schools of thought on this question. One is the authoritarian view, which follows the pattern of religion and demands that you follow certain dictates because an authority figure says so. Another school, the common one today, is the rebel's view; it regards rules as an arbitrary restriction on your freedom, as a subjective construct with no basis in reality and which gets in the way of self-expression. Both of these views make rules into something antagonistic to artistry and musicality; both of them make rules artificial and, in fact, unfair.

A rational perspective disregards both of these views. Instead, it begins with the question: what are you trying to do? It begins with the perspective that in studying counterpoint one has the goal of *making something*, of creating a beautiful little musical composition, but in this case one that is deliberately delimited and controlled in its possibilities so that you can master musical techniques on each level of complexity.

Rational creativity means a process which holds the purpose in mind and uses logical thinking and analysis to achieve it. In this case, our purpose is to learn the nature of various note-combinations and gain skill in controlling them—and we achieve it by thoughtfully and intelligently trying things out, by drafting and honing an ultra-simple, miniature musical composition. By keeping things simple, we are better able to understand them. Later on, we will understand complexity by means of simplicity.

Irrational creativity means a process which rejects logical thinking and analysis, and which instead adopts whim—unexplained emotional impulse—as the absolute. This subjective attitude usually takes the form of a foot-stamping rebellion demanding "Why can't I just write whatever I feel like?" Of course, with such an approach, one learns nothing, least of all the process of translating one's inner state into a work of art. If you want to express yourself, you need more than a desire, you have to gain control of the means of expression.

Most people today feel very antagonistic toward the suggestion that they should consider musical sounds intelligently and analytically. People often want to just let the sound wash over them and surrender to pure emotion. In a dismissive attitude toward analysis, you might hear the sounds go by and think, "yeah, yeah, I get it." But no you don't. Passive hearing and conceptual understanding are two different things. Any ape can sit there while sounds impinge on its ears. Only a man can understand them conceptually and learn to do something with them.

Global, overall, general perception is automatic and requires no effort. Discriminated, analytical, locally focused awareness of specific detail is not. Only the man who takes the music apart and puts it back together again understands it. The default, passive state is just allowing it all to go by.

Composing music in the full artistic sense (beyond simple exercises) involves an element of inspiration and spontaneity; even our simple exercises have that element to some extent. But these are not the whole process. There is also the stage of working with material to shape it into the form that actually expresses what one is inspired to express. As Thomas Edison said, "Success is 10% inspiration and 90% perspiration." It applies just as well to artistic invention as to mechanical.

The attitude that takes artistry to be 100% inspiration (or intuition or spontaneity) is a setup for failure. This attitude is anti-thought, anti-analysis, anti-method—and that rejection of the mind shows in the resulting incoherent junk.

If you hear the injunction to "loosen up, relax, take it easy"—that is the sound of a passive mind trying to shut down some implication that he should do more than just let the sound wash over him.

Guido wrote in the Prologue to his *Antiphoner*, explaining the importance to reading music of the active use of one's intelligence: "It is indeed quite another thing to recall something with understanding than it is to sing something by rote; only the wise can do the former while persons without foresight can often do the latter."

Rules of composition are not an arbitrary dogma. Contrary to the approach of so many thinkers, they are not found in the Bible as the revealed word of God. Rather, rules grow up naturally from experience. Composers tried out different note-combinations, and over time accumulated observations about which ones have which sorts of effects; this includes a strong distinction between those combinations which are beautiful, harmonious and fluid, versus those that are harsh or jarring.

In today's era of subjectivism and emotionalism, the biggest barrier to the teaching of counterpoint is a student's tendency to react to elements out-of-context. The typical pattern is: some blemish enters into a draft of a counterpoint line, such as an unresolved discord between the lines or a melodic skip of an augmented second; the teacher points it out as musically bad in this context, explains why and starts to seek an improvement—but the student insists "It sounds cool" or "But I like it."

What is happening in this situation? The student's mindset seeks the opposite of an integrated, harmonious flow. He seeks any unusual sensation to trigger a jolt to the mind. He wants the newness and shock of a totally isolated, out-of-context sensory reaction. The "cool" sound is out of place and is not part of a connected progression. It sticks out as a breach or interruption of continuity. But the youngster feels a thrill for that outrageous flash of stimulus.

This is sensationalism; it is like evaluating a movie as good because it made you feel a sudden fright—regardless of whether that gasp, that momentary blip of emotional reaction, was connected into a plot or a meaningful theme holding the film together.

Sensationalism in music values the odd, strange new sensation; it values any stimulus that makes itself stick out, any jerk of externally-triggered action inside a passive mind. Sensationalism means a human mind seeking not an intelligent comprehension of an integrated whole, but a reaction to a local, isolated particle of stimulus.

Rationally, and in marked contrast to this, our standards are based on continuity and integrity of progression. These standards accept only those elements that are appropriate to, and consistent with, the full musical context.

Learning counterpoint by the Fux method is like learning tennis. Different teachers have slightly different methods, but there is a common basis of general basics. In tennis, there are such rules as how to hold the racket, keeping your eye on the ball, and so on—these are general facts that are common to all good tennis instruction. But there can be and are varying degrees of emphasis from teacher to teacher on certain details or derivative elements such as how to use the feet or how to prepare for a shot mentally.

Similarly with counterpoint, there are common basics but also variations with regard to less essential details. In learning counterpoint the aim is to develop increasing auditory discrimination and ability to control the musical elements, to understand how lines can and do fit together, to hone one's ability to combine musical lines. There are broad fundamentals common to all elementary counterpoint teaching, such as how to begin and end and such as how to prepare and resolve dissonances. Yet there will be differences in the details that one teacher brings in versus another, such as whether to use leaps over the barline; there are merits to avoiding leaps over the barline as it generally creates much smoother lines, but it is understandable if a teacher would omit this rule or, perhaps, not think of it.

None of this makes the topic subjective or arbitrary; it just means that the teaching method is not a rigid dogma—it is not like some intrinsic set of commandments ordained by God—but a living process that one adapts to one's real practical purpose. The means, in other words, are tailored to accomplish the ends. Without the fundamentals, the goal cannot be accomplished. There will be some options along the way but these operate on the basis of and within the context of the fundamentals.

In short, heed the word of Goethe: "The most insidious of all errors is when good young minds think they will lose their originality by recognizing as true what has already been recognized as true by others."

### 3RD SPECIES: SCALAR MOTION

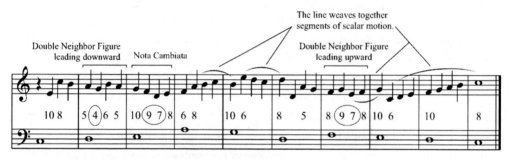

7.4 *Third species studies scalar motion by adding a second line in quarter notes.*

Third species counterpoint divides time values further. The counter-line is built of quarter notes, for a time ratio with the cantus firmus of 4:1. It may also be written in waltz meter (3/4); then the cantus firmus proceeds in dotted half notes, while the new line moves in quarters, for a ratio with the cantus of 3:1.

In a good third-species line, long scale motions in quarter-notes create an energized sense of momentum and active progress. In a poor line, the quarter-note motion becomes tedious and lacks any sense of direction.

Third species continues the study of neighbor tones and passing tones. In the example above, the passing tones are not marked because, so long as the starting and ending notes of a scalar motion are consonant, any dissonances along the way are integrated as passing tones.

Third species introduces a couple of fancy ornamental motions (see below). But really this species extends the study of passing and neighboring tones to work with more extended *scalar motion*, because in order to create a flowing line with so many notes, it must be built out of stepwise runs which interlock and interweave with one another and lead ultimately into the final note. In this species it is especially important to lead into downbeats with stepwise motion.

✳ The last note of the counter-line is, as always, a whole note on the tonic.

✳ The counter-line should begin with a quarter rest in order to offset it from the cantus.

✳ As in second species, the *first tone of each measure must be consonant* with the cantus. The remaining tones may be dissonant, as passing or neighboring tones.

✳ Since this species has so many more notes, more changes of direction within the line are appropriate and necessary.

This species also introduces two idiomatic figures which you see illustrated above: the double-neighbor figure (bars 2 and 7), and the "nota cambiata" (bar 3). Both of these permit a leap from, and/or into, a dissonance, but because of the way the notes wrap up together in overall stepwise patterns, the "breach" does not upset the beauty of the music. The nota cambiata, in its strictest form, would not allow a dissonance on the third beat, but even this license integrates smoothly into the progression because of the various stepwise connections.

These two idiomatic figures begin to indicate to us the sort of elaborations of the basic patterns of counterpoint we find in more advanced composition, and which we will learn about in the theory of Heinrich Schenker.

## 4TH SPECIES: SYNCOPATION

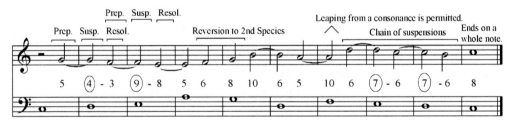

*7.5 Fourth species studies syncopation by adding a new line in tied half notes.*

Fourth species counterpoint deals with *syncopation*. The term "syncopation" derives from the Latin *syncopationem* meaning "shortening" or "contraction." Even earlier, the term derives from the Greek *synkoptein* "to cut up." Syncopated notes are those that create accents out of step with the meter. Under simple and ordinary musical circumstances a note begins on a strong beat and continues into a weak beat. But a syncopated note *begins on a weak beat and continues into a strong one.* This is one of the most expressive rhythmic patterns because of the dynamic interplay of the voices, and because of the motion into the tension of a dissonant suspension giving way to the relief of its resolution.

Syncopated notes are offset from the steady, regular notes of the cantus and play against them. Syncopated notes introduce rhythmic conflict with the basic pattern established by the meter, and lend liveliness and energy to the music.

So fourth species counterpoint uses half notes tied over the barline. This is like using whole notes (as in first species), only shifted over one half measure. The syncopated notes are staggered from the steady notes of the fixed voice.

The simple patterns of first species counterpoint underlie the complexities of syncopation. It is possible to create a normalized, "square" version of the fourth-species line, a simplification or essentialization which renders the line without the rhythmic staggering. This helps reduce the complexities of syncopation to a simpler pattern that is easier to understand. Here is the simplified version of the example above:

7.6 By removing the syncopation, a fourth species line can be reduced to first species. This is a reduction of figure 7.5.

As you can see and hear this makes a respectable first-species counterpoint, but the line lacks the liveliness and momentum provided by syncopation.

One of the most important types of syncopation is the *suspension*. A suspension means just what the word suggests: a holding over. We use the term mainly for the situation in which a note holds on longer than is usual in the meter, *thus causing a dissonance.*

Dissonance is the unstable element in music. It must be treated properly if it is to integrate into the harmonious flow of the lines. The simplest and most complete pattern for the suspension has three elements: preparation, dissonance, and resolution.

The preparation is a consonant note preceding the dissonance (as in the first bar of figure 7.5). The note then holds over into the next strong beat where it becomes dissonant because of the change of the note below it (downbeat of bar 2). Then comes the resolution—the "giving way" or "yielding" of the dissonant note—by a downward stepwise motion (second half of bar 2).

The dissonant note resolves downward, which is a decrease of tension and energy. Upward-resolving suspensions do exist but they are a special case which is not so basic.

It is *absolutely essential that the note resolve by step.* The term "resolution" comes from the Latin *resolutionem* meaning "process of reducing things into simpler forms," and originally in the sense of "solving" (as of mathematical problems). To resolve was "to loosen or settle."

A skip from a dissonance is not a resolution, merely a departure that leaves the clash hanging. The brain integrates music by stepwise connections; this is why leaping out of (or into) a dissonance is mentally jarring. A proper resolution makes the tension yield into a repose, by a downward stepwise movement.

Consonance does not have this constraint; as the stable element, it can be treated more freely.

A *chain* of suspensions is a repeated series of the same type, such as 4-3, 4-3, 4-3 or 7-6, 7-6, 7-6 (see the last few bars of figure 7.5). These can work well and give a sense of musically rolling ahead, but for the sake of variety don't use more than three in a row. The 9-8 is a special case; use only *one at a time* because a series of 9-8 suspensions is the equivalent of parallel octaves and causes the lines to fuse.

Some further considerations: work to use tied half notes through the whole exercise, but if you get into a difficulty or need to introduce variety you may "break the species" for one measure (as in bars 4-5 in figure 7.5). This means using half notes without ties instead of with. The half notes are governed by the rules of second species.

Notice that with regard to placement of dissonances, *fourth species is the opposite of second species.* In second species, the downbeat is always consonant while the weak beat may be dissonant. In fourth species, the weak beat is always consonant while the downbeat may be dissonant—there are no dissonances on the second half of the bar.

To get the rhythmic pattern established right off the bat, a rest always occupies the first half of bar 1. And in order to give final resolution and to "square up" the rhythm at the end, the last measure of the exercise is a whole note on the downbeat and there is no tie from the second-to-last measure.

## ORNAMENTED 4TH SPECIES

Some flourishes are available for ornamenting the resolution of suspensions. Half notes tied over the barline already add liveliness to the melody. Our new ornaments will accentuate and give "snap" to the syncopation. There are five types:

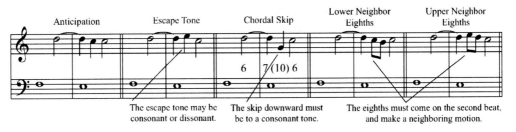

*7.7 The methods of ornamenting the resolution of suspensions*

These ornaments may be applied to any suspension whether consonant or dissonant, but they ornament the motion from dissonance to resolution and therefore always lead into the note of resolution; they come right before it on the weak beat. The anticipation permits a repeated note. The escape tone is an incomplete upper neighbor and may be consonant or dissonant. The chordal skip interpolates a consonance between the suspension and the note of resolution; a downward skip is less bumpy than an upward one, and follows the "fill the gap" rule. Ornamental eighth notes come in a pair and always move by step in the pattern of a neighbor figure.

Mix in some of these ornaments, but don't overuse a single type. They are for touches of interest and their effectiveness depends on being used sparingly. Overdoing it will make the line nervous, frenetic, and repetitive.

For practice take a complete fourth-species exercise (such as the one at the head of this section, figure 7.5) and add ornaments to it.

### 5TH SPECIES: ORGANIC MELODY

Regarding this stage of study Fux wrote:

*"This species is called florid counterpoint. As a garden is full of flowers so this species of counterpoint should be full of excellences of all kinds: a plastic melodic line, liveliness of movement, and beauty and variety of form. Just as we use all the other common species of arithmetic—counting, addition, multiplication and subtraction—in division, so this species is nothing but a recapitulation and combination of all the preceding ones. There is nothing new that need be explained, except that one should take the utmost care to write a singable melodic line—a concern I beg you always to keep in mind."*

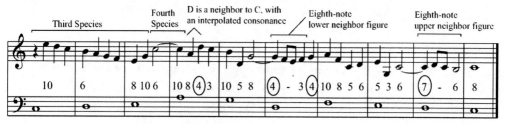

7.8 *Fifth species studies the varied flow of melody by adding a new line that uses all the previous species.*

Fifth species counterpoint is the combination and culmination of all previous species. Half notes, quarter notes, and syncopations all occur. Each note value is governed by the rules of the species to which it belongs.

In this species we draw upon the techniques we have learned and use them in a more creative exercise. The control of the musical elements that you have gradually built up will now enable you to adopt in fifth species, with its flexibility and wider range of possibilities, a more artistic and esthetic approach. Fifth species allows room for more unique individual self-expression.

This does not mean: drop everything we have learned up to now and write "whatever you want." It means: *use* everything we have learned up to now to write your own coherent creation.

The main issue in this species is learning to *control the rate of motion*, the flow of time values, to create a line that builds momentum and leads inexorably to the wrap-up provided by the final note. Here are some rules of thumb:

❋ Begin with a rest to set the counter-line off from the cantus. A half-rest prepares for half-note motion; a quarter-rest prepares for quarter-note motion.

❋ Use a varied combination of half notes, quarter notes and suspensions.

❋ Suspensions are particularly useful in producing liveliness and movement, tension and repose. Ornament suspensions to give even more momentum.

❋ Use eighth notes *only* as a neighbor ornament of the resolution of a suspension. Otherwise, they are too fast and confuse the basic rate of tempo with a sudden, unprepared acceleration.

❋ Don't use a single note value for too long (two or 2.5 bars) because it makes the subsequent change jarring.

❋ Be sure to use enough skips and changes of direction. They make the line interesting and give it richness.

❋ As always, be wary of melodic leaps over the barline as they tend to make the downbeat very heavy. Music flows well when it moves *through* the barline, smoothing it over instead of making a break.

❋ The following events can break the continuity: notes of too long a duration such as whole notes or dotted half notes; changes from half to quarter notes on the downbeat which gives the feeling of a start of a new section; using quarter-note motion into a half note on a weak beat, which usually feels like a sudden, awkward lurch.

❋ Be careful of half notes starting on the second quarter of the bar. They are syncopations but don't match with the general pattern of 4th species' tied half notes. Halves starting on the second quarter of the bar often don't flow very well—they usually give a feeling of a sudden stop, or a subsequent abrupt acceleration.

You must be very analytical about the rhythmic effects in your exercise—what works and what doesn't and why. Only a process of listening and naming the issues explicitly gives you control of the nuances of rhythm. And only this process will enable you to create a melody that spins ahead naturally and organically to reach its climax and then its final resolution. A good melody carries the listener naturally and satisfyingly through its course, and its ending gives a rewarding sense of completeness.

## AN EXAMPLE BY BRAHMS

An overall summary of the art of two-voice counterpoint we have been learning is best given in the form of a concrete example. To illustrate the principles as applied on a sophisticated level by a master, here is a brief passage from Brahms' First Violin Sonata.

From Sonata No. 1 for Violin and Piano in G Major, Op. 78 by Johannes Brahms

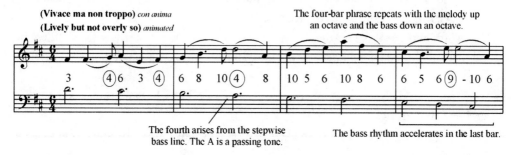

7.9 *This music by Brahms shows the use of counterpoint in sophisticated, passionate personal expression.*

The upper line, the violin melody, is essentially a "fifth species" line. Its notes fit together, flow, and rise and fall beautifully. The lower line, the main notes of the piano part, is a descending scale in longer notes, a steady structural line above which the melody floats. The bass rhythm accelerates in the last bar, sweeping into the next phrase. The bass notes in this last bar interlock with the timing of the melody notes, making a rhapsodic effect.

The violin and piano lines form a sensuous harmony with one another. Out of 22 intervals sounding between the two voices there are 13 imperfect consonances, about 60% of the intervals. All of these 3rds and 6ths lend great sweetness and warmth to the music.

This four-bar phrase repeats, with the music expanding dramatically. The first iteration is soft, ending with a crescendo into the reiteration which becomes quite strong. The second time through, the melody is an octave higher to soar in the violin's high register, reinforced by the piano playing the melody in a lower octave. The steady descending scale is dropped down deep in the piano's bass register. In full context, with the preparation that precedes it and the development that follows it, this tune is thrilling to hear and makes for totally unforgettable emotional experience.

## 1ST SPECIES IN 3 PARTS: RICHER SONORITIES

We return to first species counterpoint, only now writing in three parts. This level teaches us to use fuller sonorities, and to create a beautifully rich sound.

Remember that no dissonances are used in first species; this is true both in two parts and in three.

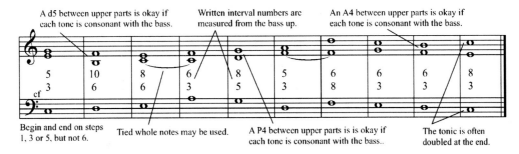

7.10 *We revisit the first species, now adding two new lines to study richer sonorities.*

In three parts, we contend not only with the relation of each new line to the fixed voice, but also with the relation between the two new lines.

The interval between the two new voices must be consonant. So, no 7ths, 9ths or diminished or augmented intervals. (See below regarding the tritone between upper voices.)

Between the staves, write the number of the interval between the line above *and the bass*. You don't need to write down the interval numbers between the upper two parts, but you must check them. (No dissonances; no parallel fifths or octaves.)

The upper lines may cross (but they don't have to). It is generally best not to cross below the lowest part because it confuses the line of the bass (plus then you would have to count intervals from a different lowest tone).

The top line must land on the tonic in the last bar. It should approach by step. However, if you need to leap to the tonic in the last bar (top line scale degree 5 to 1), that is not out of the question as long as the notes are consonant.

|  |  |
|---|---|
| 5 | 6 |
| 3 | 3 |

7.11 *Figures of the full sonorities*

There are two possible *full* sonorities, sonorities in which each voice has a unique note. Other sonorities are possible with octave (or unison) doubling. The full triadic sonorities are richer in sound; using them most of the time helps avoid the coldness or thinness of the doubled or "incomplete" sonorities.

Be careful with fifths—only perfect fifths are consonant.

Don't double the leading tone, it sticks out like a sore thumb.

| 8 | 5 | 8 | 6 | 8 | 10 |
|---|---|---|---|---|---|
| 5 | 5 | 6 | 6 | 10 | 10 |

7.12 *Figures for sonorities with doublings*

Several dissonant intervals have their clashing effect mitigated or eliminated when they are between upper parts. Thus, the perfect and augmented fourths and the diminished fifth may be used between upper parts (not with the bass). This is *not* true of the other dissonances; seconds and sevenths, for instance, still clash stridently even when they are consonant with a pitch sounding below. So P4, A4 and d5, but no other dissonances, may be used between upper parts.

So, fourths between the upper parts are *not* dissonant. Their character is altered when other notes are sounding below. Fourths create discord only when they are between the bass and an upper part.

If there is a tritone between the upper parts in the second to last bar it must resolve properly. The notes move by step. The augmented fourth expands out to a sixth. The diminished fifth contracts in to a third. In both cases, scale degree 4 moves down to 3, scale degree 7 (the leading tone) resolves up to the tonic.

The outer voices are more prominent. This doesn't mean the middle voice is mere filler; it should have quality and character as well. But special attention must be given to the highest and lowest parts.

Tied whole notes may be used. They are least obtrusive in the middle voice.

Continue to avoid similar motion into a fifth or octave in the outer parts. In an inner voice, though, they can be okay depending on the context. Parallel 5ths and 8vas are still no good because of the lurch in sound they cause.

All lines must end on the notes of the tonic triad (no sixth above the bass).

## CONCLUSION

This concludes our exposition of the basics of the art of counterpoint in the Fux method.

We have learned the way the consonances create a strong, intelligible framework. We have learned the methods of introducing and resolving dissonances. We have learned the way in which lines can be shaped and coordinated to avoid any ugliness or jarring interruptions, but instead to create smoothly integrated beauty of sound. We have learned to control the ebb and flow of lines in time, to lead to a climax and then to wrap up with satisfying closure, so that our miniature composition has a good sense of plot and holds together very well. We have seen the basic patterns of musical composition, and we have learned to control the musical elements for expressive purposes.

This knowledge is the result of the learning process embodied in Fux's systematic series of "*Gradus ad Parnassum*," the graded stairway by which we climb Mount Parnassus to, like Apollo, meet and dance with the Muses.

## SPECIES COUNTERPOINT SUMMARY IN ONE PAGE

| | |
|---|---|
| LINE SHAPE | Line is 8-12 notes long, all whole notes.<br>Use **2-3 skips** and **3-6 changes of direction**.<br>**Fill the gaps** created by skips.<br>Lead to one clear climax.<br>Do not leap by, or outline, a seventh, tritone or A2. |

METHOD:
1) Fill in the last two notes.
2) Plan the overall line shape.
3) Choose the climactic note.
4) Flesh out the line, leading to the climax and ending.
5) Critique your work and make improvements if necessary.
Throughout, write the intervals between the staves.

1ST SPECIES                                     CONSONANCE

New line consists of **whole notes**.
The shapes of the lines should complement each other but be different.
Use **exclusively consonances** (1, 3, 5, 6, 8) between the two voices.
Approach **fifths and octaves** by contrary motion. *No parallel P5s or P8vas.*
Maximum of three consecutive instances of the same interval.
Don't begin on the sonority of a 6th. End on the tonic note, by step.

2ND                          PASSING AND NEIGHBORING TONES

New line consists of **half notes** and may begin with a half rest.
The **downbeat must be consonant** with the fixed voice.
The second beat may be dissonant as a **passing** tone or **neighboring** tone.
Use leaps within the measure but stepwise motion over the barline. No repeated notes.
No chromatic motion. Be careful of **natural vs. melodic** forms of the minor scale.

3RD                                     SCALAR MOTION

The new line consists of **quarter notes** and may begin with a quarter rest.
The first note of each bar must be consonant with the fixed voice.
The other beats may be dissonant as passing or neighboring tones.
The **double neighbor** figure, and the "**nota cambiata**" figure may be used.

4TH                                     SYNCOPATION

New line is written in **half notes tied over the barline**. Begin with a half rest.
The first half of each bar may be consonant or dissonant.
The **second half of the bar must be consonant**. (The opposite of $2^{nd}$ species.)
If the downbeat note is dissonant, it must **resolve down by step**.
If the downbeat note is consonant, you may skip from it.
Don't use more than three suspensions in a chain. Use **only one 9-8** suspension at a time.
Five ways of **ornamenting a resolution** are:
    anticipation, escape tone, chordal skip, lower and upper neighbor eighths.

5TH                     CONTROLLING THE FLOW OF TIME VALUES

Mix quarters, halves, and tied halves; each note is **governed by the species it belongs to**.
Rhythm should **flow through the downbeats**; avoid making the downbeat too heavy.
Don't use a single note value for more than 2 ½ bars.
Longer notes should coincide with stronger metric position, except with tied halves.

| | |
|---|---|
| 1ST IN THREE PARTS | Full triadic sonorities (5/3 and 6/3) usually flow best.<br>Do not begin or end on the sonority of a sixth above the bass.<br>P4, A4 and d5 are usable between upper voices but not with the bass.<br>Generally avoid doubling the leading tone.<br>Occasionally, tied whole notes may be used.<br>No Parallel P5ths or P8vas. No similar motion to P5 or P8 in outer parts. |

# 8

---

## HARMONY

As composers continued to write polyphonic music, and to accumulate observations about how to combine lines, they began to grasp and use a new idea: the *chord*.

Consonances, we have seen, are the main structural element of music. Dissonances are important and valuable, but secondary; they are to be introduced only in such a way as to integrate smoothly around the consonances. Early on these issues were dealt with, as they had to be, in terms of the distance between two notes at a time, in terms of the *interval*—and this is indeed how the first rules of polyphony were formed.

But as composers continued to work with many voices, a pattern began to emerge: they found that they could deal with a *package* of intervals sounding together. They could extract from all the possible combinations a simple principle which helped them deal with a set of notes sounding at the same time. This was the triad.

Jacob of Liege, in around 1330, referred to the "divided fifth" with a major or minor third on the bottom. This was a very early indication of the triad. We saw that Zarlino, in 1558, defined the major and minor triads as the central sonorities of tonal composition, and made these centers the essential distinction for brighter versus darker emotions. Johannes Lippius in 1612 coined the term "triad" by analogy to the holy trinity; his work was part of the shift from fundamentally polyphonic thinking to *harmonic* thinking in the modern sense.

"Chord" is a term for "string," as on a violin. But it had another meaning as well, in several languages: "chord" is a shortening of "accord" in the sense of "bring into agreement" or "reconcile." "Accord" in turn, had come from the Latin "ad-cordis," meaning, "to be of one heart." That is indeed where the musical chord came from: it is a means of bringing multiple melodic lines into expressive harmony with one another.

The triad, the basic form of chord, consists of a root note with a third and a fifth above it. For example, scale steps 1-3-5, or the notes C-E-G or D-F-A. A triad is a three-note simultaneity, stacked in thirds. The major and minor triads are the most complex sonorities which are still consonant. All consonant sonorities can be understood as forms of the triad, and all elements of dissonance can be understood as ornamentation of the triad in one way or another. Thus this concept provided a powerful new way of handling notes sounding at once.

Composers found that holding a set of notes in mind as a chord helped them coordinate many voices more efficiently than thinking only in terms of individual intervals. The new concept reduced the number of units that had to be held in mind at once. It simplified the composing process by creating a more advanced tool. Standardized patterns of chord connection could be memorized and drawn upon, thus boiling down the vast variety of possible voice combinations into a manageable amount.

## Voice-leading

With the advent of the device of the chord, a new concept was formed which translated the rules of counterpoint into the context of the harmonic way of thinking: *voice-leading*. "Voice-leading" means simply the way to lead the voices so that they form the chords you want. Voice-leading is a simplification of counterpoint into standardized chordal formulas.

The concept of polyphony came about from the practice of combining voices. The concept of "voice-leading" came about from a perspective starting with chords, asking the question: given that I want, say, a C major chord followed by a G major chord, how to I connect the notes of the first chord to the notes of the next? Really polyphony and voice-leading mean the same thing, but with a different approach in mind. Polyphony is a concept from the mindset that starts with lines and makes chords; voice-leading is a concept from the mindset that starts with chords and then figures out how to assign the chord tones to separate lines.

Counterpoint is the science of polyphony, and was geared toward coordinating the motions of many voices which moved independently, which contrasted with one another and created an interplay. The science of harmony and voice-leading, in contrast, used chords and their connections as the means of simplifying and boiling down the wide variety of possible contrapuntal motions.

Voice-leading patterns are one form of economy of thought made possible by the concept of chord. For instance and for starters, if we consider the connection only of root position triads, we can summarize all the progressions in three simple patterns, and all the voice leading in a few simple rules.

Summary of all Voice-Leading Patterns for Root Position Traids

| Root motion by 2nd (or 7th) | Root motion by 3rd (or 6th) | Root motion by 4th (or 5th) |
| --- | --- | --- |
| To avoid parallel 5ths & octaves, upper voices move contrary to the bass. Two upper voices move by step. One moves by a third. | Two common tones hold. One voice moves by step. | Two upper voices move by step. The common tone holds. |

*8.1 Chordal harmony enables the classification of progressions into a small number of simple formulas.*

When chords in inversion are introduced (having a non-root note in the bass), and when dissonant sevenths are added, the voice-leading becomes more complicated. But you can see that packaging linear motions in categories by chord is a great help to managing the flow of lines. Using chords, one can memorize and draw upon the formulaic patterns of chord connection. This is greatly superior to treating each moment of music as a unique confluence of voices, unrelated to other moments.

However, also observe that almost no real music moves in a purely chordal fashion like the simple patterns of harmony show. This is the way in which the formulaic patterns of progression are only abstract simplifications. They do not have much musical value as such. Real music is richer and more complex. But the chord patterns provide the composer with a means of understanding linear motions on a new level, summarized in a relatively small number of standardized patterns. So they are helpful.

The emotional effects of the chord progressions can similarly be summarized. The effects relate back to the basic elements, the intervals and their qualities. This involves both the interval from chord root to chord root, but also the qualities of motion in the voice-leading. The progression of root motion by 2nd gives propulsion and sense of direction; it has the energy of the dissonant 2nd and the converging power of contrary motion. Root motion by 3rd is soft, smooth, gentle in quality; it has the tenderness and warmth of the third and the subtlety of very little change in the upper voices. Motion by 4th or 5th has the strength and power and stark clarity of that interval, conjoined with the smooth movements of the upper voices.

These effects will be modified, of course, by the qualities of the chords (major, minor, etc.) and by their positions in the scale, especially the relation of chord root to tonic.

## CHORD FUNCTION

The advent of the harmonic way of thinking introduced a new dimension to Zarlino's principle of tonality. Zarlino's was a principle of unity which set a particular note (and the triad built on it) as the center of a composition, the center around which all of the music moved. A single melody developed a sense of tonal direction when its shape led eventually to settled closure on the tonic note. The feeling of direction toward the tonic also became an attribute of polyphony, as multiple lines moved together, converging at a cadence. The concept of chord now enabled control of the harmonic progression as well. The new concept was that the harmony could progress in its own distinctive way, contributing to the sense of direction to resolution.

Harmonic progression is a matter of using chords according to their role in the musical scale. The function of a chord can be, for instance, a stable landing chord, or a mere passing chord.

Just as a scale-step gets its unique audible quality from the position of that note in the scale —because of the unique network of intervals surrounding it in context—so, too, a chord gets a large part of its psychological impression from its position in the scale. A chord containing the leading tone is affected by the pull of that note to the tonic. A chord containing the tonic is affected by the stability of that note. The primary fact about a chord is the *scale degree of its fundamental note, its root.* A chord built on the tonic (scale-steps 1-3-5) is the most stable. A chord built on scale-step 2 (steps 2-4-6) has the unstable energy of that note. And so on.

We capture the function of a chord by assigning a Roman numeral to it. The Roman numeral identifies the *scale degree of the root of the chord.* The I chord is built on the first scale degree, II on the second, and so on. (Using Roman numerals avoids confusion with the Arabic numerals of figured bass notation.)

The bass line is the controlling element of the harmony. The musical quality and function of higher tones is affected to a great extent by the bass note sounding below which makes the foundation.

The nature of harmonic progression and the nature of the bass line are intimately connected. While melody is characterized primarily by stepwise motion, the bass line is characterized primarily by leaps. Its distinctive function is to leap to the roots of chords, which means most of all to leap by perfect intervals (4,5,8). For a bass line to leap by these intervals is a very strong and powerful motion because of the stark quality of these intervals. (Recall that the octave is a 2:1 ratio, the 5th is a 3:2 ratio, and the 4th is a 4:3 ratio.)

The main harmony set in opposition to the tonic, the main antipode, was the chord on the dominant (V). Because of its close mathematical relation, the fifth step is the secondary main note of the scale, the secondary center of gravity like the moon in relation to the Earth. Thus the simplest, most elementary harmonic progression is:

$$I \;\rightarrow\; V \;\rightarrow\; I$$
$$\text{Tonic} \rightarrow \text{Dominant} \rightarrow \text{Tonic}$$

Jean-Phillipe Rameau, a French theorist of the 18th-century Enlightenment, picked up on Zarlino's principle and devised a formulaic, chordal system of music. He stressed the pattern:

$$I \;\rightarrow\; IV \;\rightarrow\; V \;\rightarrow\; I$$
$$\text{Tonic} \rightarrow \text{Dominant Preparation} \rightarrow \text{Dominant} \rightarrow \text{Tonic}$$

Rameau regarded other chords as substitutions of these (for instance, II as a substitution for IV, or IV as a substitute for I—since each substitute chord shares two notes with its match).

There is an important perceptual fact about this progression. Observe which scale degrees it provides to the ear.

❊ The tonic chord gives the ear scale-steps: 1-3-5.
❊ The dominant chord gives steps: 5-7-2.

What is missing? Scale degrees 4 and 6. In order to fully flesh out the scale—in order to provide the ear with the full musical context—one further chord is needed. This is the role of the *dominant preparation* chord. The IV and the II chord are both dominant preparation chords—they both contain the needed scale degrees 4 and 6. The primary relationship remains the progression I-V-I, but now the V can be intensified by the preparatory chord.

Thus in tonal music, as a preparation and intensification of the dominant, the IV (or II) has its main functional place *before* V-I, not between V and I. The alternative, I-V-IV-I, which is used in the blues, lacks a strong sense of direction and pointed purposeful progression; this is one means by which the blues has a more relaxed, loose and laid-back mental effect.

The use of Roman numerals to identify chords was popularized by German music theorist Gottfried Weber, whose *Theory of Musical Composition, treated with a view to a naturally consecutive arrangement of topics,* was published in 1817-21. (For historical perspective, this was 26 years after Mozart died, and about two years into the third and last stylistic period of Beethoven's life.) Weber's book was one of the first on musical theory translated into English and published in America (in 1846).

Because of the systematic and comprehensive nature of the book, it was beloved by academics. Even though Weber's name is almost entirely forgotten today, a great deal of American music theory derives from his compendium.

First, Weber designates a chord by giving the note name of the root, plus a figure. Thus, C7 means a seventh chord built on C. This is the origin of the method of chord designation later used in jazz.

Second, he devises a method of designating chord in relation to key. "We will hereafter make use of a method of designating all the various harmonies of a key.... Instead of employing the... letters we will use the Roman numerals to denote the degrees of the scale on which chords have their fundamental tones."

He specified the quality of the chord in the symbol: a major chord was given a capital Roman numeral, a minor chord a lowercase one; other qualities were shown with further symbols.

Weber's system of chord identification provided some economy and some insights, but led to a fairly mechanical procedure of assigning Roman numeral and figured bass to every chord in a piece. This method has been widely practiced, but fails to take into account the different levels of importance of different chords in context—one chord might be a major structural pillar of the piece, while another is merely a brief transition.

Heinrich Schenker, a later German theorist, refined the approach. He regarded the specification of chord quality in the Roman numeral as redundant and unnecessary, and preferred the clarity and standardized simplicity of using only capital Roman numerals. One can rely on one's understanding of the operative scale to supply the information of chord quality.

Furthermore, Schenker found it misleading to give every chord a symbol in mechanical fashion. Instead he thought some chords were pillars or crucial structural elements, which deserved to stand out with Roman numerals showing them to be part of a fundamental progression. Other chords did not have this function; they were subordinate elements of the harmonic flow, and therefore did not deserve to be spotlighted with a Roman numeral. We will learn more of Schenker's method and perspective shortly.

## CADENCE

The idea of the chord also enabled a clear classification of the types of cadence.

Forms of Melodic/Harmonic Cadence

| Perfect Authentic | Imperfect Authentic | Half | Plagal | Deceptive |
|---|---|---|---|---|
| V - I | V - I | I - V | IV - I | V - VI |
| The melody lands on the tonic. | The melody lands on the third or fifth, not the tonic. | The phrase lands on V (preceded by any chord). | The "Amen" cadence. | Acts like a PAC, but with a surprising shift in the bass. |

8.2 Chordal harmony also enables a classification of cadential formulas.

Different forms of cadence give different expressive effects.

The two forms of *authentic* cadence, progressing from V to I, create strong closure. An authentic cadence is the period at the end of a sentence, which gives a firm answer to the question posed by any prior half cadence. The *imperfect* authentic, in which the melody does not land on the tonic, gives a more suspended or floating feeling—a sense that this is only one closure, not the ultimate and final one. The *perfect* authentic cadence, in which the melody lands on the tonic, is indeed the absolute and total closure and conclusion; it gives the strongest possible feeling of completeness and finality.

The *half* cadence, which arrives on the V chord, creates a landing which is still open; it is settled in some way but not completely and therefore gives a unique combination of rest and anticipation of what will come next. The half cadence is the "?" at the end of a musical question—a mark defining an end, but an open end.

The *plagal* cadence gives a gentle sense of worship, of repose, of yielding, of broad majesty and solemnity. The term "plagal" points to the use of the fourth scale degree, as the root motion is IV-I. The term originally came from Greek *plagios* meaning oblique or sideways.

The *deceptive* cadence, moving largely like the perfect authentic cadence, creates an expectation of closure which is then suddenly swept away and rendered incomplete by the stepwise movement of the bass. Instead of a place at which the music lands, the cadence creates a lift, a feeling of levity and a springboard for further motion. It is a particularly subtle, poignant and moving effect.

## FIGURED BASS

In the Baroque period, it became standard practice to employ in musical ensembles a core group which provided rhythmic continuity and filled out the harmony. This was necessary at the time partly to deal with the practicalities of sickness and other reasons for incomplete ensembles, and to make performances more securely viable if the musicians had weaknesses of technique or were unfamiliar with the music and unable to read perfectly at sight. With the core group of accompanists chugging along, such failings would not interrupt the flow or cause a breakdown of the performance. The core group consisted of a bass instrument such as the cello and a harmonic instrument such as the harpsichord or guitar. (Notice that the rhythm section of jazz ensembles—piano, bass and drums—has a similar function.) The term for the Baroque period arrangement is "basso continuo" or "continuous bass" because it provided not the tune or counter-melodies, but the bass line and the steady rhythmic continuity.

We know from our study of counterpoint the practice of writing the intervals between the voices as a means of keeping track of the relationships. This form of notation evolved into a *shorthand means of indicating chords for the keyboardist* in the continuo group. Below the notes of the bass part were written numbers indicating the sonority to be played above it. This meant that the full accompaniment part need not be written out; it could be realized at sight by interpreting the figures below the bass.

Here is the continuo part for the opening phrase of Sonata II by Arcangelo Corelli, published in 1683. The accompanist would be given only the bass line with figures, and would play from that a realization such as what you see written in the upper staff. The accompaniment on its own is rather dull; it merely fills out the harmony and keeps things going. The real interest is between the melody and bass. (The violin melody is indicated in the small notes above.)

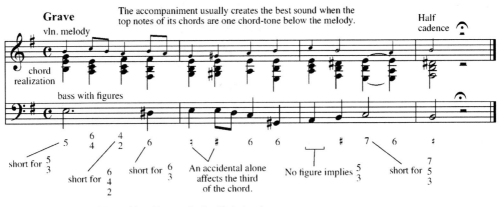

*8.3 Chordal harmony enabled the use of figured bass as a shorthand for keyboard accompaniment.*

Clearly, the invention of the device of the *chord* enabled a great amount of practical musicianship. The patterns of voice-leading provide simple formulas for learning to coordinate the flow of voices more easily. The forms of cadence can be classified, and the patterns used for the appropriate type of closure needed; instead of each phrase-ending being a totally unknown, unique event, it can be shaped using the models provided by the cadences. Accompaniment becomes a much easier undertaking; the study of chords feeds composition to such an extent that, given the figures and bass, a keyboardist can realize the harmonies at sight, improvising an accompaniment. The chord puts many useful tools into the composer's hands —and it does so by helping him hold a set of relationships in mind as one package.

These innovations led to the creation of an entirely new style of music.

## HOMOPHONY

The Corelli passage above is an example of the new style enabled by the chord: *homophonic* style. The word derives from "same voice" in the sense that the voices generally move together in the form of chord changes, but the essential meaning of the term is the pattern of a single prominent melody supported and enhanced by a subordinate accompaniment. The effect is to spotlight the main melody and enhance our perception of its character by providing a background that throws it into relief.

In homophonic style, the principle structure is the relation between the *outer voices*—the melody and bass. These two lines form the primary framework, while other lines (the inner voices) become highly subordinate and merely fill in the rest of the harmony. And essential to this new way of thinking was the differentiation of the character of melody and bass.

Melody continued to be what it had always been, organized by scalar or stepwise motion. But the bass line now took on the function of not just another melody, but the provider of foundational notes of chords. Since chords in the tonal system have as their primary root relationship not the step but the 4th or 5th relation, a more leaping, disjunct (but still integrated) character came to be the essential trait of the bass line. While the melody characteristically would move in steps (with some leaps mixed in for variety), the bass characteristically would move in skips from chord root to chord root (with some steps mixed in for smoothness).

Part of the development of homophonic style during the late Renaissance was a renewed focus on the intelligibility of the words being sung. This became a real preoccupation and source of controversy around the year 1600. Composers like Monteverdi rebelled against the interweaving lines, the interplay of melodies, the dynamic interaction of multiple melodies passing in and out of prominence through the course of a polyphonic vocal work. Instead, they demanded clarity of the words—which meant, in principle, dropping polyphony and adopting a homophonic style.

The demand for clarity of words sounded emphatically from a group of intellectuals and artists in Florence which called itself the Florentine Camerata. The group, meeting regularly at the home of its patron, Count Giovanni de' Bardi, discussed and sought to give direction to trends in the arts. The period of the group's strongest influence was around 1580.

The Florentine Camerata looked to Greek models for its artistic ideals; Greek plays, the Camerata stressed, had been sung rather than spoken. In music, the Camerata demanded clarity of words, the expression in music of the affection of the poetry being set, and a single prominent melody. These ideas led to experiments in vocal-theatrical music, and created a new genre: opera. In opera the singing is of course supported by subordinate accompaniment of the orchestra and chorus—a massively important instance of the new homophonic style. The first full opera in the modern sense was Jacopo Peri's 1597 "Daphne," which has not survived; his later work "Euridice" from 1600 is the earliest surviving opera. Peri's work was directly inspired by the ideals of the Camerata.

Composer Claudio Monteverdi operated on the cusp of all these trends. The preface of his Fifth Book of Madrigals, published in 1605, was a sort of manifesto of the new ideals. Monteverdi is known as the originator of the technique of basso continuo, including marking the figures beneath the bass for the accompanist to read from. Monteverdi's "l'Orfeo," premiered in 1607, has the distinction of being the earliest opera that has remained in performance to today.

In the church, the splendor of polyphony had been prized as a form of glorification. But in the secular or "popular" sphere of music, homophonic style seems to have been the norm. Josquin des Prez, who flourished in the later 1400s and early 1500s, wrote in homophonic style for his secular music, but polyphonic style for his church music.

Even the traditional and conservative Catholic Church became part of the new trend toward homophony and clarity of words. In reaction to the Protestant Reformation, a council of the Catholic Church met in Trent from 1545-63, issuing condemnations of the Protestant movement and reasserting the doctrines of the Roman church.

The Council dealt with church music as well. In one of its canons it asserted:

*"Since the sacred mysteries should be celebrated with utmost reverence... so that others may be filled with devotion and called to religion: ... Everything should be regulated so that the Masses, whether they be celebrated with the plain voice or in song, with everything clearly and quickly executed, may reach the ears of the hearers and quietly penetrate their hearts. In those Masses where measured music and organ are customary, nothing profane should be intermingled, but only hymns and divine praises. If something from the divine service is sung with the organ while the service proceeds, let it first be recited in a simple, clear voice, lest the reading of the sacred words be imperceptible. But the entire manner of singing in musical modes should be calculated, not to afford vain delight to the ear, but so that the words may be comprehensible to all; and thus may the hearts of the listeners be caught up into the desire for celestial harmonies and contemplation of the joys of the blessed."*

These and related sentiments led to changes in the style of the music of Catholicism—in a movement away from polyphony and toward the homophonic style. This showed up in the music of, for instance, Orlando di Lasso.

Thus the late Renaissance saw a concerted reaction against the complexities of polyphony, a turning away from the interplay of many lines overlaying one another. Instead the clarity of words came to be prized, together with the new style of music which went with it: the homophonic style, the style of chord changes, the style of melody with subordinate accompaniment.

## Chorale

The transition from polyphonic to homophonic style coincided with the broad upheaval of the Protestant Reformation.

In 1517, priest and theologian Martin Luther posted to the chapel door at the University of Wittenberg "95 Theses" challenging practices and doctrines of the Catholic Church. This was the start of a sweeping rebellion whose very name derives from the word "protest."

A legate of the Pope told Luther to recant his position; Luther refused. In 1520 the Pope threatened Luther with excommunication in a document titled *Exsurge Domini* (Arise, oh Lord)—which, two months after he received it, Luther publicly burned.

Luther was excommunicated in 1521, and in that same year he was summoned by the Emperor to a hearing at the city of Worms. At the trial, Luther declared:

*"Unless I am convinced by witness of Scripture or plain reason (for I do not believe in the Pope or in Councils alone, since it is agreed that they have often erred and contradicted themselves), I am overcome by the Scriptures which I have adduced, and my conscience is caught in the word of God. I neither can nor will recant anything, for it is neither safe nor right to act against one's conscience."* (Charles Beard's *Martin Luther and the reformation in Germany*)

As a result of this refusal, the Emperor condemned Luther as an outlaw and a "notorious heretic."

The Catholic Church had practiced a form of worship in which the clergy presented the service to a mass of listeners who passively received the inspiration. The Reformation rebelled against such an elitist approach. The Protestants insisted on a revolutionary idea: people could study the Bible directly, learn about religion, and participate in worship as individuals independently of Church officials. This was a "democratic," individualistic idea which defied the oppressive authority of the age-old Catholic Church. The Bible had always been in Latin—the exclusive tongue of the Church. Luther translated it into German so that anyone could read it. Catholic priests had been forbidden to marry; Luther married and set a precedent for ministers who had private lives, and were not the sequestered servants of God living in a monastery. He began a tradition in which ministers were more integrated with and involved in worldly life.

For the practice of its new form of worship, the Protestant Church required a special type of music: music that could be sung by the congregation itself in active participation. This meant the music had to be suited to the ability of the untrained public, so the melodies had to be simple, and florid polyphony was not appropriate. Music of the intricate and complex texture of polyphony required a trained, professional choir of skilled musicians.

The result was a straightforward and basic hymn setting using block chords under a familiar, rudimentary tune.

Johann Sebastian Bach, an employee of the Lutheran Church, was a master at composing chorales which elevated this basic format into a fine work of art. His chorales brought the smooth richness of polyphony to basic congregational tune setting.

### Oh Sacred Head, Now Wounded
#### (from the St. Matthew Passion)

J.S. Bach

8.4 *The Protestant chorale hymn became the miniature model for studying chord progressions and voice-leading.*

The Protestant chorale, a compact miniature form, used full harmony but without much complication by florid counterpoint. These qualities made it the perfect vehicle for studying harmony and harmonic progression with chords connected by smooth voice-leading. And indeed it has been used for that purpose ever since.

### CONCLUDING SUMMARY

The "chord" or triad—a root-note with a third and fifth sounding above it—was an important innovation of the late Renaissance. The major and minor triads are the richest, most complex sonorities which are still consonant; so dissonances can be understood as ornamentations in and around them.

The chord enabled composers to deal with simultaneous note combinations more efficiently, placing less of a tax on working memory by boiling down the vast array of possible flows of voices into a small number of possible chord-connections.

Chords made it possible to devise simple, formulaic patterns to summarize voice-leading. For instance, in connecting two triads whose roots are a third apart (such as a C major chord and an E minor chord), the upper voices hold two common tones, while the remaining voice moves by a step and back to its starting note. That's 12 notes and all of their interval connections, summarized in one sentence. The "prefabricated" patterns of chord changes enabled composers and their students to grapple more quickly and easily with their material.

A classification of cadences—methods of phrase closure—became possible. The V-I, "authentic" cadence is the strongest form of closure because of the root relation, for instance —like the period at the end of a sentence.

Keyboard accompaniment could be notated in shorthand figures above the bass line, eliminating the need for laborious literal notation. The keyboardist could play the accompaniment at sight without the need of having all the notes written out—since he knew the patterns of chord connection. This saved a lot of time and effort.

Like the notes of melody, chords could be understood by their function in the scale. The impression of a chord depends not just on the quality of its sonority (such as a major triad or minor one) but on which scale-steps comprise it. The basic factor is the scale-step of the root of the chord, which we designate with a Roman numeral.

All of this enabled a revolutionary style of music, one which, among other things, gave greater clarity to the words by homogenizing the rhythm. The new style was *homophony*—a single prominent melody accompanied by subordinate voices which merely filled out the harmony in a simple way without detracting attention from the tune. This enabled the prominent tune to be thrown into relief against the background padding provided by the accompanying voices. This new style enabled the creation of a completely new genre: opera.

# 9

## Primacy of Line vs. Primacy of Chord

From the flowering richness and sensuality of the Renaissance through the symphonic majesty of 19th-century Romanticism, the greatness of man found expression in music. That expression was made possible by advances in our understanding of music as an organic integration of notes over time—as a synthesis of individual lines from notes, then as a synthesis of a tapestry from lines. That music required and called upon understanding of melodic shape, the scale, the organization of musical elements in time, the arts of counterpoint and chordal harmony. It required knowing, calling upon, and maximizing the principle of tonality—of unity, direction, and motion to resolution.

Palestrina's spiritual purity and soaring exaltation, Vivaldi's intensity, clarity and propulsion, Mozart's grace and inventiveness, Beethoven's majesty and might, Chopin's sensuality and vigor, Puccini's outpouring of passion—all this was enabled by the growth over centuries of ever-greater conceptual knowledge.

But a trend developed which undercut all of this art by negating its foundation. The trend consisted of a new way of thinking which took the last result of the whole development of music theory—the chord—and treated it as the foundation, starting point, and essence of the art form. This new way of thinking expanded the latest innovation into the all-consuming principle, ignoring and replacing the true roots of the field.

In this chapter we will first trace the history and development of this "primacy of chord" viewpoint, including its solidification in the theoretical system of Jean-Philippe Rameau. We will delve into the motivation behind the viewpoint, and the consequences that result from it.

We will reassert the evidence that melody (and musical line more broadly) is actually primary. And we will introduce a culminating innovator on the topic of linear synthesis, Heinrich Schenker, who by reviving the "primacy of line" perspective corrected the conception of music, and who used that perspective to make a quantum leap in our understanding of musical cognition.

## The Rise of the Primacy of Chord

The original Greek concept "harmoniai," the root of our term "harmony," meant the synthesis of notes over time into a melodic line with continuity and coherence. A number of historical developments precipitated a change in the meaning of the term, such that today it is associated primarily with simultaneous combinations of notes. This was not a harmless change of terminology, but a fundamental re-orientation of thought which lost sight of music's foundation.

The change took place gradually, and partly as a result of real facts which were misinterpreted.

Audiences were amazed by the powerful richness of polyphonic and, later, homophonic music. The depth of sound in these musics was a distinctive achievement of the Western world, and a marked advance in power of expression.

The new invention of the chord (during the Renaissance) was very useful. It improved a composer's ability to handle notes mentally. It enabled a shorthand notation for keyboard accompaniment. The functions of chords in the key could be controlled to contribute to the feeling of tonal direction. The chord enabled the creation of a new style of music, homophonic style, which became essential to a powerful new genre: opera.

Conceptions relating to simultaneous sounds seemed to explain the emotional content of music: chords could be major or minor, sonorities could be consonant or dissonant. But this selection already reflected a narrowing of focus since these things alone do not determine emotion—they are dependent on the musical context for their meaning and effect. This selection already reflected a neglect of the fact of *time*—of the temporal nature of musical perception, cognition and experience.

The transition from counterpoint (rules of polyphony) to voice-leading (rules of homophony) was part of the trend. Where counterpoint had thought in terms of a confluence and interplay of diverse voices, voice-leading thought in terms of chord changes and how to connect the notes of one chord to the next. Where counterpoint sought to give each voice unique shape and interest, voice-leading sought to keep each voice as simple as possible with the goal of making a smooth connection between chords. It is not that one of these is inherently superior; however this is part of a shift from a dominantly "horizontal" (linear) conception to a dominantly "vertical" (chordal) one.

Thinkers began to take for granted and then increasingly forgot the conception of the synthesis or "continuity and consecution" of melody. They still wrote and listened to melody, to be sure, but the way they thought about music was changing.

Intellectuals such as Johannes Lippius, writing around 1600, became preoccupied with chords—their various kinds and permutations and relations; linear considerations became of derivative interest. This shift was not thought of as a revolution, nor was it very abrupt. But as time passed the transition accelerated.

In 1701 mathematician Joseph Sauveur published, in his treatise *Principes d'Acoustique et de Musique*, his discovery of the *overtone series*. When a string vibrates, it does so as a whole but also simultaneously in halves, thirds, quarters, and so on. Each of the fractions is smaller than the last and vibrates with less energy, so its sound is correspondingly fainter.

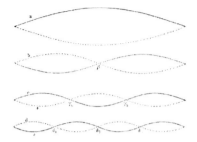

9.1 The visually separated components of a single string's vibration

Thus a single musical tone, which we perceive as a simple unity, was discovered to be composed of many constituent vibrations which were related to one another by a simple mathematical principle. The vibrating string produces an array of frequencies in the ratio 1:2:3:4:5:6:7:8:9:10 etc.

This is the overtone series in music notation:

9.2 The overtone series, the array of partials in a single musical tone

We perceive a musical tone as a single, elementary sensation. But in fact a musical tone is composed of a set of *partials* which are closely related by mathematical ratio, and which fuse in our perception.

People found the overtone series incredibly impressive. It came in origin with the prestige of a scientific, mathematical certainty. It was thought to be an objective basis of music and came to be called the "chord of nature." The overtone series, people began to think, is a fact existing outside of us which exhibits the same structure as our harmonies.

Only it doesn't. The overtone series contains elements in the upper partials which don't comport with our musical system. Certain tones of the series (partials 7, 11 and 13) are not in tune with the established intervals. The declining mark in the diagram (figure 9.2) for Bb indicates the tone being slightly flat in relation to a usual, (slightly wider) minor seventh. Its pitch is between standard A and Bb. The rising mark next to F indicates that this note is sharp compared to the usual fourth—it is between F and F#. The basis of human musical perception is pitch relations which are reducible to small whole-number ratios. But these out-of-tune notes stand in ratios which are not reducible in that way—their ratios contain large prime numbers. This explains why they don't comport with the rest of our system despite the fact that they sound in the so-called "chord of nature."

Furthermore, chordal music uses sounds which do not appear in the overtone series: minor chords, diminished chords, augmented chords, suspensions and various forms of seventh chord and ninth chord. And what about the musical scale? It is inherent in the human brain, but is not present in this "chord of nature."

If the standard of objective musical validity is that the pattern exists outside of us in the physical world, then what about all the noises we hear around us? They exist outside of us, but don't have such a neat mathematical structure. What about human speech? Or birdsong or whale song? Those sounds are not seized upon as being the magical essence of the art of music—because they take place over time.

There is a selection bias operating in the excessive adoration of the overtone series. Thinkers have picked out one fact of nature that fits their preconceptions, while ignoring others which do not.

The overtone series is a true and good discovery and does mean something, but its meaning has been misinterpreted. It is one more instance of mathematical relations in music. But it should not be taken as *the* archetypal case—the principle is wider than that. The objective basis of music lies not in the "chord of nature," but more broadly in the phenomenon of mathematical relations among tones—relations which, because of the inborn nature of the human hearing system, have certain psychological effects on us.

But this perspective was never asserted; the discovery of the "chord of nature" and the interpretation of it as an objective basis of music unfortunately became a significant step in the distorted perspective men were developing on music.

There was a further, decisive stroke, however, without which the transformation of the concept of melody into the concept of chord could never have taken hold or become so pervasive. No one had formulated such an inversion on principle, and no one had given it the power of being developed into a complete system of musical thought—until Jean-Phillipe Rameau.

## RAMEAU

Jean-Philippe Rameau was a French music theorist who is said to have originated the theoretical framework of modern harmony. His 1722 *Treatise on Harmony* did indeed shape the future course of thought on the subject.

In order to understand the content of Rameau's thought, we must learn the underlying philosophical base from which he approached the subject. Rameau was a devotee of the philosophy of René Descartes, the dominant voice of a school of thought called *Rationalism*. As the name suggests, the school advocated reason—this philosophy was a part of the historical Age of Reason—but essential to the ideology is a certain conception or definition of reason. Reason, according to this school, was not a primarily extrospective faculty, looking out at the world, but primarily an introspective one, operating abstractly in a sphere of its own.

Descartes was impressed, as so many were, with the achievements in mathematical physics by such men as Kepler and Galileo. However Descartes created a philosophy which set aside the observational base and the extrospective focus of science, and replaced it with a devotion to the creatively free *inventions* of the intellect.

Descartes focused on abstract mathematical deduction rather than inductive observation as the essence of philosophy. He held that the standard of truth was not an idea's correspondence to reality, but some qualities of the idea in the mind—that it was "clear and distinct." He is particularly famous for his premise "I think, therefore I am" (*cogito ergo sum*)—which makes the first and primary certainty not the observable world around us, but thoughts inside the mind.

This "wrapped up inside your head" philosophy is also evident in the title of his work *Meditations*—and in the fact that its format is a dialog between Descartes *and himself!*

Rameau was a fan of Descartes and followed this method.

Rameau's *Treatise on Harmony* begins not with any survey of human music, but "On the Relationship between Harmonic Ratios and Proportions"—those of the overtone series. This conception of a stack of notes sounding at once in harmonic ratio is the central fact which "may be used to make music perfect."

What happened before we knew about the overtone series? That is a question Rameau does not ask. He skips any consideration of melody or the centuries of history which developed polyphony and the science of counterpoint. He takes no cognizance of how the concept of "chord" originated. As translator Philip Gossett noted, "Rameau refers to all musicians preceding Zarlino as the Ancients. He does not discriminate between Greek music and plain [Gregorian] chant, nor does he show any awareness of Medieval or Renaissance polyphony."

Rameau details the types and properties of chords, harmonic cadences, etc. He derives principles of composition from the previously laid out abstractions. And the final section, the culmination, the climax of his book is not melody but: accompaniment!

The second sentence of the Treatise is: "Music is generally divided into harmony and melody, but we shall show in the following that the latter is merely a part of the former and that a knowledge of harmony is sufficient for a complete understanding of all the properties of music."

In Rameau's thought, the conception of a fundamental tone, with harmonic tones sounding above it, became the central model and starting point. Thus he decisively establishes the conception of "harmony" in the modern, non-melodic sense.

Like everyone who holds that chords come first, Rameau had to make concessions to the fact that music takes place over *time*. Even though his main conception of music is a single bass note with harmonic tones above it, followed by another, and so on—he does deal, as he must, with the issue of how to connect chords. Lines are treated as derived from and determined by the chord progression. (Where does the chord progression come from? No answer.)

Rameau counts on the major and minor scales in all of his thought. But what is his justification for doing so? He wants all theory of music to be deduced from the "chord of nature" but sneaks in the scale principle. Where did he get the concepts of scale or key? What is their basis and what is the justification for using them? No answer, they are just there. As Thomas Christensen wrote in the Grove Dictionary of Music: "Rameau was always insistent that major and minor scales were generated by the fundamental bass, partly in order to prove the primacy of harmony over melody and partly to justify the pedagogical efficacy of his fundamental bass. But he found he could not demonstrate this in any systematic way."

Rameau's solitary positive contribution to musical thought is the idea of looking at chords in terms of the root and to consider the chord in relation to the key (which, we may point out, is an issue of temporal context). For example, he stressed the use of the IV chord as a preparation of the dominant. But this is small potatoes in terms of understanding musical cognition or expression. And the value of this insight is more than swamped by Rameau's massive inversion of the hierarchy of knowledge.

The essence of Rameau's thought is not the introduction of any new technique or musical concept, but the systematic re-orientation of the field to make it a deduction from the overtone series rather than a conceptualization of human musical practice.

Fux and Rameau published their books in almost exactly the same year: Fux's *Gradus ad Parnassum* came out in 1725, Rameau's *Treatise on Harmony* in 1722. Fux taught linear counterpoint using a method which helped the student master musical elements first on a simple level, and then on increasingly complex levels, working step by step so that the student at each stage could deal with the material fully without being overwhelmed or sacrificing detail or artistry.

Rameau, on the other hand, has the temerity to insist that students begin learning music by writing in four parts: "Once four parts are familiar to us, we can reduce them to three and to two. Composition in two parts can give us no knowledge, however, for even if we understood it perfectly, which is almost impossible, there is no fundamental [bass] to guide us."

He elaborates that:

*"harmony may be taught only in four parts. Everything in harmony may then be found in just two chords (as we have indicated everywhere) and it is very simple to reduce these four parts to three or to two…. In conclusion, we affirm that though it has been impossible to understand fully the rules given until now concerning harmony, the source we have proposed will certainly lead to an understanding which is all-embracing."*

Just where is this mystical "understanding which is all-embracing" to come from? How is a student supposed to learn to handle the complexities of four-part writing if he cannot even handle the simplicity of two parts? By *what means* is he to know how to handle four parts as a beginning? By imitating the teacher without understanding?

Rameau might as well suggest that a writer begin with a 1000-page epic novel, and then learn to write short stories by simplifying. He might as well suggest that kindergartners begin learning differential and integral calculus, because then in elementary school they could simplify it down to algebra, trim it to arithmetic in high school, and then at university finally reach the stage where they can count. It is outrageous—but a perfect expression of Rameau's inversion of the hierarchy of knowledge.

The greatest theorists of music, such as Zarlino and Fux, regarded theory as the mere servant of practice; they placed composition and performance as the main values and looked at theory as an assistant, a means to those ends. Rameau, in contrast, prided himself on, and wished to be known for, his theory more than his composition—despite the fact that he wrote more than 40 dramatic musical works (operas, ballets, cantatas), as well as many instrumental works. This prioritization is consistent with and an expression of Rationalism, a primary devotion to abstractions. (The fact that he was so productive—and that some of his music is rather songfully melodic—reflects the split between Rameau's theory and practice. The future would do what he said, not what he did.)

Curiously, Rameau's first opera, *Hippolyte et Aricie* (1733), was the first work to be described as "Baroque." According to the Grove Dictionary, some "found the music overcomplex, unnatural, misshapen." The term "baroque" had originally described a misshapen or imperfect pearl. It came to be the name for the entire style period to which Rameau belonged.

The famously "misshapen" music came from the same mind that produced this grotesquely misshapen theory.

## CAUSE AND CONSEQUENCES

Rameau's system met with success and was looked upon by future thinkers as a fresh foundation, as the new, scientifically modern system of music.

His thought became especially dominant in academia. Philip Gossett, Professor at the University of Chicago, wrote in the introduction to his translation of Rameau's Treatise:

*"It would be wrong to conclude that the significance of Rameau's treatises was not appreciated by his contemporaries. Indeed, these works were dissected, condensed, and rearranged in order to make them palatable to those unable to follow the tortuous lines of thought in the original books...*

*"Rameau here constructed and rationalized a theory of tonality that was to remain basic for Western music during the next two centuries...*

*"[He] remains the first to have conceptualized those principles of tonality which were so thoroughly revolutionizing harmony in the eighteenth century."*

The translator forgets that the practice of tonality had preceded Rameau by hundreds of years, and that it was Zarlino who had congealed the concepts.

Species counterpoint was dropped as the starting point for learning music. Instead, teachers jumped right to chords and voice-leading in four parts as Rameau had suggested. Ironically, counterpoint became an advanced course for graduate students which involved imitating the style of J.S. Bach.

Weber's method of analyzing chords with Roman numerals, which had grown out of Rameau's thought, also became a mainstay of music teaching.

Learning chord-connection is a fairly mechanical, rote process. Unlike species counterpoint, it is not very artistic or creative; it doesn't activate one's intelligence or cultivate discrimination and planning a course from climax to cadence in the same way. Basically, in the new method, music students were trained to simply add garnishes to formulaic chord progressions. The result was that students didn't know how to produce anything but stilted marches of chords. Culturally, this is part of the reason for the absence of composers who could write organically integrated, flowing, symphonic music.

The new, chord-centered teaching also resulted in an oversimplified notion of what goes into the art of the great composers. People learned Roman numerals and some voice-leading, and concluded something along the lines of, "so *that's* all there is to Mozart." Chordal analysis became a means of dismissal; labeling a musical element chordally was taken to explain it away as obvious and something anybody could do (and yet somehow no one does).

What is the motivation for the chord-centered approach? What got it started and kept it going? Partly there were some understandable facts which lent themselves to misinterpretation, as we have seen. But a woefully wrong premise like this could not become so pervasive, among experts and laymen alike, without something more behind it.

Rameau's thought, that product of the "Age of Reason," became successful by catering to those who do not wish to think. He provides the lazy mind with the ultimate mechanical shortcut to pretend mastery of the field.

Think of the kind of care, sensitivity, historical awareness, discrimination and artistry in the work of the thinkers in the linear tradition: Aristoxenus laid out the methods of dividing the pitch spectrum to produce a scale for synthesizing melody by "continuity and consecution," by the laws of "harmoniai." Guido d'Arezzo devised methods for improving one's mental facility, composing ability, and singing ability together—methods including staff notation, solfege, consideration of the emotional effects of the various modes. Zarlino began with the law that consonance is primary and ended with a grand-scale conception of music as a unified percept unfolding over time, which first establishes a tonal center, then fans out away from it, and then converges upon it again to create a magnificent feeling of striving and surging forward in purposeful motion. Fux gave great composers from Haydn to Strauss the method for giving direction to their passion—by first learning to compose on the simplest level with a vision of the motion to climax and cadence, and then step-by-step growing one's facility to the level of total mastery and control of the expressive power of music.

Rameau gives his student the chance to skip all of that effort while seeming to reach the same level of artistry and mastery. Painstaking intelligence drops by the wayside in favor of rote imitation of preconceived formulas.

Most students who go through chord-centered curricula don't understand why things are done that way (unsurprising since the method makes no sense), and simply feel bored. But the scheme is perpetuated by those who *want* the chord-centered way of learning, because they want to jump to the last results as a shortcut. They want to get the products of using rich sonorities and they want to be like, and have the same status and prestige as, a Rachmaninoff or a Dvořák—but without the long process of effort involved in learning the symphonic principle, the coordination of lines. They prefer to go for crude, gross effects without bothering with details and refinements. They do not want to exercise the patient, methodical judgment of learning counterpoint, but they do like the musical equivalent of a "get rich quick" scheme.

Observe also that for people who prefer to stare and not to think, visual perception is the model for everything real. In such a mentality, a prejudice exists for things which exist *all at once*, as material objects do. People who passively rely on visual perception feel that in order for something to be fully real, in order to trust it, in order for it to be objective, it must exist as a material thing and *as a simultaneity*. Chords do, and the overtone series does. Melody does not.

An unthinking person does not accumulate information to gain a sense of the past—of what happened and why; he does not relate the past to the present and he does not project the future; he has no goals, nor any plans leading to future values. It is not surprising that he would give insufficient attention to the fact of time in music.

The "just give me the chords and I'll run with them" attitude is an example of the anti-conceptual mentality, the mentality that unquestioningly accepts whatever is around in the culture today, with no awareness of or concern for where these things came from. It is the mentality of a person who treats the chance contents of his memory banks as, in effect, the word of God—as an unquestionable absolute. Such a mentality does not consider how the content got there or what its basis in reality is.

Rameau, who seems to have exhibited this mentality, had avoided the effort of learning or using the hierarchy of knowledge—the step-by-step historical progression building our understanding from elementary melody on up. Then he grabbed and ran with the finished product (richness of sound by means of chords) without regard for where it came from.

This is a form of intellectual theft—a form of taking something and using it without having earned the right to it. It is like the desire of a thief to have money, but in disregard of who made the money and who rightfully owns it. The cause of the value is negated while the value itself is irrationally, avariciously grabbed.

A person may listen to melodies, sing them, and love them. Yet when he thinks about music he can be quite dismissive of melody and focus intensely on harmony, studying it as a serious and important science. There is a certain premise (or pretense) here that Harmony is a substantial and "hard" science, in contrast to melody which is neglected and taken for granted as non-scientific and subjective. Sometimes melody is even despised as a low or vulgar factor which falls short of the splendor of rational science.

Notice that in today's informal, layman's parlance, people will sometimes say "I don't like that dissonant music." But because of the modern orientation to simultaneity, the meaning doesn't come across quite right. Today we tend to think of a dissonance as some notes that clash at once; but the original conception pertained to the use of melodic concords and discords. What that person is trying to say is: these modern sounds don't make sense, they don't fit together over time, they don't integrate into a coherent progression, and the result is a sound that is not harmonious or melodious, it doesn't make sense to me and therefore I reject it. But this idea has become impossible to communicate because our language no longer has words pertaining to synthesis or temporal "continuity and consecution." Unfortunately, Western thought has essentially lost the concept of "harmoniai." It has been transformed into its opposite: instead of naming the synthesis of tones in the flow over time, it came to mean chords and the science of chords.

Moreover, the term "harmony," despite the reversal of its meaning, still carries the prestige it acquired through all the ages with its opposite, melodic, meaning. When we read Plato and Aristotle or the other Greeks and see them refer to "harmony" how many of us are clear about what the concept meant to them? Instead the ideals of the great philosophers are connected, in the modern Western mind, not with melody and its expression, but with chords—of which the Greeks had no inkling whatever.

Centuries of Greek and Roman culture included "harmonics" in school curricula as the means of teaching mathematics. The question of how to divide the pitch spectrum, how to tune instruments and establish a scale, provided the perfect area for learning about proportions and measurement. Because of the change from the ancient to the modern meaning of harmony, this venerated tradition, too, became associated with chords rather than lines.

All the objectivity of modern science, all the prestige of ages-old mathematical knowledge, all the poetic majesty of Greek philosophy, even a misguided notion of speedy practicality— all of these have their weight thrown onto the wrong concept.

This is how the modern concept of harmony has co-opted and robbed the original meaning of "harmoniai" and taken the place of the true core of the art of music: melody.

## Au contraire: Melody Comes First

Today we tend to take chords for granted, as though they were eternal acoustical facts, as though we've always known about them, as though they existed ready-made in reality like fruit hanging from a tree. But for most of human history, there was no such thing. Men had not so much as the faintest inkling of the chord, neither as a sound nor as an idea. Man has been around for well more than 40,000 years, but the chord is only around 500 years old—it has existed for only about 1% of human history.

The chord was an invention of the late Renaissance, and it was a totally new, unheard-of, unprecedented idea and artifact. It was the product of a complex development of practical knowledge, and a new level of conceptual product, and a *means of summarizing* prior observations about intervals and lines. The chord is not a naturally occurring phenomenon, but an advanced human tool. It is not a simple primary, but a complex derivative.

The first form of human music, from the dawn of man, was melody. The singing voice has existed as long as man has; our earliest instruments such as the flute played melodic lines. Throughout the world for millennia the only form of music was melody, sometimes accompanied by percussive sounds such as hand-claps or drum-beats, and sometimes slightly elaborated in "heterophonic" style (as when one sings a melody and plays an ornamented version of the same tune on an instrument). Harmonic improvisation, if it occurred, left no historical record before the 9th century in Europe.

This was followed by a centuries-long development of polyphony, a process of learning to combine lines into a rich fabric, flowing together in beautiful synthesis. In the course of this development, composers learned very slowly, by trial and error, how to fit lines together and how to coordinate their motion. They gathered rules of thumb and formulated an entire art of counterpoint to manage such a synthesis.

The concept of "chord" came very late, as a means of summarizing the patterns of voice motions; the very word is a shortening of "accord," meaning to bring lines into accord with one another. Chords give nothing more than simple, formulaic, pre-packaged patterns of voice-leading—and these did not exist and could not have existed without the prior art of counterpoint.

The instruments suited to playing chords—the organ, clavichord, harpsichord, piano, guitar, accordion—were all invented much later in history than the melody instruments.

When we listen to music, we attend to, follow and remember the melody; in more polyphonic or symphonic music, we let the ear follow one line such as the oboe, then pick up and follow the violins, and so on, always attending to lines and how they relate to one another. The harmony in music, to put it strongly, is a sort of expressive by-product. Harmony means the sonorities produced by the lines flowing together. The particular quality of a sonority does matter, and is part of the total package of expression. But no simultaneous sonority exists or is perceived or remembered in isolation. It is merely a qualitative impression at a given moment, at the mercy of context for its meaning and appropriateness.

Cognitively, a melody is a *thing*; a harmony is a mere impression. A melody is a perceptual entity, a chord is nothing more than a momentary sense quality. Harmony adds to richness and expression, but no one hums a chord in the shower, or gets a chord stuck in his head.

A single melody by itself is music; a single chord by itself is not.

A melody activates the brain's capacity to integrate sensations over time, and it has a fully complete emotional meaning even without accompaniment. Think of the stately majesty of the British national anthem "God Save the Queen" (known in America as "My Country 'Tis of Thee"), or the saucy, snappy verve of Gershwin's "I Got Rhythm."

But a single chord does not activate the brain's capacity to integrate sensations over time. It does not create a new synthesized entity. Nor does it have a self-contained emotional meaning. A single chord simply registers in the mind as a bright sound or a dark one, a clear sound or a muddy one, a rich one or a thin one, a stable one or an unstable one. The cognitive significance and emotional meaning of a chord depends on its role in context over time; a major chord can be part of a dark feeling as the dominant in a minor key, for instance.

A simple, self-evident primary is precisely what a chord is *not*. By the time a child is old enough to be taught music formally, he is already familiar with melodies he has heard. But chords must be taught by an artificial process.

We teach chords by teaching how to build them, using the interval relationships among the notes, which one must sing and explain in succession. No one can sing a chord at once; to use your voice to grasp the arrangement of notes you must sing the notes one after another.

If we are given the sound of a chord, we have no way of understanding it except to break it down into its components. In identifying chords by listening, a student must learn to isolate out each note, to move his attention over each tone one at a time; this enables him to gauge the distances. At a certain point, he becomes familiar enough with the composite sound and its inner relations, and can recognize it instantly—but that is a skill acquired by means of linear, temporal cognition.

To place harmony as the primary factor of music flies in the face of a metaphysical fact: time.

Rhythm is an inherent attribute of melody. The pattern of notes making up a tune includes the time-values, the relative durations of the notes. Change the proportions of the time values, and you mess up the tune. A chord, on the other hand, is as close as you can come to something outside of, or without time. It has to last some duration, of course, but to communicate its sound one simply plays it and says "that's it." The duration does not matter—let it sound for a fraction of a second, or let it ring for half a minute, and you have still conveyed the same sound impression. Now, if you want to raise the possibility of a chord repeated in rhythmic fashion, well then you have created a substrate for a melody, but still lack the substance.

## MELODY PRECEDES HARMONY

The concept of melody is prior to the concept of chord.

Line is first in our perception and our production of music.

Lines are the content of music. Harmony is secondary, derivative, subservient.

Melody comes first historically and in the order of learning—thus it is first in logic. The concept of harmony depends on, and cannot be understood except in the light of the fundamental fact of linear cognition.

## ISN'T IT BOTH?

When people address the question of the primacy of line versus chord by insisting "it's both"—meaning that music has both harmony and melody—they are really expressing the primacy of chord view.

The fact that a lot of music has melody and also harmony is a truism, not a defense of chords being the central fact of music. The question is one of proper definition and clarity of principle. In history, in perception, in logic, lines come first. Chords are nothing more (and nothing less) than an advanced tool growing out of, and summarizing, simple patterns of the confluence of lines.

A person insisting on equality of melody and harmony wants to be "above the fray" of disagreement on the issue. But that actually means defending the status quo, acquiescing in the assumptions and perspective of today, which is strongly influenced by Rameau. Today the "primacy of chord" opinion runs so deep that people no longer see it. To raise controversy about it disrupts something people have become familiar and comfortable with.

Fundamentally, those who take the stance of taking no stance just don't want there to be any question about the issue. They want the question to go away, because at root what they refuse to consider is a *linear view of consciousness*. That is the real root of the disagreement.

A proper understanding of music must acknowledge that an "equal partnership" between melody and harmony is equivalent to imagining a building whose first and fiftieth floors are in the same place. It is a contradiction.

A proper understanding of music must reverse Rameau's reversal. It must acknowledge the root and base of the field. It must not seek equality where there is none.

## SCHENKER

The mass of misguided thought launched by Rameau was swept aside by the clear vision of a man who once again understood music in terms of its fundamental nature: linear synthesis.

Heinrich Schenker, a Viennese pianist, music teacher and writer, provided the antidote to the inversion of melody and harmony. And, fortunately, the dissemination of his ideas over the past century or so has begun to gradually correct Rameau's reversal in men's understanding.

Born in 1868 in Poland and raised in the twilight of 19th-century Romanticism, Schenker developed a revolutionary new theory of music which strongly reasserted the importance of linear connections, and which provided profound new insights into the nature of human musical cognition.

Schenker edited quality print editions of scores by Bach, Handel and Beethoven, for which he scrupulously studied original sources to understand as closely as possible the composer's intentions. This abiding concern of fidelity to the composer's conception animated all of his work.

Schenker published numerous books and articles of his own laying out his ideas with more or less encyclopedic thoroughness.

Schenker was not mesmerized by the "chord of nature." In the preface to *Counterpoint*, he speaks of artists "transcending the spare clue provided by the overtone series." He describes Rameau's views, for subtle reasons, as "the most fateful confusion" and "an error of a gravity that had not previously been equaled."

Schenker writes that he "must certainly endorse" a statement that "the study of music must begin with melody." He is deeply aware of the importance of auditory integration over time, referring to "the difficult art of synthesis—truly the only source of all musical laws." His theory is one of organic unity: art is a process of "selection and synthesis" and of "the continuous natural growth of phenomena from the basis of a few principle laws." Music should be understood in terms of "the power of growing outward from within" just as a seed grows outward into a tree. Schenker regarded the scale as the fundamental basis and integrating framework of music, and scale degree as "the generator of [musical] content."

## BREAKING THE RULES?

Schenker, as we shall see, not only restored the primacy of line, he also solved the problem: How can laws of musical order have permanence amid changing styles?

The rules of counterpoint had been formed to deal with composition of vocal polyphony in the Renaissance style. But not far into the Renaissance, great strides were made in the construction and playing of instruments. Music using the unique capacities of instruments, and the unique abilities of virtuoso players, was undeniably of great value. And yet this new style differed radically from vocal polyphony's long tones moving in smooth lines. Instrumental technique is easily able to produce music that the voice is poorly suited to—such as extremely fast notes and wide-ranging leaps. Sonatas, symphonies and concertos employed amazing and powerful instrumental effects that would be impossible to execute, or even conceive of, in a purely vocal idiom.

Consider this example by Vivaldi, which illustrates the new instrumental idiom:

9.3 *Instrumental music developed a style very different from vocal polyphony, which seemed to break the rules of note-connection.*

But the new instrumental style seemed to break all the rules of counterpoint. It called into question what had been accepted as the principles of rational order in music. There were times when many leaps took place in the same direction, when leaps were not filled in or compensated for by scalar motion in the opposite direction, when the instrument leaped into or out of dissonances, when the notes moved in parallel fifths. To theorists of music, who prided themselves on understanding and explaining the patterns of order in music, these seemed to be unanswerable facts. They could not deny the musical validity or artistic, expressive power of the flourishes and virtuosity used in good instrumental music, but they were at a loss to explain it in terms of the only intellectual framework they knew.

As Schenker wrote in *Counterpoint*,

*"The pressing need finally arose to resolve once and for all the contradiction between, on the one hand, the ways those masters [Schubert, Schumann, Wagner, Brahms and others] set their tones according to new psychic forces, and, on the other hand, the former theory—especially contrapuntal theory—which made the discrepancy between the two worlds (practice and theory) really appear too wide and great."*

Particularly with the advent of philosophical Subjectivism, people of a certain type took this as the excuse to declare "anything goes"—that the old system of musical order had been exploded, disproved, overturned, invalidated. In place of the careful and narrowly circumscribed principles of order and consecution in vocal counterpoint, people moved in the direction of thinking "I can write whatever I feel like"—that there were no more laws to the art of music, that it was entirely a matter of "self-expression" not in the form of rationally purposeful, passionate yet structured artistry, but in the sense of freewheeling, anti-analytical, irrational impulse or whim.

Schenker solved these problems. In contrast with the Rameau-ian primacy of chord perspective, he reasserted the primacy of line and the fact of consecution over time. He solved the problem of instrumental technique by showing that the *complexities of instrumental music were elaborations of the simpler underlying patterns of species counterpoint.*

Schenker distinguished between counterpoint, which was for the purpose of learning or acquiring mastery of materials, and free composition, which was for the purpose of applying those skills in creative expression. Counterpoint exercises are strict, operating with deliberately but artificially limited constraints to make the learning process clear and step-by-step. Free composition need not hold to every detail of the counterpoint exercises, but the crucial central tenets of counterpoint, those which are fundamental, do hold and are manifest in a more complex fashion in free composition.

He showed how the new innovations did not explode or overturn the prior laws of order, but rather *used* those laws, counted on them, depended on them as the basis of intelligibility. Inside the flourishes and arpeggios of instrumental music were the clear and elementary linear patterns of vocal polyphony.

## LEVELS OF STRUCTURE

Rameau, and the Roman numeral tradition started by Weber, had viewed music as "flat"— as though all notes and chords were of equal importance, as though they were all on the same structural level. Schenker viewed the various notes and chords in a piece as having radically different levels of importance—some were mere ornaments on the surface, others were part of the musical flow in a deeper way, and some represented key structural pillars of the piece.

Schenker first conceptualized music as having *levels* of structure; he formed the conception of three levels: the foreground, middleground, and background (or immediate, intermediate and remote). He looked at the complex surface of the music as an elaboration of the simpler underlying structure.

The flip-side of this perspective is to look at music in terms of the hierarchy of our comprehension, which integrates patterns in stages, reducing them to ever-simpler forms in order to hold the package of musical elements as an organic whole.

Schenker developed a new method of graphical notation, an adapted form of traditional music notation which shows not just the literal note-to-note motions, but also the fabric and hierarchy of interconnections over time. He developed and honed this method to a high degree of perfection, so that it is capable of showing connections on many levels of a composition down to the most profound structural fundamentals.

The following analysis illustrates Schenker's kind of insights and his methods of showing them. The first staff gives the opening measures of Bourrée I, from the Third Cello Suite by J.S. Bach, in its literal version. The later staves show some of the structural elements holding the music together. The second-to-last staff shows the main structural notes and their connections. The last shows the contrapuntal pattern from which the Bach melody is derived— or, conversely, the simpler form to which it reduces. Overall, this figure (9.4) is a small illustration of Schenker's fundamental insight that music has levels of structure, as well as of his means of indicating the network of connections in a piece.

This is merely a sample in microcosm of Schenker's insights, which in their most impressive form illuminate the integrity of an entire composition. For more, see Schenker's own work, especially his *Five Graphic Music Analyses*.

The syntax is two short parallel sub-phrases.

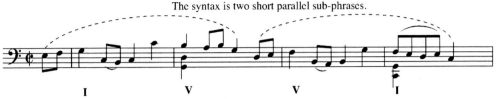

I              V              V              I

The harmony moves in the first phrase from cognitively closed (I) to open (V), and in the second phrase from open (V) to closed (I).

A leap of an octave opens a wide pitch space, which is then filled in by a long descending scale-line inside the melody; this line cuts across the parallel phrases and helps hold the music together.

Part of the parallelism of the phrases is this pattern.        Which reduces to/is an elaboration of:

Using Schenker's graphical notation to show the local network of connections:

The upper line makes a descending scale motion between two stable tones of the tonic triad, 5-4-3 (G-F-E).
The spine of the melody is supported by a bass motion I-V-I.

(Open noteheads
indicate not rhythm
but structural importance.)

The music can be boiled down to a simple species counterpoint pattern.

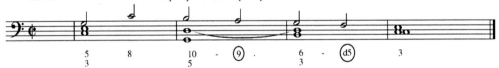

$\begin{matrix} 5 \\ 3 \end{matrix}$    8    $\begin{matrix} 10 \\ 5 \end{matrix}$  -  (9)  .    $\begin{matrix} 6 \\ 3 \end{matrix}$  -  (d5)    3

*9.4 An application of Schenkerian analysis to a simple phrase by Bach, showing various aspects of the music's integrity.*

The melody of this Bourrée does not superficially follow the elementary progressions of species counterpoint—because it is a *compound* melody made up of threads which *do* follow the elementary progressions. The cello's line arpeggiates across the strands of the underlying contrapuntal fabric. Thus Bach's melody (in the top staff above) can be seen as an elaboration of the simple pattern of species counterpoint shown in the bottom staff. The complexities do not contradict the laws of species counterpoint, they build upon them.

The delicate interconnections of these fibers make the piece subtly and gently beautiful. The major key makes it clear and bright, and the particular sonorities chosen (prominent imperfect consonances, for instance) make it sweet and warm in sound. The dance rhythm brings life and energy and movement, with a clearly emphasized strong beat. The cello's three-note chords on the downbeats of bars 2 and 4 give a broad feel to the rhythm.

The complexity of the melody is intelligible because it is an elaboration of an underlying pattern of clear, simple motions. Or, the inverse way of saying the same thing: the florid complexity can be boiled down, reduced to something elementary, and this is the basis upon which the brain and mind integrate and hold the music as a unified whole.

Thus Schenker discovered and systematically developed a theory of music based on the principle that *we understand the complex by means of the simple.*

The same is true of the inverse process: creation—we *create* the complex by means of the simple. (Remind you of Fux? It should.)

Part of Schenker's idea of levels of structure is the fact that a simple structure such as a chord can be elaborated or extended in what Schenker called "composing out." The *voice exchange*—in which two voices swap notes through passing motion—is one example.

The outer voices exchange notes.

9.5 A voice-exchange is a means of expanding a single harmony. The first and last chords are both C Major; the middle chord is a means of passing between. The top voice moves from E to C, the lower voice from C to E—hence the term "voice exchange."

This sort of pattern, Schenker identified, is not best understood by merely attaching Roman numerals to each chord. Rather, the middle sonority is derived from passing tones—it is a passing chord, a means of transitioning from the tonic triad to its later inversion. This movement is an extension or composing-out of the stable sound of the tonic triad. Thus, a static sonority can be infused with living energy and motion. The music maintains one basic sound, one main effective harmony, but prolonged, extended, and made to *move*. This creates a sense not of sitting in place but of development of material—a sense of the push forward, of progress. This is the way in which music is a living, growing thing in Schenker's conception, even as that motion relates back to a unifying stable sonority.

Through Schenker's vast experience over his productive life he came to the conclusion that all integrated tonal music is ultimately an elaboration of a super-fundamental, ultra-simple underlying pattern or archetype he called the *Urzatz.* "Ur" comes from from the name of the ancient city in Sumer (modern Iraq), one of the oldest known cities; "ur" has come to mean "original," "prototypical," "archetypal" and to have the connotation of "eternal." The German word "Satz" is multifaceted. It means: sentence or proposition, movement (in the sense of a musical movement), grounds, setting, leap or bound.

The Ursatz is the ultra-fundamental structural pattern of a piece. It consists of two elementary lines, one melodic the other a supporting bass line. The fundamental melodic line, called the Urlinie, marches by scale from a stable note of the tonic triad down to the tonic. The particular form depends on the substance of the composition in question. The most common Urlinie is the melodic progression through scale degrees 3-2-1. More rarely, 5-4-3-2-1 or even a progression down a full octave. These motions would be supported by a straightforward "Bassbrechung" (bass leaps "breaking" the fifth): I-V-I.

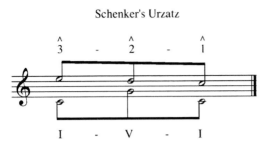

Schenker's Urzatz

$\hat{3}$ - $\hat{2}$ - $\hat{1}$

I - V - I

9.6 *Schenker found this elementary "eternal-motion" to be the seed or the deep structure of tightly integrated music.*

The Urlinie motions are not local, foreground motions, but deep structure forming the large-scale backbone of a piece. The piece can be looked at as a unique elaboration of a consistent archetype—or as reducible back to this elementary pattern. Thus Schenker's motto: "Always the same, but never in the same way" (*semper idem sed non eodem modo*).

Schenker concerned himself with the major-minor tonal system and the music of the great composers who worked using that system. The focus of the principle of tonal direction or gravity is central to Schenker's thought. However, his observations about linear connections provide insights to any music employing the diatonic scale, even if it does not use the full harmonic system of tonality. However, the sorts of connections Schenker identifies are found most intensively in tonal music. Tonality is the most tightly integrated of any musical system; other music is looser, less tightly interconnected and organically integrated. Therefore, Schenker's insights about musical integrity are most revealing for the tonal masterworks.

The one significant shortcoming in Schenker's theory of music is its neglect of emotion. He was a practical man, who thought expression and artistry were important, but he was unfortunately influenced by a prior German thinker, Eduard Hanslick, who held that emotion was not a scientifically legitimate concept with regard to music. So Schenker magnificently explained the nature of musical cognition, and elaborated it in encyclopedic fashion, but he completely avoids dealing with emotion-concepts.

Schenker reasserts the primacy of line, and his theory of structure is absolutely correct, but his thought doesn't include Zarlino's cognizance of the importance of feeling, pleasure, and sensuality. Shenker was utterly brilliant and gave us fundamental insights about music; he certainly doesn't rail against emotion in music, but his thought is post-Hanslick and studiously avoids the topic of feeling, which is a pretty serious omission.

Although Schenker did not think of music in terms of emotion, he did give insight to the underlying phenomenon, namely the motions of the soul. As Robert Snarrenberg wrote in the Grove Dictionary: with the idea of the "Zug" (a structural "march" of melody through the scale-steps from one stable tone to another),

*"Schenker was able to describe melodic movement with great precision: departures, arrivals, detours, reversals and so forth. The Zug is a norm for interpreting the ebb and flow of free melodies, just as even pace is a norm for interpreting the rhythm of free melodies…. prose permitted description of what it is like to follow that path: how the linear progression moves in a particular direction and in a particular location within the texture of the piece, how it is paced, whether it is hesitant or*

*storming, tumbling or dragging, how directly or indirectly the goal is reached, and whether setbacks, delays or detours are encountered."*

In marked contrast to Rameau's wish to be known for his theory more than his compositions, Schenker was eminently practical in mindset. "Schenker intended his publications to aid performers more than scholars. Annotated editions and commentaries on performing practice were meant to be of direct practical utility, while the theoretical and interpretative writings were meant to help performers refine and train their musical intuitions." (Snarrenberg)

Schenker's system of thought represents a "righting of the ship" with regard to the relation of line and chord. And his theory is a profound advance in our ability to grapple with the patterns that hold music together.

Recall Zarlino's sentiment that a composer had to maintain unity of mode through a work, otherwise the "end of his composition would come to be dissonant with the beginning and the middle." Schenker's theory is a tremendous advance upon and completion of that idea: his perspective regards a central tonic and its harmony as the persistent background consonance retained by the brain, to which all other elements relate as blending or clashing, with the result that the ultimate completion is the resolution of all discords back to the original core.

Schenker had a great perceptiveness into what particular connections hold an integrated piece together—and he had an extensive ability to explain and show those multi-layered, delicate fibers of connection. He is one of the greatest of that rare breed, the musical scientist who penetrates to the core of the art form, giving profound insight into the phenomenon of organic linear synthesis in music.

## CONCLUDING SUMMARY

Let us review and condense the material we have learned through the course of this book.

Linear synthesis is the fundamental of music.

A musical line or melody becomes coherent by means of its shape moving from beginning to climax to cadence. The pitches of a line are interconnected by means of stepwise relationships; leaps are integrated only to the extent that the notes leapt from, and leapt to, are connected in some stepwise relation to other notes of the line.

Melody moves not by gradual fluctuation of pitch, like the rise and fall of the wind, but by definite motion from one discrete point of pitch to another. Essential to melody is the fact of the distance from one note to another, the pitch interval. Different intervals produce different expressive, emotional, or affective qualities in the mind.

The audible quality of an interval is the human form of perception of certain mathematical relationships. There are three basic categories. Perfect consonances, which make the simplest ratios such as 3:2, produce a strong, stark, clear sense impression. Imperfect consonances, which make the next simplest ratios such as 5:4, have a warm, tender, rich quality. The disso-

nances have the most complex ratios and produce a clashing, intense quality. Some dissonances, such as the minor seventh (16:9) are fairly mellow. Others, such as the major seventh
(15:8), are more discordant, piercing and pained.

A special category must be set aside for *stepwise dissonances when the notes are heard in succession*—since this relationship is the basis for linear connections over time. When the two
notes of a major or minor second are heard in succession, and when these notes integrate into
an overall diatonic framework, they are the means by which the brain integrates notes into a
line. This is a satisfying and pleasurable form of connection.

Aside from this case, all dissonances (successive and simultaneous) produce a buzzingly
nervous, unsettled, unstable sensation in the mind. A dissonance, by itself, is the musical
equivalent of a contradiction; the brain cannot resolve the note-relationship. This is an
unpleasant form of cognitive failure.

This is why dissonances must resolve. In order to be processed successfully by the auditory
system, dissonances must be introduced in the proper way, and must give way to consonance
in the proper way. A dissonant note resolves when it moves by step to a consonance.

Sophisticated music employs not just one line but many lines flowing together at the same
time in an integrated fabric.

An entire art or science of counterpoint evolved to manage this integration. One of its fundamental tenets is: consonance is primary; consonance provides the framework or structure
within which dissonances can be made intelligible. Dissonance is secondary; it is the ornamental element which accentuates and intensifies the satisfying clarity of consonance.

"Polyphony" is the name for the confluence of many independent, contrasting voices.
"Homophony" is the name for a single prominent melody with harmonic accompaniment.

The correct conception of homophony, however, is not "melody with chords," but a single
prominent line accompanied by other subordinate lines which provide a background of harmony, with the bass line serving as the chief and foundational line for the support of the main
tune. This is the conception consistent with the basic nature of music—namely linear synthesis—as well as the conception mandated by the way in which harmony arose historically.

Chords are not free-standing entities unto themselves, ready-made in nature; they are
human creations which have value and purpose, but only as a packaging together or summary
of linear information. Chords provide composers with an advantage in coping with the limit
of working memory; instead of holding a profusion of interval relationships in mind, a composer can hold a lot of relationships mentally in the form of a chord progression with certain
voice-leading. But chords should not be treated as something more basic than they are. They
are not a simple primary but a complex derivative.

Music is primarily linear, not chordal—even when it uses chords, they are subordinate to
linear factors. The impact and meaning of a chord depend on the full musical context over
time. Chord progressions are merely a means of coordinating or holding together, as a
package, a bunch of bits of linear motion. A line is a retainable entity, a chord is merely a sense
impression. A line is a form of synthesis; a chord is not.

Voice-leading, the means of connecting notes from chord to chord, is not a new concept but a mere simplification of the laws of the art of counterpoint.

As a bottom line: if a person cannot write beautiful polyphony, he has no business using chords.

The correct and profound conception of "harmony" has to do not with chords as such, but with the overall phenomenon of the relation of tones to the scale that forms their context. The scale is the basic and controlling form of musical context.

Music has levels of structure. Some notes are mere surface ornaments while others are part of its main structure or skeleton. At the deepest level, very simple patterns underlie even the most far-flung complexity, if it is intelligible complexity, that is. We understand the complex by means of the simple.

Our process of auditory comprehension integrates music in stages—in a hierarchical fashion. In listening, our auditory system progressively breaks down or reduces more florid or complicated elements into simpler patterns and thus we grasp the notes as one unified structure. When sounds lack such a structure, they cannot be comprehended in a unified way and they do not constitute an organic synthesis.

Music takes place over time, and the relations of timing are a very crucial aspect of its nature. Rhythm means action coordinated in time, using the uniform unit that is the beat or pulse as the measuring unit. Meter, a regularly recurring pattern of strong and weak beats, provides a hierarchical structure to time measurement, like the marks on a ruler provide a hierarchical structure to length measurement. There are larger units (such as bars) subsuming smaller divisions, and finer cuts (subdivisions) nested within broader ones.

The feel of a rhythm depends in significant part on whether the meter is duple or triple. A duple meter, with the alternation of strong and weak beats as in a march, arouses more angular, left-right-left motion. A triple meter, with every third beat accented as in a waltz, arouses rounder, more flowing, arc-tracing motion. These effects result from the binary nature of man's body: his muscles, which function in opposing groups, and his limbs which operate in alternating pairs. The issue is not purely physical, however; there is an analogous phenomenon of change of place in the mind. The act of creating or mentally reciting a poem is an example of mental action coordinated in rhythm.

Rhythmic action enables the integration of smaller component actions (whether physical or mental) into a single, unified, larger action. Thus the essence of rhythm is the experience of the efficacy of one's own action-integrating capacity; the concomitant pleasure is nature's reward for that success. Thus there is a profound connection between rhythm and life.

Just as meter is the measuring rod for time, the musical scale is a measuring rod for pitch; the scale is a series of increments providing a framework within which note relationships become intelligible. The diatonic scale is made up principally of the simple perfect consonances, the perfect fifth (3:2) and fourth (4:3); there are more of these intervals in the scale than any other. This is in contrast to, for instance, a stack of six half-steps, which has more half-steps than any other interval; thus it lacks a base in the clear simplicity of perfect consonances.

The diatonic scale is one built out of the 4-note interval pattern: Whole-step, Whole-step, half-step, or pitch ratio 15:16:18:20. The diatonic scale is distinguished from a scale based in micro-intervals such as the quarter-tone, and from the various symmetrical constructs such as the chromatic, whole-tone, or octatonic series. The diatonic scale is able to provide the mind with an orienting framework because it is *not* symmetrical; the array of note relationships around each scale tone is unique and distinctive, giving each tone an unmistakable position and role within the scale, and enabling the mind to orient itself in the musical context.

The diatonic scale is required by the human brain. It is not a "Western social construct" but a timeless universal inherent in human musical perception.

A great deal of complexity can be integrated into an overall diatonic framework. Chromatic tones, for instance, can enter in as ornaments coloring the feeling of the scale. And some notes have the function of carrying the listener to a new key (modulation). Modulation to closely related keys, those which require the alteration of only one note, are smooth and subtle. Modulation to distant keys, those which require the alteration of many notes of the scale, are more bold, disruptive, and dramatic.

Within the basic fact of diatony there are many forms of intelligible scale, such as the church modes and the inflected forms of scale which are more complex but retain the basic framework of steps 1-3-5.

The emotion music evokes depends to a great extent on the form of scale it employs. The fundamental distinction is between those scales based around a major triad (4:5:6), which are brighter, and those based around a minor triad (10:12:15), which are darker. There are quite a number of different forms of scale depending on how the various other notes relate to the central triad; each of these variations creates a slightly different slant on, or gives a slightly different flavor to, the basic bright or dark feeling.

Each note of the scale has a characteristic quality of its own, which is a result of the total network of interval relationships between that note and all the other notes of the scale. There are stable and unstable tones—some tones are resting tones while others are "tendency" tones which pull toward the resting notes. There are warm, tender, sensuous tones. There are more pained, piercing tones. There are bright tones and dark tones.

The ultimate expression of the nature of the musical scale is tonality—a grand-scale, intensive system of unity in music.

Tonality, an innovation of the Renaissance and the foundation of several centuries of magnificent music, is the principle of creating and using the gravitational pull of the tonic note to evoke a feeling of journey in music, a sense of goal-direction. Tonality is the expression in music of the fact of volition, of man's power of self-direction—of his ability to foresee a goal, work toward it, and reach it.

Tonality is the method of the tightest possible synthesis of all elements of a composition around a central note which is the integrating point of reference. All elements of music were marshaled to contribute to this effect: the use of the tendencies of the notes within the scale to resolve toward more stable notes, ultimately to the tonic itself; the use of resolving dissonance, especially the powerful tritone; the use of functional harmony; the use of scale-step V as the antipode to I, and as its primary competitor for the center of gravity; the control of motion to cadences—control of both the march of pitches and the timing of the progress and arrival; the use of modulation—change of key—to depart from the home scale and travel far afield, exploring and opening out, then returning to the home scale with a tremendous feeling of resolution and completeness; modulation also offers different possibilities for the character of the journey such as how long it takes, how far afield one travels, how smooth the course is and how much struggle is entailed.

Thus we see how melody, its intervals, the scale, rhythm, polyphony, counterpoint, harmony, and tonality all express the same basic principle: the integration, the synthesis over time, of many distinct elements into one unified whole, grasped and used by man's mind.

What is the practical result of this? What is the concrete product of such implicit and explicit knowledge?

## A SYMPHONY OF BEETHOVEN

Beethoven's Fourth Symphony begins with a long sustained tone in octaves, played softly and unadorned by the winds. The stark, desolate sound poses a question: What will fill the void? That question is hardly answered as the tone recedes into the background; we hear from the strings in unison a line of slow, eerie, evenly paced notes, conjuring an atmosphere of apprehension that intensifies the question, "What is coming?" The music is sparse, austere, darkly mysterious. We sink into its tense gloom for several minutes—until suddenly there comes a tremendous, bold burst of sun and the orchestra races forth with a vivacious melody. The anxious despair is swept away, cast off with abandon by a firm assertion of ebullient, dancing joy.

We hear the alternation of graceful gentleness and masculine strength, lightheartedness and mysterious apprehension. The sense of propulsion is irresistible.

The clarinet plays a solo which the bassoon promptly chases; the two instruments play the same melody, staggered in time, rolling over one another, tumbling forward not in a jumble but in perfect order in time and harmony.

Stormy outbursts give way to the quietest possible fragmentary wisps of melody, a delicate filigree of question marks—and with a burst the ebullient theme announces itself again in a great declaration, and the movement drives to its close.

After a pause, we hear in the second movement a tune of tenderness and sweetness, a respite from the struggle and stress of the first movement. This gentle, very slow waltz is interrupted periodically by a stronger motto which then yields back to the tender music. The theme undergoes progressive variation—one moment a plain tune, the next a busy filigree. The movement begins to dissolve, the tender theme evaporating; but it finally closes with a brief, strong, solemn cadence.

We next feel the heaviness and vigor of a curiously syncopated waltz—a dalliance which keeps passing, temporarily, into a mood of ominous foreboding. The music keeps its omnipresent sense of forward motion, of steady progression.

The finale is the epitome of *fast*. It races, it rolls, it drives, it dances. Energetic syncopations and the interplay of the instruments boost the rhythm. Quick modulations to new keys keep the journey moving apace.

As the music expands out, developing its themes, it travels harmonically far afield from the home key. The inventiveness and transformation of the themes is stimulating, the fragments are tossed about; but the sense of control is palpable.

An undercurrent of churning agitation and continually mounting tension propels the whole project. It builds an almost intolerable anticipation and, finally, drives ahead to climactic satisfaction—decisive and absolute.

A titanic intelligence operates in this music. We sense a mastery of the mind's domain, a power over of the forces of the psyche—the power of linear synthesis. Not just the single line but the weaving together of a wide range of linear elements into a harmonious progression, the power of forming and working with the patterns that are the themes, the facility of forming and transforming these abstractions.

The music has the integrity of building everything out of the theme, with no extraneous elements. It is a purified, perfected manifestation of the process of rational thought, albeit in the form of tones rather than words, stripped of any irrelevancies or dead ends or unresolved elements. It is the thrill of a cognitive process devoid of any pointless digression.

A tremendous force of *Will* is in this sound—the power of a continuous progression to a goal, the sense of the inevitable, unstoppable purposeful motion of a mind in the process of actively using its contents, building them in a great project of summation that fulfills and resolves all the elements, that wraps up with the inevitability and completeness of profound mathematical truth.

That truth dramatizes the enormous emotional range of a heroic being: there is no trace of confusion or terror, no moment of boredom, only the drama of an exploration of the full gamut of the psyche of the mature hero: from ebullience to cataclysmic fury, from solemn serenity to sweeping rapture, from mysterious wonder to epic triumph. All this is integrated in a tremendous symphonic sweep that is the embodiment of man, the *whole* being—man the inseparable unity of rational intelligence and passionate moral integrity.

## BIBLIOGRAPHY

Recommended Relevant Books

For the general reader:

*What to Listen for in Mozart*
Robert Harris

*The Vintage Guide to Classical Music*
Jan Swafford

*Horace's Odes and the Mystery of Do-Re-Mi*
Stuart Lyons

*Romantic Manifesto*
Ayn Rand

*Hermann von Helmholtz* (biography)
Frances Alice Welby, Leo Koenigsberger

For the more technically ambitious reader:

*Music in Western Civilization*
Paul Henry Lang

*Source Readings in Music History*
Oliver Strunk

*On the Sensations of Tone*
Hermann Helmholtz

*The Study of Counterpoint* from Gradus ad Parnassum
Johann Joseph Fux, translated by Alfred Mann

*Counterpoint in Composition*
Felix Salzer & Carl Schachter

*Five Graphic Music Analyses*
Heinrich Schenker

*The Story of Notation*
C.F. Abdy Williams

*The Harmonics of Aristoxenus*
translated by Henry S. Macran

*Psychology of Music*
Carl. E. Seashore

## TIMELINE OF THE DEVELOPMENT OF MUSIC THEORY

**BC**

Greece

| 500s | Pythagoras | (legendary) discovery of mathematical ratios of intervals |
|---|---|---|
| 400s | Socrates | thinking method: ask questions |
| ca. 400 | Plato | metaphysics of two worlds, high and low |
| 300s | Aristotle | logic, science, this-worldly philosophy |
| 300s | Aristoxenus | summary of Greek music theory, including scales; melodic synthesis |

**AD**

Medieval Period

| ca. 400 | Augustine | transforms Plato's philosophy into Medieval Christianity |
|---|---|---|
| ca. 600 | Gregory | organizes Christian church; (allegedly) collected church songs |
| ca. 800 | Charlemagne | unified Europe, temporarily revived learning and culture |
| ca. 900 | Unknown | first known polyphony, notated in *Musica Enchiriadis* (Handbook of Music) |
| ca. 1000 | Guido of Arezzo | staff notation, solfege; centered teaching on the major scale |

Renaissance

| 1200s | Aquinas | infused Aristotelian philosophy into European thought |
|---|---|---|
| ca. 1440 | Gutenberg | the printing press |
| 1517 | Luther | Posts 'Ninety-five Theses,' initiating the Protestant Reformation |
| 1558 | Zarlino | *Le istitutioni harmoniche* (Institution of Harmony): rules of counterpoint including dissonance resolution, definition of triad, principle of tonality |
| 1500s | Palestrina | culmination of Renaissance polyphony |
| ca. 1605 | Monteverdi | asserted homophonic style, began practice of basso continuo; opera |

Enlightenment

| 1687 | Newton | *Mathematical Principles of Natural Science* |
|---|---|---|
| 1700 | Christofori | invents the piano |
| 1701 | Sauveur | the overtone series |
| 1722 | Rameau | *Treatise on Harmony*, system asserting primacy of chord |
| 1725 | Fux | *Gradus ad Parnassum*, systematic counterpoint method |
| 1760s | Haydn | settles large-scale forms such as Sonata form |
| 1776 | Jefferson | Declaration of Independence |
| 1803 | Beethoven | *Eroica* Symphony – revolutionary new scope of expression |
| 1859 | Darwin | *The Origin of Species* – man's natural origin |
| 1863 | Helmholtz | *On the Sensations of Tone* – summary of science of music |
| 1877 | Edison | invents the phonograph |
| 1906 | Sherrington | *The Integrative Action of the Nervous System*; the synapse |
| 1920s | Schenker | levels of musical structure, concept of organic coherence, method of graphical analysis, re-asserts primacy of line |

Modern Era

| 1781 | Kant | *Critique of Pure Reason*, system of philosophical Subjectivism |
|---|---|---|
| 1854 | Hanslick | *On the Musically Beautiful*, musical emotion as illegitimate (Formalism) |
| ca. 1900 | | beginnings of Jazz; principle of Africanism |
| 1912 | Schoenberg | *Pierrot Lunaire*; the principle of atonality; "liberation of the dissonance;" Serialism; principle of nihilism |
| 1913 | Stravinsky | *Rite of Spring* causes a riot in Paris; principle of primitivism |
| 1914-45 | | World Wars |
| 1956 | Chuck Berry | "Roll over Beethoven" – Rock 'n' Roll, lowbrow rebellion |

Information Age

| 1920s | | use of radio becomes widespread |
|---|---|---|
| 1971 | Ayn Rand | *Art and Cognition* – neural integration applied to music |
| 1990s | | expansion of the Internet to the general public |